RECORDER TECHNIQUE

Intermediate to Advanced

**3rd edition,
considerably revised**

ANTHONY ROWLAND-JONES

Peacock Press

Peacock Press
Scout Bottom Farm
Mytholmroyd
Hebden Bridge
West Yorkshire
HX7 5JS

Earlier editions published by Oxford University Press:
First published 1959
Second edition 1986
Reprinted 1991

British Library Cataloguing in Publication Data
Rowland-Jones, Anthony
Recorder Techniques: intermediate to advanced. —— 3rd ed. —— (Instrumental
technique books)
1. Recorder (Musical instrument)
I. Title II. Series
788'.53'0712   MT350
ISBN 0-907908-75-6 (pbk.)

Printed in Great Britain by
Lightning Source. UK

Acknowledgments:

I should like to thank Professor Peter Nolan for reading and
commenting on the proof of this book. I should also like to thank
Diana Wyatt for her careful typesetting with the 'considerable
revisions', and all at Peacock Press for their patience with
my many telephone calls and faxes. And my wife Christina for
typing all the new bits and the index.

Front cover image © Helen Hooker

In this book masculine pronouns are used
for both male and female genders.

AUTHOR'S PREFACE

The first edition of *Recorder Technique*, published by Oxford University Press in 1959, was based on a series of articles which first appeared in *The Recorder News*, the journal of the Society of Recorder Players, and which were then copied in the *Newsletter* of the American Recorder Society. At that time, the recorder was generally regarded as a school instrument, and was held in low esteem by most professional musicians, recorder parts in its own repertoire generally being played on transverse flutes. It was therefore visionary of Alan Frank, the music books editor of OUP and himself a clarinettist, to include the recorder in OUP's instrumental technique series to join those already published for the oboe, the clarinet and the flute. No other book intended for adult recorder players was then available. Each of the original articles dealt with a different aspect of technique, such as breathing, tonguing, fingering and dynamics, and the book followed the same pattern, and still does so. In this third edition, however, at the risk of some repetition, I have made the approach to these aspects rather more progressive and integrated. It is their inter-relationship which builds up the understanding of technique that enables a player to respond with skill and imagination both to the potentialities of his instrument and to the demands of the music he chooses to play.

The small format of the series precluded the use of music examples. These were published separately by OUP in 1962 as *A Practice Book for the Treble Recorder*. Again with enthusiastic amateurs in mind, this book draws its material mainly from the standard repertoire of the recorder rather than providing daunting finger exercises, scales and arpeggios which must be the daily labour of aspiring professionals. *The Practice Book* ('PB') links in with the chapter headings of *Recorder Technique* ('RT') in its selection of pieces which, to be played well, call upon different skills required by the recorder player in breathing, tonguing, fingering, dynamics, ornamentation, and other considerations affecting the interpretation of a piece of music.

1962 also saw the appearance of Edgar Hunt's *The Recorder and its Music*, recently revised for its current publication by Peacock Press. This book expanded considerably on the chapters in the first edition of *Recorder Technique* on the history of the instrument and its repertoire, a subject which is also considered by several writers, including myself, in *The Cambridge Companion to the Recorder* (ed. J.M. Thomson, Cambridge University Press, 1995); references to this book are abbreviated to '*Companion*'. In 1978 OUP published my *Introduction to the Recorder*, referred to as '*Intro*', a tutor with practice material designed for adult beginners in music on descant or tenor, and/or treble, recorders, up to the stage of participating in consort music or embarking upon their first accompanied solos. This book, now out of print but which will shortly also be available from Peacock Press, superseded the original *RT* chapter 'Beginning to Play the Recorder'. The second edition of *RT*, published by OUP in 1986, therefore had the sub-title 'Intermediate to Advanced', which remains the scope of this third edition.

Each new edition of *RT* has given me the opportunity to make considerable changes. In teaching adult recorder players individually and in groups for over fifty years I am

Contents

To Christina

constantly encountering new problems, and discovering and receiving fresh ideas. Furthermore, during that period there has been an enormous increase in scholarship in the field of early music, with far greater attention given to the writings of musicians and teachers from the time of Ganassi, author of the first recorder tutor, *Fontegara*, in 1535, and onwards to the flautists Quantz and Tromlitz. Much of this is of relevance to historical techniques of recorder playing, and that consideration accounted for the greatest differences between the first and second editions of *RT*, especially in the chapters on articulation and ornamentation. It also accounts for revisions in this, the third edition, particularly with regard to the growing use of recorders modelled on Renaissance originals to play the music of that period.

Another phenomenon of the later decades of the twentieth century was the realisation that the recorder, partly because of its simplicity, was peculiarly adaptable to extended techniques cultivated by 'avant-garde' composers. The second edition of *RT* contained several references to avant-garde techniques, without studying the subject in depth. In revising *RT* for the present edition, I have not enlarged upon this aspect of the recorder's capabilities and repertoire, partly because it would have resulted in a considerably extended *RT*, and partly because many of these compositions are too difficult to be mastered other than by professionals and exceptional amateur players. Those interested in this field should seek out a good teacher who can perform these works in public recitals. They should also read Eve O'Kelly's *The Recorder Today* (Cambridge University Press, 1990), and study the pioneering work in this field, Michael Vetter's *Il Flauto Dolce ed Acerbo* (Moeck, Ed. 4009), Celle, 1969), Volume III of Walter van Hauwe's *The Modern Recorder Player* (Schott, Ed. 12351), London, 1992) and other books referred to in 'Some Suggested Reading' (Appendix 2). I strongly endorse the point made by these writers that rigorous practising of extended techniques not only enables recorder players to understand and enjoy contemporary recorder compositions but, by revealing the ultimate capabilities of their instrument, especially in its dynamic range and expressivity, also greatly increases their interpretative powers in performing music from earlier centuries.

Although *RT* and *PB* refer in general ways to phrasing, and the *PB* examples show phrasing marks, neither book is primarily about interpretation. But, except in music written for the sole purpose of virtuoso display, interpretation is the be-all and end-all of technique; technique is the servant of interpretation, a means to an end. Interpretation, and performance practice in different periods and places, is the subject of very many books and articles. Ultimately good interpretation can only be the outcome of much listening to music, understanding it, and playing it – especially playing it with the guidance of an inspiring teacher or conductor.

Nevertheless, in the book which I regard as a culmination of this series, I do attempt to show how, in examples drawn from the recorder and keyboard repertoire, knowledge and skill in technique serve the process of interpretation. This book is *Playing Recorder Sonatas*, published by Clarendon Press, Oxford, in 1990, and permanently available from OUP on demand. This third edition of *RT* makes many references to it as '*PRS*'. Following roughly the same order as *RT* and *PB*, it considers a Handel sonata with special emphasis on sound and expression, a Telemann sonata (dynamics and Italian style), one by Lavigne illustrating French style and inequality, Herbert Murrill's Sonata and the *Furioso* from a

Handel sonata to consider articulation and slurs, and an early seventeenth-century Italian sonata calling for ornamentation and improvisation. Ten other sonatas are looked at less comprehensively in order to illustrate other problems of interpretation. For example, while *RT* gives various fingerings for high F sharp on the treble recorder, *PRS* uses a Sonatine, written in serial form in 1966 by the Viennese composer Robert Schollum, to show how these fingerings can be used in a variety of contexts both to facilitate playing and – more importantly – to achieve the most effective interpretation of those phrases in which the high F sharps appear.

I have a strong recommendation to make to recorder players who, after finishing *Introduction to the Recorder,* have, ideally with a teacher and constantly gaining experience in consort and chamber-music playing, worked all the way through this combined *RT* and *PB*. It is that they should then for the time being make no further deliberate attempt to acquire new technical skills. With their teachers, or *PRS*, or both, they should concentrate on the process of using their technical knowledge and ability for the purpose of responding to their growing perceptions of the significance of the music they play, its historic background and the composers' intentions. The objective is to achieve greater expressivity and more developed rhetorical powers in their playing (see *PRS,* Ch. 1). Recorder technique is a dangerously fascinating subject, and the smaller recorders in particular lend themselves to displays of empty virtuosity which can be indulged in when playing early seventeenth-century canzonas and sonatas, Vivaldi concertos, the nineteenth-century csakan repertoire (see pp. 142–3) and many twentieth-century compositions. Younger recorder players often allow themselves to be seduced into nimble-fingered virtuosity while they are still unable to express and communicate the meaning and beauty of a simple folk-tune or a Schubert song arrangement. Technique as an end in itself, without musicianship, is a dead end.

Many amateur recorder players, perhaps possessing just one treble recorder, may well derive all the enjoyment they are seeking in having cultivated their playing to the level implied by the title of this book. But, with practice and experience, they may hone their technique and develop their musical understanding and adventurousness to the 'advanced' level associated with professional playing. There are many worlds to conquer. I have added at the end of this third edition of *Recorder Technique* a short section (Appendix 3) describing the delights waiting to be discovered in these further regions.

Anthony Rowland-Jones
Cambridge
September, 2003

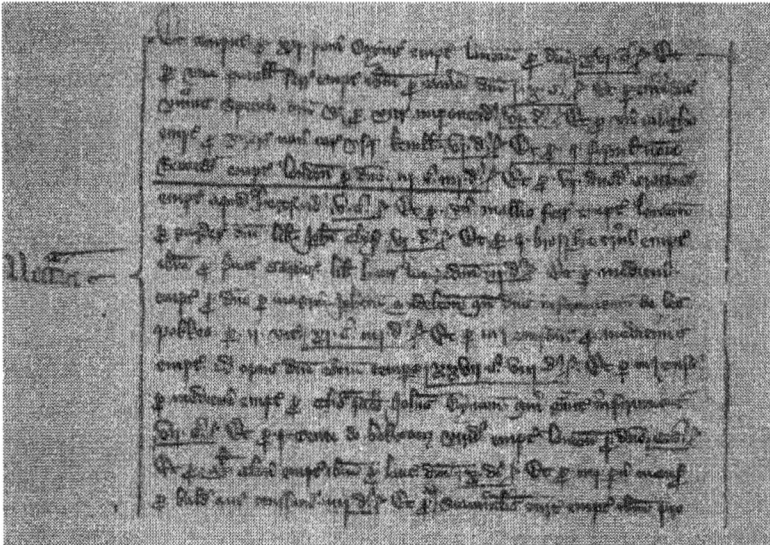

Here, reproduced by courtesy of the Keeper of Public Records, is the earliest known documentation of the word 'recorder' – spelt with an '-our' ending, now represented by '-er'. It is at the London Public Records Office in the household accounts (folio 16v) kept for the Earl of Derby, later King Henry IV, and entered on 30th September, 1388. The underlined section reads 'and for one flute by name of Recorder bought in London for my lord, three shillings and four pence' – a tidy sum, being about £500 nowadays. It seems that the recorder has always been taken up by cultivated and enthusiastic amateurs, for whom this book is mainly intended. Below is the word 'recordour' itself, enlarged:

I

KNOWING YOUR INSTRUMENT

There comes a point in the process of learning to play the recorder where, in a sense, you have to go back to the beginning. A recorder player, however skilful his technique, cannot play at his best unless he knows his instrument's qualities, strengths and weaknesses. This opening chapter is intended to increase your knowledge about recorders generally and how they are played, and to help you establish a rapport with your own instrument, or instruments, a prerequisite to good performance.

A recorder is basically an open tube blown at one end in which sound is produced by the impinging of an airstream shaped by a windway upon an edge (the 'labium edge') formed by the chamfering of the surface of the tube. This principle of sound formation is used for the flute, with the difference that a flute player shapes the airstream with his lips. A sheet of paper, such as a page of this book, can be made to produce an edge-tone: hold it about a quarter of an inch from the lips, in a horizontal position. Now blow softly a very thin stream of air directly on to the edge, and, with adjustment, a quiet wavering squeak will result. This squeak is caused by the formation of eddies on each side of the sheet of paper which produce regular alternations of pressure and set the air around vibrating – for further details and diagrams consult books such as *Music and Sound* by L.S. Lloyd (Oxford, 1951), and, for a full scientific analysis, John Martin's *The Acoustics of the Recorder* (Moeck, Ed. 4054, Celle, 1994). In the flute and the recorder these vibrations are modified by being 'coupled' to a tube the sounding length of which may be altered by opening and closing holes in it with the fingers and thumb. The recorder uses eight such holes, although the lower two holes are doubled to facilitate the production of semitones, at least in modern and some late baroque instruments.

Experiment further with the edge of the sheet of paper by blowing even more softly and holding it a little further away from the mouth. This will produce a very quiet edge-tone of low enough pitch to be identified on the piano, illustrating the principle that the softer one blows the lower the note, and vice versa. This principle is used to obtain high notes on the flageolet (which normally has six finger-holes), and on the tabor-pipe, which, with a long narrow bore that facilitates the production of harmonics, can produce two octaves from three holes by the use of stronger articulations and overblowing. Unless the cross-sectional area of the windway can be controlled (as in the lips of a flute player), overblowing means more air, and more air creates more sound (see Chapter II), so on the flageolet the upper octave must needs be louder than the lower. The formation of harmonics on a wind instrument can, however, be achieved without any increase of breath input by opening a small hole (octave-hole or 'speaker') between the source of vibration and the first finger-hole; on the recorder this is usually done by partially opening the thumb-hole. The superiority of the recorder over other end-blown flutes lies in its ability to play notes of the upper octave more softly than those of the lower octave. Recorder players must exploit this facility to the full in response to the needs of the music they play.

RECORDER TECHNIQUE

The windway of a recorder is formed by the insertion of an incised plug or block (whence the German name 'Blockflöte') into the blown end of the tube, which is generally made beak-shaped (whence 'flûte-à-bec') to fit between the lips. This block is made of a wood such as red cedar which does not swell much with moistening. The opening of the windway opposite the edge is chamfered slightly to direct the air in the best way against the edge; this process is called 'voicing'.

It is in the skill and understanding with which the craftsman matches the voicing to the nature of the piece of wood he is working with, and to its future maturing as a musical instrument, that the hand-made wood recorder is so superior to a machine-made instrument, although misjudgement or bad luck could result in a hand-made recorder being a very poor thing. The most critical factor in voicing is in the way the edge divides the air into two parts, one vibrating in the bore, the other escaping along the top of the instrument. An uneven division of air favours the tone of the lower notes of the instrument and minimises differences in quality between the notes of this register, but this voicing makes it difficult to get good high notes, which are better produced with an equal parting of the airstream. The distance between the opening of the windway and the labium edge, known as the 'cut-up', is also a factor in tone production, the higher register being favoured by closeness, although too close a voicing stifles the tone: if this distance is made greater the lower notes are favoured, although too great a distance means that less air is made to sound, so causing 'fluffiness'. The cross-sectional area and profile of the windway affects tone because this determines the amount of breath needed to make a note. Many other facets of construction affect tone-quality and volume, such as the height and angle of the window walls, the breadth or narrowness of the window and the labium (is it flat or curved?), the shape of the windway (parallel or converging,wide or narrow, high or shallow), the thickness of the walls of the bore, the undercutting of the finger-holes, and, especially, the profile of the bore. This profile may be round or oval, cylindrical or conical, or (as with most recorders) a highly complex combination along the bore of cylindrical, and less or more inwardly tapering and outwardly tapering sections; the bell end of the bore at the foot of the instrument may have a slight flare, and some recorders have a 'choke bore', i.e. the lower part of the bore before the bell is shaped with inward and then outward conicity.

It is important to consider these factors because the maker of the instrument will have had a particular tone-quality in mind in constructing his instrument, and a player is at odds with his instrument if he does not identify and nurture this tone. The best tone may be achieved with lowish breath input and pressure, or, if the windway opening is narrow, with a rather higher breath input and pressure. The player must experiment to know where the instrument responds best across its range. If the recorder is properly looked after (see below), tone may improve with age, but it will deteriorate when the thumb-hole becomes worn and needs re-bushing, or when the edge and chamfers need sharpening, and revoicing by the maker is required (see below).

Although voicing in relation to bore is paramount, tone-qualities are also associated with the material of which the instrument is made. As Francis Bacon put it, 'When the sound is created between the blast of the mouth and the air of the pipe, it has nevertheless some communication with the matter of the sides of the pipe, and the spirits in them contained'

(*Natural History*, cent. II § 167). Wood is undoubtedly the most satisfactory material for making recorders. Bacon suggested that 'it were good to try recorders and hunters' horns of brass, what the sound would be' (cent. III § 234). The effect would in fact not be pleasant, since brass has a ringing tone of its own which would react favourably to some notes and unfavourably to others, resulting in inequality and hardness. Ivory tends to produce an elegant but perhaps rather hard tone-quality. Despite their weight, and sometimes (even after long seasoning and careful selection) a tendency to crack, very hard woods make the best recorders, although they are more difficult and time-taking for an instrument maker to work with, and therefore more expensive. They can be voiced with sharp, firm, long-lasting labium edges; softer woods deteriorate more quickly, and absorb or dampen sound. The best wood for recorders has no knots and a close, parallel grain that allows a surface to stay smooth even under conditions of frequent wetting and drying, without cracking, splintering or swelling. Even microscopic splintering or mis-shapenness at the windway, edge, bore, or finger-holes will cause imperfections of tone. The woods that most nearly meet these requirements are expensive hardwoods, such as box, palisander, rosewood, olive, and blackwood or ebony. Slightly softer woods such as maple, plum, pear, and cherry are also suitable for recorder making (for types of wood used in making recorders see Appendix 2). Woods such as maple can be made impermeable to moisture by heat treatment followed by impregnation with paraffin wax. Such instruments are more stable and less likely to crack, but they are somehow less satisfying to play upon than naturally seasoned wood with its greater individuality and vitality. Although one may have a preference towards, say, box or rosewood, some makers assert that the hardwoods listed above do not each produce a characteristic tone-quality, i.e. that the differences in tone between instruments made by the same maker depend entirely on the subtle relationship between voicing and the nature of the piece of wood used for each instrument. Other makers, however, feel that there is a generic difference between all their instruments made from say, box (the eighteenth-century favourite, though it is liable to crack) and, say, rosewood (a modern favourite, although some people's lips are allergic to it).

A further vital factor affecting a player's approach to his instrument is the fingering system for which the instrument is designed. With the demise of 'German fingering' (0 123 4−−− for B♭, but 0 123 −567 for B♮) modern recorders are all now constructed to achieve good intonation with the first and second octave normal fingerings familiar to readers of this book (see inside back cover of *Introduction to the Recorder* or the fingering chart provided with a new recorder). This is not necessarily the case with recorders which are replicas of Renaissance instruments or of even some baroque instruments (see below).

'Normal' fingerings are in any case as much a compromise as equal temperament in keyboard tuning, and makers will expect players beyond the elementary level to accommodate intonation to changes of key. For example, normal C♯ may be good as the leading note in D major, but slightly sharp as the major third in A major. Moreover, the instrument maker may not have succeeded in the extremely difficult task of getting all the normal fingerings true to equal temperament (if that is what he is aiming at): an 'alternative fingering' then has to become the normal fingering for that note. For each instrument the best fingering for each note must be discovered: hopefully it will accord with normal fingering for most circumstances. Notes above top F" are liable to need a particular fingering for each recorder. This is the case especially with bass recorders and Renaissance recorders. Unusual fingerings required for each instrument should be noted on a card and kept with the recorder for reference. These considerations apply not only to intonation but also to tone. A note may be in tune with normal fingering but poor or obtrusive in tone-quality. Such a problem may possibly be cured by a slight change in breath input, but occasionally the player is better off by always using an alternative fingering for the bad note. This often applies to bass instruments; and small recorders such as the sopranino in F and the little garklein in C are difficult to construct absolutely in tune, although intonation and tonal faults are less noticeable on high-pitched instruments.

Having to make corrections for intonation or tone may be tolerable on bass and high instruments, but you would be overburdening yourself if you had to remember continually to make substantial adjustments on your main solo instruments. The maker might be prepared to re-tune the instrument if you are absolutely certain that it is a poor one (and you need to get a reliable second opinion about this). Or you can, if you are sure of yourself both in ear and hand, re-tune your own instrument (see references in Appendix 2). Otherwise you would do better to obtain another instrument rather than engage in a constant struggle against odds. But it is the case that many players have to go through a love-hate relationship with their instrument before coming to terms with it. Assuming that their instrument is reasonably good, they at first accept what it tells them in response to 'normal' fingering. As they get beyond the first stage of recorder playing, they become more critical and make more demands on the expressiveness of their instrument. Then they begin to realise imperfections: possibly their own sense of intonation improves (although the opposite happens to some players who become convinced that, for example, their recorder's high E' is in tune when it is not). This is the point at which advice from an experienced player is essential, as to whether to persist (which is usually the case) or whether to change instruments (rarely). They then discover, or are shown, how to put things right, sometimes by quite small modifications in breath input or tonguing, without re-fingering. Finally, these modifications become instinctive, and players will automatically make them upon handling a particular recorder, without consciously remembering what each instrument needs. This is an important part of recorder playing, for no recorder is perfect.

The qualities of recorders vary considerably from one maker to another, since the variables in designing and building a recorder are enormous. This is why consorts of instruments by one maker often sound better than consorts of instruments by different makers. Yet the same maker making two treble recorders in the same material is likely to produce two different-sounding instruments. Even plastic machine-made recorders by the same producer contrive to have individual qualities. It is one of the joys, as well as one of the problems, of recorder players that instruments are so different.

Historical differences in recorders

Most recorders available in shops are based on principles of design not greatly different from eighteenth-century models, so-called 'modern baroque'. They are available in six or more sizes in F and C at modern orchestral pitch (a' = 440 Hertz). This should be 'warmed up' pitch, and not the flatter note produced when a recorder is cold (for example in a shop). Eighteenth-century pitch was, at a rough approximation, a semitone lower, and makers today are making instruments at 'low pitch' a' = 415 - although even that differs from many historical originals: but this is the pitch now generally accepted for performances of baroque music (see Fred Morgan's article in *Early Music*, cited in Appendix 2). Woodwind instruments generally produce a richer, deeper, more rounded tone at low pitches, while violins and pianos become more brilliant and louder at higher pitches. A modern recorder will never sound quite like a baroque recorder because of this pitch difference, and for many other reasons.

While modern recorders have F and C as their lowest notes, Renaissance, and possibly also medieval recorders, were often pitched in G, A and D, at least down to tenor (in C). Praetorius (1619) refers to a bass in B♭; and several other sizes can be obtained from modern makers. In the eighteenth century, music was written for the sixth-flute (descant in D) the fourth-flute in B♭ and the voice-flute (alto/tenor in D). Although such instruments in principle require no special techniques not covered in this book, they present challenges in reading or transposition which a fully-trained recorder player must eventually master (see pp. 112–13 and Veilhan's book cited in Appendix 2). Musicians in the eighteenth century, and more so in earlier periods, must have been adept at reading in many different clefs, and Renaissance and even baroque musicians would have abhorred our multiple ledger lines (see, for example, p. 78).

Baroque recorders

Apart from pitch, and the wider range of instruments available, the baroque recorder varies from 'modern baroque' in its voicing and fingerings. The reforms made by the Hotteterre family and other makers of the seventeenth century resulted in recorders being made with a cylindrical head, and a body and foot with a narrower, double-conical bore (tapering, then widening). This in itself favoured high notes and increased the compass to cover the high ranges much used by Bach and Telemann (e.g. the second movement of the second Brandenburg Concerto – *PB*, Ex. 45). This late baroque type of recorder is made in three parts, with strengthening at the two joints being both a necessity and an ornament – the bulges and rings which delightfully reflect the decorative tastes of the time. The three sections enabled makers to use shorter pieces of wood, aiding selection and accuracy of internal finish. The voicing favoured the higher harmonics in the positioning of the edge in relation to the windway opening. The characteristic of baroque recorders most affecting technique, however, is the vertical shallowness of the windway exit, which offers greater resistance to breath pressure. This causes less air to be used in making a note, resulting in less sound (see Chapter II). Makers partly compensated for this by widening the breadth of the windway and labium edge, which required them both to be arc-shaped, matching the exterior curve of the head section and avoiding leaving too little thickness of wood at the sides of the windway, which, even so, was often protected by encasing in ivory. Players likewise compensated by using higher breath pressures. There are two great advantages of this design. The first is that it is less difficult (less 'clickish') to cross register-breaks. The second, even more important, is that it results in greater flexibility, i.e. a note can be played louder or softer without going out of tune, so increasing the recorder's expressive range with less recourse to some of the intonation-control techniques discussed later in this book. Baroque instrumental music, like baroque opera, is highly expressive and emotional, and even on a baroque recorder the volume range that should be used is beyond the flexibility available in using only normal fingerings. A baroque-designed instrument is ultimately therefore no easier to play than a 'modern baroque' recorder, but its flexibility encourages a style that comes less naturally when playing the modern recorder.

The baroque recorder tends to be rather reedier in tone than its modern derivative, which has a more open tone. The volume is likely to be less than the modern recorder at full breath input, although volume in itself is not always an advantage – what matters is penetration of tone. The modern recorder has many advantages if it can give a good tone-quality at low breath input, and yet, with shading, a strong tone at high pressure. What is lost in flexibility is gained in variety. On the purely practical side, the modern design with the vertically deep windway exit, apart from being easier to make, does not have such a propensity to clog up with moisture as happens with baroque voicing. A baroque recorder needs constant care to prevent fluffiness, particularly on those all-important high notes which it is designed to play so beautifully. Professional players, most of whom naturally choose the baroque recorder to play baroque music, may need to have a second treble recorder ready and warmed up for use in the second part of a recital because of the danger of clogging up, particularly if the atmosphere is humid. Many recorder makers now make 'baroque' recorders based closely on eighteenth-century models, with baroque voicing. It is vital for the player to know how his recorder is voiced or he could play all the while at the wrong breath pressure. These makers do not necessarily, however, copy baroque fingering. The first difference is that baroque makers up to the time of Bressan (fl. 1685–1731) seem rarely to have used double holes on the bottom two fingerings (see pp. 114 and 130), although Hotteterre (1707) mentions their availability. This is because half-holing techniques during the Renaissance and baroque periods were much more widely used on all fingers than we use nowadays. Modern makers of baroque recorders are usually prepared to provide double holes.

The other fingering differences are rarely copied, for players and makers generally agree that they are a disadvantage. Hotteterre's fingering chart shows finger 6 down for most notes, presumably copied from the normal technique of the one-keyed flute. This is partly to support the instrument (baroque instruments do not have the modern advantage of a thumb-rest – see below), but the instrument would have been built to be in tune with that 'buttress' fingering. Later baroque fingering charts show B♭ as 0 123 4–6–, i.e. without the little finger, whereas modern fingering, and that used by most makers of baroque instruments, has the little finger down for low B♭, facilitating the intonation of B♮ and high B♭'.

Renaissance recorders

The greatly increased interest in Renaissance music, especially instrumental music, has given an impetus to the production of recorders based on sixteenth-century models and on illustrations. The outstanding differences between baroque and Renaissance recorders is that the latter are usually built in one piece (but often copied with one or even two joints), and, generalising (for there are many variations), have a wider, more cylindrical bore (see Virdung's illustrations of 1511). This, together with the more open voicing, facilitates the production of the lower notes, but reduces range – though high notes of dubious quality can be discovered. The tone-quality is open, not reedy, and the volume is, again considerably generalising, 'beefy' and loud, more obviously so in the lowest notes. Sometimes the tone may sound a trifle coarse, but is less noticeable in ensemble playing – recorders were not generally considered to be solo instruments in the Renaissance period. Yet the voicing used in modern copies allows a sweet tonal response at lower breath inputs, perhaps because sixteenth-century writers demand that recorder players should respond to different moods of music as much as if they were singers and the music had words. At higher levels of tonguing, Renaissance recorders tend to 'chiff', giving a percussive articulation to each note: it is uncertain how common this usage was, though it sounds effective in Renaissance dance music. It can easily be avoided by using light tonguings, and, as we can see from Sylvestro Ganassi's recorder tutor *Fontegara* (Venice, 1535), and later sixteenth-century manuals, these were even more strongly advocated in the Renaissance than they were in later periods.

Copies of Renaissance recorders do to some extent use historical fingerings, and these are mentioned in the chapters on fingering in this book. The main differences are in E♭, F♯, G' (though not always), C♯', and D'.

On the sixteenth-century wide-bore recorder, E♭' or E' were regarded as the highest notes, and it is often impossible to get F" even though G" may be obtainable. Some instruments, however, were made with slightly narrower complex bores, as Ganassi found fingerings for two and a half octaves. In the early seventeenth century, top C" on the descant was evidently expected to be available, as the solo variations by Van Eyck frequently require it. Models of Renaissance recorders are made with the more complex bore profile which provides this note, but with a rather less extrovert sound. Perhaps this sound, which is pure, round, and rather dispassionate, and one ideal for consort music, should be thought of as the more usual late Renaissance and earlier seventeenth-century sound.

Because they require more air to respond to the voicing and fill the wide bore, larger Renaissance recorders might at first make the player feel a little breathless. It is therefore necessary to fill the lungs more deliberately, and to look for more phrasing points in the music at which one can take a breath if needed. This is especially true of the big bass instruments, which almost seem to swallow the player's breath.

Renaissance pitch was perhaps not greatly different from modern pitch, although it was far less standardised and tended to be higher. Most copies of Renaissance recorders are therefore made at a' = 440, though high-pitch recorders are available, usually a semitone above modern pitch.

Renaissance tenor and bass recorders have keys for the bottom note with the keywork protected by a perforated wooden cover called a 'fontanelle'. This can be removed when the keywork needs servicing. It does mean, however, that bottom C♯ (F♯) is missing. These instruments are also heavier and differently balanced, in comparison with baroque recorders. Support becomes a problem, for the tenor in particular, and a thumb-rest, though desirable, is not authentic. If the bass transverse flute is an example, Renaissance wind players seemed quite prepared to put up with some physical discomfort as part of their playing. This somehow fits in with the outgoing quality of Renaissance recorders, yet, on the other hand, *squisitezza* (exquisiteness) was equally demanded of the Renaissance player. Playing Renaissance instruments in Renaissance music calls for a different mental approach, which ultimately can only be achieved by developing a historical sense, and by listening to and understanding music of the period (see Appendix 3).

Medieval recorders

Our knowledge of the recorder in the fifteenth century, and more so in the fourteenth century, remains hazy despite the considerable recent research referred to in Appendix 2. So far, archaeology has unearthed only two complete medieval recorders. One, now belonging to the Gemeentemuseum at The Hague, was discarded into the moat of a fortified manor-house near Dordrecht, and the other found in a latrine under a house in Göttingen, a university town in Lower Saxony. Both are damaged and unplayable; the Dordrecht recorder has tenons at each end to which were once fitted a foot or bell, and a mouthpiece section, and a slice of the Göttingen recorder has split off from the mouthpiece. Although both are of fruitwood and roughly soprano size, they differ considerably in design, the Dordrecht recorder being cylindrical and the Göttingen one having a contracting conical bore. Both recorders probably date from the late fourteenth century. Further fragments of fourteenth-century instruments have been found in Germany, one at Würzburg and the others at Esslingen, near Stuttgart.

The English word 'Recordour', which has no parallel in other languages, is first documented in 1388 when a quite costly recorder was purchased in London for the Earl of Derby, later King Henry IV (see p. 4), but it does not appear in English literature until some time after 1400. The earliest unambiguous representations of recorders in Spanish and French painting and sculpture date from the decades 1390 to 1410, but a few uncertain representations in English and German stone and wood carvings can be found from the earlier fourteenth century. Iconographic representations of the recorder become more common as the fifteenth century progresses, particularly in Catalan Spain. Interestingly, most of the English examples are of tenor recorders, while early representations from other countries are usually of cylindrical soprano-sized recorders. Recorders of alto size with flared bells are shown in a fresco by Francesco Cossa in Ferrara completed in 1470. But none of this tells us how and when recorders were played, although paintings from the fifteenth century nearly always show them in combination with voices (recorders may have played a highly decorated version of a singer's melody while he rested), and with soft instruments such as the harp, lute and fiddle.

Conjectural reconstructions of the Dordrecht recorder suggest that at least this medieval recorder had a sweet, unpowerful tone-quality, and, having a narrow windway and labium, was played with a fairly high breath pressure, well suited to outdoor performance. The range was probably an octave and a half. The finger-holes are large, which facilitates 'half-holing', better referred to as 'partial venting'. This technique is shown in playing of a double pipe in a fresco in Assisi by Simone Martini from 1330 (p. 68), and is referred to by Ganassi and in other manuals. Very flimsy evidence regarding articulation suggests that medieval players used the same light tonguings as were used in the sixteenth century, that is to say groupings of 'd', 'l' and 'r', avoiding stronger tonguings such as 't', 'k' and 'g'. Each note was articulated, even at fast speeds. It seems likely that slurring did not become a common practice until after 1600.

Characteristics of recorders other than descant or treble

A reader of this book who has followed all the advice in *Introduction to the Recorder* will probably possess a treble (alto) recorder in F and a descant (soprano) recorder in C. To achieve versatility in recorder playing, he would need to extend this range. This section therefore identifies problems involved in playing the other sizes of recorders generally available, and is followed by a section on choosing a recorder, which can be applied to buying any new recorder. It is quite usual at this stage for a player to want a better treble or descant than the cheap one he may have started with.

Tenor recorders

A descant player who also plays treble will have little difficulty playing tenor recorder. In fact the tenor is easier to play than the descant. The chief importance of both instruments is as members of the recorder consort – but while there is a substantial repertoire of music in three or more parts without descant, very few consorts are without tenor. It plays the third part in the 4-foot SATB consort and the top line in the 8-foot consort with bass, great bass in C and contra-bass in F (consorts are described by the sounding length of an organ pipe for the C which forms the consort's lowest note, or the next C below the consort's lowest note, so a consort with a tenor recorder on the bottom line would be a 2-foot consort). The descant has a small solo repertoire of its own, including Van Eyck and the eighteenth-century sixth-flute concertos (for descant in D) as well as a growing repertoire of more recent music; the tenor recorder is much softer, and its tone merges with other instruments, making it of more limited value as a solo instrument with keyboard or strings (though it sounds well with guitar). Although the main role of both instruments is in consort or other early music groups, the descant is harder to manage; it is often required to lead, but it needs to be played at low breath input to avoid coarseness, shrillness, and imbalance in the ensemble, and yet remain expressive and under complete control. The tenor's subdued and creamy tone is much simpler to achieve, and it is an easier instrument to control. If a player's interests were limited to consort music, he would be as well rewarded in playing only the tenor as in playing only the treble.

The one problem encountered with the tenor, especially for players with small hands, is in stretching the fingers to cover the holes. Some makers offset the third hole to the left of centre, which helps to solve the problem, though it mars the appearance of the instrument. Many provide a key for bottom C. This has the disadvantage that, unless a double key is provided, C$\sharp$ is missing. It also makes intonation control with the little finger difficult to manage. It is better to try to stretch, and become used to it, than to have a C key.

Tenor recorders tend to lack clarity of tone on their highest notes, although these are not greatly used in consort music. Attempts were made by Thomas Stanesby about 1732 to improve and revive the tenor (with its advantage of being in C like oboes) to challenge the treble as the main solo recorder; but the treble size of recorder gives the best compromise between pungency and sweetness of tone, between carrying power and blending with other instruments, and between richness in the lowest notes and delicacy in the highest. It is important for a treble player first tackling a tenor to realise and accept the fact that it is an instrument of fewer potentialities than the treble, despite what can be ravishing beauty of tone.

Sopranino recorders

It is more than likely that soon after (or even before) becoming a player of treble, descant, and tenor recorders, you will have succumbed to the charm – and comparative cheapness – of the sopranino recorder in F. It is, however, of limited value. As 'flauto piccolo' it makes a number of delightful appearances in the eighteenth century to accompany the soprano voice, mainly in ornithological contexts, or even, grotesquely, the bass voice (e.g. 'O ruddier than the cherry' in Handel's *Acis and Galatea*). Vivaldi wrote three spectacularly difficult flautino concertos. It appears in Monteverdi's wide-ranging instrumental ensemble for *Orfeo*. Modern recorder ensemble music, or arrangements, sometimes require the treble player to switch to sopranino, with considerable effect, and immense excitement is similarly produced in the last movement *(Tarantella)* of Gordon Jacob's Suite for recorder and strings (*PB*, Ex. 41).

Apart from the possibility of poor tuning already mentioned, the main technical problem with the sopranino, and even more with the tiny 'garklein' in C above it, is the bunching of the fingers, especially for a player with broad finger-tips. For an A'–G' trill – 123 456*7, for example, fingers 5 and 7 have to be pulled away from 6, while still covering their holes, in order to allow the trilling finger room to operate. Yet the brilliance of the upper octave calls for display, and therefore for quick and accurate fingering. The tone of the low notes is, of course, thin, though vibrato can give them warmth.

Bass recorders

A bass recorder (more correctly 'basset') in F is needed to complete the normal consort quartet. It is incredible how one bass recorder, sounding comparatively weak on its own, adds a richness of sound, moulds good intonation, and makes the ensemble more coherent, even when there is more than one higher instrument to a part. Given a bass recorder which is reasonably in tune (and many are not), the bass is no more difficult to play than a tenor for the purposes of most consort music. But it does involve reading the bass instead of the treble clef, and the possibility of having to read up an octave if the part goes below bottom F. To play the bass well calls for a great deal of musicianship.

High notes on the bass recorder above D' or Eb' tend to be impure in tone-quality and are likely to need modified fingerings (these are mentioned later in this book). Many basses can be coaxed up to the middle of the third octave (Bb" or B♮") with the use of 'leaking' fingerings.

Renaissance makers cleverly used oblique drilling of the holes to enable the thumb and six fingers to cover their holes directly, using a key only for the bottom note, protected by a massive fontanelle. The key is beautifully shaped rather like a swallow-tail to accommodate both left- and right-handed players. (Medieval and Renaissance angel recorder players are about equally divided as to which hand is in the lower position). Modern makers have less compunction about using keys, so that perhaps only the middle fingers of each hand directly cover their holes. This eradicates problems of stretch. Generally speaking, the fewer keys the better (but see below). They affect the resonance of the wood, and can be noisy in operation, need maintaining, and spoil the simple design of the instrument. Bass recorders, even though made of lighter hardwoods such as pearwood or maple, are heavy, and there is a problem of support, usually solved with the use of a sling as well as a thumb-rest. The sling should be adjusted so that the instrument can rest on the right thumb and lower lip without pressure, and so that no support whatsoever is given by the fingers used for playing, or by the left thumb.

Basses are made either with a metal crook (or 'bocal'), or with direct blow into the windway which is then sometimes situated at the back of the instrument facing towards the player. Some makers bend the recorder through about 45°('knick-bass') to avoid undue stretching of the right arm. I strongly advocate a direct blow F-bass, for the distance and directness from the mouth to the tone-creating edge is critical to achieve quick speaking and good tone control. There must be a key for the lowest note, as the hole is out of reach of the little finger, but it should be double to obtain both F and F♯. A further key, or double hole, is desirable to obtain G♯, as the G♯ obtained by half-holing 6 is weak in timbre. These three keys can serve a useful additional purpose for tone and intonation control in the second octave; they may even help to make an upper note speak which otherwise would be unreliable or else missing altogether. Manipulating these keys can initially cause strain on the little finger, which has to get used to operating in different positions – this is more difficult than using half-holes on the tenor because of the resistance offered by the necessary springing of the keys. If the springing is too firm it is a simple job for an instrument maker to adjust it.

Great basses in C, an octave below the tenor, are needed if a bass part goes below F, and they also take the tenor line (played as if tenor recorders) in the 8-foot consort. Even one great bass will add considerably to the sonority of a consort, although ideally the bass instruments in a consort should outnumber the treble instruments, to prevent the upper parts dominating. With an instrument four feet long, a crook cannot be dispensed with, so allowance has to be made for a small delay between tonguing and note-production: the player has to blow fractionally ahead of the beat. With such a large instrument, support is a problem, for a sling, while transferring weight, does not control the swing of the instrument. It is best to fit some form of foot spike so that the recorder rests on the floor (watch that the spike does not slip – a rubber end helps) and then to adopt a sitting position in which either the recorder is vertical, or if not, it leans against the inside of your thigh. The vertical position (between the legs) makes it more difficult to see your music. Either way, the music stand has to be carefully adjusted and placed before you begin to play, especially if you wear variable-focus spectacles.

Several makers produce the contra-bass in F, an octave below the F-bass, including one who supplies a cheaper – but no less effective – model which is square in cross-section, like a large organ pipe, rather than round. The contra-bass is over six feet high, has a long (adjustable) crook, and is supported on the ground. A great deal of blowing is needed to produce remarkably little noise from such a giant – it seems at first to swallow air from your lungs. The articulation delay is more than that of the great bass in C, and needs to be well 'thought through', especially with the lowest notes which are very slow-speaking. The effect of these large instruments in a consort is stunning.

Praetorius mentions and illustrates in his Plate IX the contra-bass recorder in F, to us confusingly calling it a 'Great bass', his 'Bass' being in B♭, and our 'normal' F bass being called 'Basset'. He does not refer to the sub-contra-bass in C, a huge recorder which existed in the sixteenth century and is now built by several makers of Renaissance recorders.

Purchasing a recorder

If you want to get the best, you will probably have to order an instrument from a world-famous maker with a long waiting list. You then run the risk that the instrument when it arrives may disappoint you. If both you, and your teacher or experienced advisers, are really convinced that a poor instrument has slipped through, send it back and ask for a replacement. The maker will not want to risk his reputation. Ideally you can arrange with the maker, if he is willing, to visit him when your turn comes up, and, with your adviser, choose from a batch.

Specialist shops in most western countries now maintain excellent selections of hand-finished recorders by a variety of makers. The shop should allow you to try several recorders by different makers, and when you know what you want, then to try several apparently identical recorders by the same maker. If the shop will not let you do this, go somewhere else.

Take with you your own instrument nearest in size, provided it is one you know to be in good pitch and tuning, and an experienced adviser. Having eliminated all but three or four instruments by the same maker test them as follows:

Pitch Compare central notes with your own instrument, cold against cold.

Tone Carefullyplay longish notes in the middle of the lower octave, and in the middle of the upper octave, preferably into a corner where the sound reflects back. If you do not like the sound, discard the instrument.

Tuning The instrument should be in tune with itself, and with your own recorder. Check first C to C', A to A' and D to D'. If you are satisfied with this test, play the sequence C♯–D♯–E–F♯'–G♯', especially making sure the last interval is not too wide on normal fingerings. Quite a few recorders are so badly out on this sequence that their imperfections are displayed without further ado.

Speech Rapidly repeated staccato C♯'s will reveal if a recorder is slow in speech. With correct tonguing, a recorder should give pure tone instantaneously when breathed into, but give the instrument a chance by using light tonguing. Try the speed of reaction and the strength of low notes such as F and forked fingerings such as B♭. Try a few high notes (E', F", G") or get your adviser to try them, for your experience of thumbing will be less than his. As the instruments you are trying are not warmed up, make allowances for possible clogging on these high notes.

Weak notes and 'Wolf-notes' Examine the lower octave again (all notes chromatically) for evenness of quality. A note may be weak beyond redemption (?B), or some notes may be unstable with an in-built vibrato of their own (?G). Bass instruments are more liable to such faults than trebles.

Volume and flexibility Make crescendos on F♯, C, and C' (others if you like) to see how loud you can go before the note breaks and, in the first part of the crescendo how much the pitch changes. Judge how resistant the voicing is. Is it what you want?

Alternative fingerings See that alternatives G', E, and D are usable as regards intonation and tone-quality.

Construction Check that the wood is of close parallel grain with no knots. Look for incipient cracks, and see there are no loose splinters of wood round the windway, edge and holes. Joints should be tight, smooth, and snug, the plug not loose to the touch, and the instrument well balanced as you feel it in your hands and under your fingers.

This check-list may seem long, but following it systematically should not take you more than three or four minutes for each instrument, and will help you to leave the shop well satisfied, even if you place the manager in a moral dilemma over the recorders you have discarded.

Care of the instrument

Good technique can never overcome the faults a recorder will develop if its not properly looked after. Pages 1–6 of Edward L. Kottick's *Tone and Intonation of the Recorder* make the same point and deal thoroughly with recorder maintenance. This section covers the main points in less detail.

First and foremost, keep your recorder in a stout box that shuts firmly. Any container that does not protect the recorder when the box is dropped is useless. Never leave a recorder on the floor or on a chair or perched on a music stand. Do not let a recorder get hot; heat dries out natural wood and makes a recorder made of impregnated wood sweat drops of paraffin wax.

After playing

After playing, *always* wipe the recorder bore dry with a mop or piece of material that does not shed fluff. Do not force a mop into a recorder nor push it into the head-piece up against the plug. A good recorder wiper is a linen handkerchief rolled diagonally and twisted gently through the bore of the instrument or put over small mop: it leaves no bits, dries moisture, and, above all, polishes the surface of the bore. Never use the slightest pressure or force, as this could deform the shape of the bore. A square of chamois leather on a weighted string is also an effective bore dryer, cleaner, and polisher. A sopranino made in one piece may have to be wiped dry with a pipe-cleaner, possibly doubled on itself; take great care to watch through the window and stop short of the plug. Bass recorder crooks should be shaken out, and left on their own to dry.

To keep the windway dry use a small, soft feather, such as a hen's feather. Take care not to let the feather push against the edge. Any accumulated deposit at the corners of the windway and the edge should be eased off, with infinite care, with the softest feather quill that will do the job. Leave the recorder in pieces to dry out. The day before a performance, or other playing session, a feather dipped in weak detergent solution may be passed through the windway to remove patches of grease which attract moisture, and immediately afterwards the windway should be washed through thoroughly with a little warm water so that no detergent whatsoever remains (it might damage the wood): shake out as much water as possible from the windway and bore, wipe the outside of the head-piece, use a dry feather in the windway, and allow the head-piece to dry out completely. This process should be carried out regularly, and at first frequently, with a shallow-windway baroque recorder. Combined with high wind-pressure in playing, this should prevent clogging. Never blow out a clogged recorder for this only spreads moisture; use a feather instead, or, if your instrument clogs while playing, suck sharply in. Warming up a recorder by breathing into it only defeats the object of dry warmth before playing. If you must do this, place your lips over the whole window/labium area and exhale gently.

After each playing or practising session, wipe the mouthpiece of your recorder where it has been in contact with the lips. This can be done with a soft moistened piece of material such as silk. Not doing it can lead to a build-up of detritus, which is especially unsightly on ivory-covered mouthpieces. To remove it, moisten it well with a wet piece of material and it can then usually be rubbed off, or, as a last resort, very carefully eased off with a finger-nail. Hold the head of the recorder downwards when you do this to avoid bits falling into the windway. When the mouthpiece has completely dried out, rub in a small drop of almond oil to nurture the dry wood.

Drying out the windway with a feather after each playing session should keep it clean, but if anything lodges in the windway, for example a piece of feather, cover the open end of the head with the palm of your hand and blow hard into the windway.

Sometimes the windway can become mis-shapen by bulging up of the windway floor, which is of course part of the softer wood of the plug. Especially with recorders with shallow, wide and arc-shaped windways of the late baroque design, this will first be felt as a need for a yet higher breath pressure to compensate for the constriction of the windway, and the instrument's tone-quality will become emasculated. Moreover, the constricted windway is more likely to become choked with breath condensation. If a windway has become domed, the changed shaped can be seen by looking through the windway into a light. Although some players, who share the craftsmanship of recorder makers, tap out the block and do a DIY operation, it is far better to return the whole instrument to the maker for what might in any case have been offered as a free first servicing. The problem can recur, but this is unlikely once the wood has settled in.

A more likely problem after several years of playing is that the sharpness of the labium edge deteriorates, affecting the clarity of tone-quality. The instrument then requires revoicing by the maker, who will at the same time check the windway and sharpen or adjust the chamfers at its exit, and if necessary recork the joints and re-bush the thumb-hole. If revoicing has to be carried out several times in the life of a recorder there could be a slight change for the worse in tone-quality as on each occasion the 'cut-up' distance from the windway exit to the labium edge will be slightly increased. Severe accidental damage to the labium edge may be irreparable.

Periodic oiling

Oil the bore of a recorder, other that one made of impregnated wood, when it is just played in and about twice a year thereafter – more frequently when the wood tends to soak up oil, less frequently with older recorders. Use a non-softening, non-acid, resinating plant oil such as banana, almond, or unboiled linseed (not olive): these oils leave a thin protecting film on the surface of the bore, helping to keep it smooth and polished. If too much oil is used it dries sticky and attracts fluff, as well as deadening the benign influence of the wood-spirits. If the outside of a recorder is varnished, oil cannot affect it either beneficially or adversely, although an old recorder with the varnish worn off does benefit from occasional oiling, and a new one looks smarter. An unvarnished recorder, in particular its head-section above the windway, needs to be well nurtured with oiling, especially when new. On no account let oil, or even your fingers, touch the tone-producing regions which must remain as pervious to moisture as possible: oil on the labium or edge and thereabouts encourages the formation of globules of condensation, destroying clarity of tone. It is important, too, to keep oil away from the plug which might be over-loosened by lubrication. It is a good idea to drop a small rolled-up ball of paper into the head before oiling to stop the mop from touching the block; up-end the head after oiling while the oil soaks in. When applying oil, warm it in the palm of the hand first so that it becomes thinner and penetrates the surface of the wood before drying. The recorder also should be absolutely dry and warm. Oil should be applied to the bore with a mop used only for that purpose.

A small paintbrush lightly dipped in oil will get at decorative turnery incisions in baroque recorders, the insides of the finger- and thumb-holes, and, with meticulous care, the upper parts of the window walls and of the wood above the windway opening – only a single stroke of the brush is needed high up here as allowance must be made for some of the oil spreading down as it soaks in. Don't oil ivory. If it needs cleaning, use a little lemon juice soaked into a soft rag.

Keywork will need occasional oiling with a sewing machine oil. Cork stops need a spot of lanolin. At long intervals leather pads will need replacing by an instrument repairer.

Joints

Joints should be airtight, and should be snug enough not to allow 'play' in the lower sections of the instrument, particularly the foot. Never hold the instrument by the foot joint, which weakens it. Instruments should both be assembled and taken to pieces by screwing gently but firmly in the direction of the lapping of the joint (clockwise), without any sideways force. With bass recorders which have complex key systems take care not to snag one key against another – some anticlockwise turning may be necessary. If cork joints are loose, they may be made to swell slightly with moistening, or can be burred with a pin: another method is to grease the cork and then warm it lightly over a match flame. Thread joints can be varied at will by winding off or adding thread; bobbins of soft and resilient waxed thread are obtainable from woodwind suppliers, or else cobbler's hemp rubbed with beeswax or soaked in melted candle wax may be used. If the inner section of a joint develops a hair-line crack, it should, as a temporary measure, be bound tightly between the lapping and the bottom of the joint with fine and inelastic wire such as five-amp fuse wire. A hair-line crack on the outer sleeve of a joint, or any larger crack, is more disturbing and the instrument should at once be returned to the maker to be repaired (e.g. to be fitted with a retaining ring) or replaced. If a cork joint becomes so worn that a section of the instrument is loose, this too is a case for hospital treatment at the maker's, not just first aid with pieces of thin paper. Cork joints can be preserved by applying lanolin, enough of which can be obtained inexpensively from a chemist to last the recorder's lifetime. Lanolin also makes a stiff cork joint easier to operate and it is a good idea to put some on the joints of brand-new instruments before assembling them. Soap or Vaseline have the same effect.

Thumb-hole wear

After a certain amount of use the thumb-hole of a wooden instrument may wear away with the rubbing of the thumb-nail on it. Experienced players do not 'thumb' violently so they are much less troubled with this disorder. With a badly worn thumb-hole it is difficult to judge the width of the space left between the thumb-nail and the edge of the instrument ('thumbing aperture') and high notes are therefore hard to form. Tone may be affected if the thumb-nail intrudes too deeply because of a worn hole. The instrument maker should then be asked to 're-bush' the thumb-hole, preferably with a hard ivory substitute.

Playing in

New wooden recorders need playing in, to break the wood gently to its task of maintaining its personality under varying conditions of temperature and humidity. However tempting it might be to go on, a player with a new instrument should stop playing after fifteen minutes for the first week or so of the recorder's life and dry the instrument thoroughly (swab and feathers) before putting it away unassembled. A new recorder should be played every day, increasing to half an hour in the second week. A month-old recorder properly played in will last out a normal playing session without danger of the wood cracking. With care, however, its tone will continue to improve as apparently it adapts itself to its owner and as the owner comes to recognise its qualities and idiosyncrasies.

Playing position

Playing position is described and illustrated in *Introduction to the Recorder*. But to recapitulate and develop:

Be relaxed in your body and arms, right down to the fingers and especially the thumb.

Never raise your shoulders, or become hunched.

Play with the recorder at 45° or less to the vertical, with the elbows beside but slightly away from the body.

Wrists should be low (think of your hands holding a soft ball of wool).

Finger tops from the main joint to the tip should be near horizontal, and fingers almost at right-angles to the instrument (as nearly as feels comfortable).

Looking down the instrument from the mouthpiece, the fingers form a sort of plateau (see *Intro* p.18 and illustration 6). This means that the position where the pad of finger covers its hole will vary in distance from the finger-tip, being furthest down for the third finger of the right hand. Picart's beautiful engraving of a recorder player's hands done for Hotteterre's 1707 *Principes* (see Appendix 2) shows a perfect playing position (see p. 114). All finger movements should be short in distance, quick, light, and economical.

Be seated comfortably in a firm chair without arms. Do not lean right back while playing: be slightly forwards to your music – or rather the audience, for the music stand should not come between you and them, dampening sound projection. But do not play the recorder from the side of the mouth, as this may impede the passage of air, and looks wrong. If you stand, adopt a stance in which you are balanced between both feet, one slightly forward and at a slight angle to the other. Standing helps breathing, but if other players are sitting, it can imply dominance. Consequently, you should stand for concerto, but sit for ensemble music (as a string quartet does). Remember that the baroque solo sonata is usually conceived as ensemble music with the bass equal in importance to the treble; if you prefer to stand, don't feel you are playing a concerto.

The recorder is supported by the right thumb and lower lip, the latter in a relaxed, slightly dropped position (see p. 33). Although the little finger of the left hand may rest on the body of the recorder to give lateral support, the operating fingers and left thumb should have nothing to do with supporting the recorder: all their attention is taken up by playing, and their movements must be unimpeded by other considerations. Basses need slings, great basses slings and floor contact; but all recorders, with the possible exception of the descant and sopranino, need a thumb-rest. Placing the thumb-rest depends on where each player feels it gives him the most relaxed support. This is usually under and between holes 4 and 5. The thumb-rest may be slightly at an angle, or even slightly off-centre. Before fixing it permanently, try it in various positions held temporarily with Sellotape or an elastic band. It is a common fault to put it too high in the first place, which allows the right-hand fingers to be held too obliquely to the recorder for efficient movement. Thumb-rests can be of cork, or cork-faced: they should not be metallic or hard where the thumb touches them. They have to be broad enough to give comfortable support in long use. Clarinet-type thumb-rests can be bought and, when you have experimented and decided on the best position, fixed with contact glue, not screws; some shops supply a small rubber cushion to fit over a clarinet thumb-rest. With a descant, the surface tension of the thumb may give just sufficient support if the instrument is light. Trebles and larger instruments ought to have fixed thumb-rests, despite their ugliness, for fine playing. Some makers supply a shaped piece of matching wood, with cork facing, for the owner of the instrument to glue on where it best suits him. Moving a thumb-rest previously fixed inevitably makes an unsightly mark.

Before playing, ensure that the finger-holes are in line with the centre of the windway. This looks best, and is probably the most comfortable position for your fingers; it will not affect tone if the holes are slightly out of line with the windway, but it will certainly do so if you do not properly cover a hole with the pad of a finger, or if a key is leaking. If you suspect the latter, take the head-joint off, cover tightly the bottom end of the bore (e.g. with your bare knee) and blow into the middle section, all fingers on as if for bottom F.

No air should emerge. If it does, shuffle your fingers and press each key in turn very hard to identify the fault. A key may need repadding.

The foot section should be carefully turned so that it best suits your little finger both for F and F♯. To be sure that the foot section is best placed for your hands, each time you assemble a non-keyed recorder hold it in a playing position with all the holes firmly covered except the right-hand little finger hole. Then bang the little finger hard down to cover both its holes. If the placing of the foot section is good, you should hear a clear percussive sound slightly flatter than G (or D for a tenor or descant). If the placing is not good, the sound will be muffled and the foot then needs turning slightly one way or the other. Then do the same banging, with the wrist in the swivel position (see p. 58), with the little finger covering just its half-hole. This should produce a clear-ringing percussive G or D. If this note is muffled, a little more adjustment will be required, until both notes sound good. When you have played the instrument for some while, you may find it helpful to make a small mark on the middle section and on the foot section at the joint so that alignment is always correct or very close to being correct. But still check it with little-finger banging.

During playing there is no need for the player to move much, except if he is leading, in which case he needs to convey to his ensemble, by small but clear movements, the start and finish of the music, time changes, and so on. If he is relaxed and lost in the music, a player will not be completely still, but will show his involvement by some spontaneous, almost unconscious movement. This should be above the waist, and should on no account penetrate to the feet, which may consciously have to be prevented from beating time. Avoid any excessive movement while playing, such as swinging the recorder around – this is distracting both to an audience and to other players. The pulse of the music, established in the second before starting, is an internal feeling, though shared by all the players in an ensemble. This realisation that a piece of music is a 'going concern' among all those involved (including the audience) is in itself very rewarding to the player.

II

BREATHING AND BREATH DELIVERY

Two factors affect how one breathes in order to play a wind instrument – first the expenditure of breath needed to make a note, and secondly the pressure required. In oboe playing, breathing is a major problem as the instrument uses a small amount of air at a high pressure, and this is true to varying degrees with most other wind instruments. Recorders, however, 'go with a gentle breath', using as much air and at as low a pressure as is needed for reading aloud or soft singing. Were it not for the fact that intake of air must be very much more rapid than exhalation, it could be said that in playing the recorder one breathes naturally. Recorder playing is just unnatural enough to cause breathlessness or indigestion if it is indulged in immediately after eating or drinking. But there is no compelling reason why a healthy person with no breathing problems (as may be caused by smoking) should undertake regular breathing exercises, of the kind designed for training professional singers, in order to play a recorder. Nevertheless such exercises may well have beneficial effects.

Breathing for recorder playing, as for singing and playing other wind instruments, should be from the bottom of the lungs, that is, the diaphragm. Sit or stand upright with the shoulders back and the head up, and become conscious of the movement of the muscle across the triangle formed by the ribs below the breastbone. Breathe in deeply through the nose so that the diaphragm is fully extended but do not raise or hunch the shoulders in the process; then, with your hand on the diaphragm, release the air in five or six separate and fairly slow exhalations, noting the muscular movement. Now open the mouth and throat, and allow the diaphragm to draw in a good breath as quickly as possible so that the lungs are nearly full. Half close the lips and let the air go out softly, slowly, and evenly. Notice that in breathing in both directions the muscles of the throat and mouth do nothing: they remain relaxed so that air can be pumped past them by the diaphragm. It is easy to fall into the bad habit of snatching a small amount of breath in quickly with the throat – that is, gasping – when a breath has to be taken during a very short interval in the music: it is vital, however, that even when time allows only a little replenishment of the lungs, the action of drawing breath should be made by the diaphragm. Try to do this even when a breath has to be taken in the midst of semiquavers, as in *PB*, Ex.3. The feeling should not be of a gulp from the throat but of a rapid filling out of the chest.

The impression one should have when blowing into the recorder is that the breath originates from the base of the lungs, a sensation of air pushed up from underneath and travelling smoothly up the windpipe, through the throat, across the mouth and into the windway of the recorder. The conscious realisation of this sensation of the passage of the air from the diaphragm to the edge helps to keep a long note steady. If you have difficulty in experiencing the sensation, artificially create conditions in which the diaphragm has to pump harder by making a stricture in your mouth with your tongue against your teeth, and feel the push of the air up to the stricture, and through to the instrument. As an aid

23

towards playing a long note evenly, this device would be more useful if it did not disturb the airflow and create eddies that affect tone (see pp. 91 and 98); it can serve a purpose, however, where very quiet long notes are required, as diaphragm control at ultra-low pressures is extremely difficult and in such circumstances good tone must be sacrificed for steady intonation. Some further assistance in keeping a long note steady can be gained by imagining that the note is being sung, quietly, to the sound 'err'. It may help to visualise the steady flow of a deep river, or the even passage of a dot along a straight line.

When playing a piece of music, a recorder player should feel most of the time that his lungs are reasonably full, though never bursting. Subject to constraints of phrasing (see pp. 117–19 and many references in PRS), no opportunity where breath might be replenished should be allowed to go unused. Most rests are breath marks, and at long rests you should breathe in and out normally through the nose until drawing in (through the mouth) a large intake of breath just before your re-entry. Aim at breathing frequently even if only a little at a time, so that occasions where a big (and noisy) inhalation takes place are rare. It is particularly important to breathe often and deeply when playing bass instruments: breathlessness causes anxiety both to performers and audience. Care must be taken with the large basses, however, not to hyperventilate, which can induce dizziness or even fainting; once the column of air in the instrument is in motion it only needs topping up, every few notes, with normal breath intakes. With a sopranino the condition might arise where a lungful of air becomes stale before it is used up, and like an oboist, the player has to breathe both out and in at the end of a long phrase.

Breathing when playing the recorder should be deliberate and planned, with the help of phrase-marks (see Chapter XI), but should always feel as natural and relaxed as possible.

Breath input

While many players tend to blow too hard – too much air, too much pressure, or both, others (perhaps to avoid disturbing their neighbours) develop the bad habit of blowing too softly in relation to their instrument's best tone-quality. It is vital to establish the optimum breath input for each note, and an optimum overall breath input for your instrument's *mp/mf*. Practise as follows: finger the note G', and, after breathing in deeply, whisper into the instrument to make the quietest noise you can imagine that passes for a musical note. Hold it *steady* (this is very difficult) for twenty seconds; don't let it get out of control at the end. Now play the same note loud like a trumpet, giving it the greatest breath input you dare, almost making the note 'break' – that is overblow with a nasty rasp into a higher octave. Hold the note steady for ten seconds (this is relatively easy) and finish by blowing it over the break. The first note will be thin and wispy, the second strident, and the two should be at least one whole tone apart in pitch. Now go back to the low breath input but make the note just loud enough to be pleasant and convincing (it will still, however, be a little breathy): this is your instrument's *pp*. A clear, loud (but still slightly harsh) note well clear of that break you have just discovered, is your *ff*. Somewhere between the two levels of input, generally but not necessarily midway, lies the most beautiful G' – find it by experiment – and this is your optimum breath input. In consort playing, however, your general level of attack should be slightly below this level, so that your purest notes come in an *mf* passage or when you announce a theme in a Fancy.

When carrying out the above process, note that it is the amount of air you put into your recorder that determines both the exact pitch and the volume of a note, not the pressure at which it is delivered. If tongue movement, which as we shall see later is an essential element in recorder technique, were to be taken out of the equation, and the tongue not moved at all, then an increase in breath would produce a corresponding increase in breath pressure, as resistance would remain a constant. So changes in breath pressure are an effect of changes in breath input, not vice versa, although the two concepts are inevitably closely interrelated. The commonly used term 'breath-pressure' is therefore misleading in the present context (but see Chapter VI, 'High Notes'). The optimum pressure at which breath needs to be delivered depends upon the resistance to airflow caused by the profile of your recorder's windway and by the position of the tongue in the mouth (see next section).

When you have found your best G', move on to other notes on the instrument, studying their behaviour under varying breath inputs. You will thereby discover the level of input at which your recorder plays best. As stated in Chapter I, different recorders are voiced to play best at different breath-delivery pressures, so be prepared to vary the general level of attack to suit each instrument you possess.

To consolidate these experiments play at low, high, and medium breath inputs and at a speed of about five seconds to each note any slow hymn-tune made up of equal length notes (e.g. 'Rock of Ages' starting on C, or see *PB*, Ex.1). Practise on all the recorders you have, and concentrate on steady breathing at low breath inputs. Play towards the corner of a room, so that the sound is reflected back at you; concentrate very hard on listening to it (would that more musicians did this!) and be extremely critical. Do your best not to allow a waver in the evenness of your sound. But for physiological reasons, it is extremely difficult to achieve an absolutely constant airflow at low breath input and pressure. 'The respiratory system is almost designed to oscillate' (I quote from a letter from Dr Valerie Flook printed in the Winter 2002 issue of *The Recorder Magazine* (p. 166)) because of the complex and uneven way in which muscles controlling exhalation contract ('a continually changing activity'). A great deal of determined practising is the only way to achieve an unwavering quiet note.

When concentrating on the sounds you produce, try to be aware of the undertones and harmonics that form a constituent part of each note. Hearing these and keeping them steady and in tune may help you in achieving your best, non-vibrato tone-quality for each note. Include in this process all the normal-fingered notes up to G″ and the common alternatives, E, G', and D.

Having established the optimum breath input for each note, practise the rapid change in breath input level required when slurring from a note in the lower octave to a note in the upper octave above the break in registers, e.g. F' to A'. To avoid 'clicks' two conditions are essential – extreme rapidity of finger movement and a sudden though small increase in the level of breath input from the optimum for F' to the optimum for A'. Some recorders behave better than others with awkward slurs over the register break: a player who can do these slurs on any instrument *pianissimo* without 'clicks' may claim to be an expert. But, as shown later in this book, there are various ways of overcoming this fundamental problem of recorder technique.

RECORDER TECHNIQUE

Breath delivery and 'fine-tuning'

The procedures recommended in the previous section will take the recorder player a long way towards discovering the characteristics of each note of his instrument and adjusting his breath input to achieve the optimum sound for his recorder as a whole and for each note. But to make music, these notes must relate to each other in the same way as spoken syllables are put together to create words, phrases and sentences, and to communicate meaning. The optimum sound of a note on its own may not be the best sound in particular musical contexts. It may need modifying, even degrading, in relation to other notes in a phrase.

Firstly, the notes must be in tune with each other and with those produced by other players in an ensemble. While the fingers are the main control mechanism for intonation (see Chapter IV), breath input has a role to play in fine tuning, even after an ensemble has warmed up and tuned together and the music is under way. An electronic tuner acts as a salutary visual aid in understanding the intonational behaviour of your own instrument. Keeping its needle steady is an excellent, if rather a cruel one, of practising long notes, especially at low breath inputs. But ultimately it is the sensitivity of your own ear, not a machine, that must be the judge. These constantly ongoing slight adjustments in breath input are essential to good recorder playing, but if they cause deviations of more than about ten cents (a hundred cents being a semitone) then fingering adjustments may need to come into play.

Almost as importantly, breath delivery controls the strength or weakness of a note (early writers called them 'good' and 'bad' notes) in respect of their relative contributions to the shaping of a phrase. The rhythmic life of a piece of music, and of its component phrases, depends on metrical repetition. Music, like poetry, has its own prosody. Alongside, or superimposed upon, the rhythmic pattern are the music's expressive demands, and, where the music has a text, its speech-rhythms, which may or may not correspond with the ordering of the underlying pulse. These factors can only be adequately illustrated in relation to particular pieces of music, which is the prime purpose of my *Playing Recorder Sonatas*, especially in the chapter on 'Sound and Expression'.

In discovering an optimum sound for individual notes, you will have noticed that some notes have a natural strength (this is usually the case for bottom and middle G) while others tend to be weak, especially those employing cross-fingerings, the half-holed bottom F♯ and G♯ (E♭), B (sometimes) and upper C♯' (often). You should therefore, again ideally with the help of an electronic tuner, first learn how to play scales which are fairly even in tone-quality throughout by applying slight adjustments in breath input, though not enough to make any note go out of tune within its context. To achieve this 'string of pearls' effect in a scalic series of conjunct notes so that every note is of equal importance, it may help to imagine that each note as you play it is the first of a group of three, like a continually extending ladder. Advanced players refine exactness of intonation to the point where they can play in the different tuning modes used in early music. Treat this, however, as a first stage process, as groups of notes in phrases, including in scalic passages, are not normally evenly stressed, otherwise there would be no meter, no rhythm, no expression. Fluctuations in breath, including during the playing of a single note, are the basic constituent of musical expression for recorder players, just as they are in singing. Feel that each phrase, each note in a phrase (especially the longer ones), is being moulded by your breath. Imagine that you are singing, or dancing, or both, as you breathe life into your music.

The tongue has a vital role to play in this process. In this chapter, I want to describe the mechanics of breath delivery, although the subject is considered in more detail in the chapter on 'Tone'. There are only two places where the stream of air emanating from the lungs can be affected by muscular action. The first is the throat (including the glottis), which controls breath vibrato and aspirated articulation for non-tongued notes (see below). The airstream then flows through the mouth above the tongue, between it and the hard upper palate. It passes between the parted teeth into the windway of the recorder and makes sound where the shaped airstream issuing out of the windway is divided by the labium. This sound is enlarged by the action of the body of the instrument as a vibrating resonator. The player himself can sense the wood of his instrument vibrating between his lips, and this gives him the feeling of acoustic contact between his mouth and the instrument.

The main function of the tongue is in tongued articulation. But it has an additional function after a note has started. If the tongue lies at the bottom of the mouth in the position to enunciate the vowel 'or', the mouth is a rounded cavity, and the tongue in no way impedes the passage of the airstream, so that a given amount of air is delivered at a low velocity. This suits the production of low notes, which can then be 'creamed up' with a slight increase in the quantity of airflow, making them louder and closer in volume to notes in the middle of the recorder's register. If the tongue is central in the mouth, the sound 'er', it delivers the airstream directly between the teeth – which should always be kept parted – in line with the windway. This is the most relaxed tongue position and assists sound production in the middle register. It is also most conveniently placed for a range of tonguing articulations by being close both to the upper front teeth and to the alveolar ridge above them (referred to as the teeth-ridge); this is considered in more detail in Chapter VIII. By pressing forward firmly on to the teeth-ridge the tongue cuts off the airstream altogether, thus ending a note, and in this position allows a variable build-up of breath pressure behind it which controls how strongly or lightly the next note is articulated.

As we have already noted, a slight release of tongue pressure on the teeth-ridge (or just above or on the teeth) allows a thin stream of air to get by, but this constriction causes eddies which degrade tone-quality. A narrow passage of the airstream can, however, be created without causing eddies by anchoring the tongue against the upper molars and shaping it close to the upper palate. This is the 'ee' position. The narrow channel causes the airstream to increase in velocity which is only slightly reduced by friction in the windway. This airstream then strikes the labium edge at a higher pressure with no increase in the amount of air delivered; this, not blowing harder, is the secret of playing high notes (see Chapter VI). The tongue then operates in rather the same way as a singer's tongue does when it enunciates different vowel sounds at various tone-qualities and dynamics (see p. 91). It positions the airstream at the right breath pressure for delivering each note into the windway, rolling it from the front and tip of the tongue. So, as well as being the prime mover in articulation, the tongue also remains constantly in action in optimising breath delivery and beauty and fullness of sound.

RECORDER TECHNIQUE

Aspirated articulation

Sometimes a note sounds best in its context if it is played with no tonguing articulation, not even the lightest graze of 'l' or 'r' (see next chapter). This is sometimes referred to paradoxically as 'h' tonguing. Although it is initiated from the throat muscles and not the tongue, the tongue nevertheless has its usual task of delivering the resultant airstream towards the recorder's windway between the lips. The lungs need to be well filled, but as the throat is less delicate and sensitive than the tongue in cutting off, holding back, and then releasing a slow-moving airstream, it needs to generate the initial movement of the airstream by enunciating 'h' neatly and quickly. The 'h' needs to push air forward at the rate required by the note. But supplying the ongoing airstream to the note, which may then either remain steady or increase or decrease in volume, immediately becomes the task of the diaphragm from the moment the note is delivered and sounded.

Aspirated articulation has a particular part to play in sounding the first note of a piece, or the first note of a phrase, especially if the music is slow. It is particularly valuable in playing slow-speaking large bass recorders, especially in their lower registers where it may well be combined with 'or' breath delivery to nurture low notes. It is unlikely to work on high notes, even with 'ee' breath delivery. As it is itself, even if enunciated abruptly, a slow-speaking articulation, care must be taken, especially with contra-basses, to carry out the action before the beat (or the point where the note needs to start sounding), otherwise the beginning of the note will not coincide with one produced in the ensemble by a quicker-speaking smaller recorder. Even with quicker-speaking tonguings the low instruments will sound behind the pulse, dragging the music, unless their players constantly compensate for their sluggishness of utterance.

Aspirated tonguing adds to the player's repertoire of techniques which help to bring recorder playing closer in spirit to singing words. A nice example is the start of the English version of Schubert's 'Who is Sylvia?' (begin it on A') in a recorder arrangement. The 'h' sound at the start replicates the opening word, and can be used again for the second phrase, 'What is she?'.

Throat control as a means of eliminating fingering sounds

A change in a note, whether by putting fingers down or lifting them off, causes an alteration in the acoustic pattern of the air within the bore of the recorder, which, however lightly and nimbly the fingers are moved, produces an audible 'finger articulation' noise when the notes are slurred. If the fingers are moved vigorously, their impact will exacerbate this effect as the escaping air is hammered back into its finger-hole. Many players accept this noise as a characteristic of recorder sound, giving a crisp start to a note, in the same way as a harpsichord player has to accept the noise of plucking at the start of each note as an integral feature of his instrument, known and put to advantage by composers. But with the recorder this transient sound can be eliminated to achieve a perfect slur.

Try slurring in the treble's lower octave the notes G–B–D–F', in slow succession at medium breath input. These are in fact the four notes which open the second treble part of the Andante of the second movement of Martinu's *Divertimento* for two treble recorders, a piece where the composer has marked slurs, stresses and staccato dots with meticulous care, or deliberately left them out. When a parallel phrase opens the recapitulation it is not marked with a slur, so, to emphasise this expressive contrast, the opening slur should be as perfect as possible. But it is plagued with fingering sounds if it is taken in one smooth ongoing breath, even though in two of the three note-changes only one finger is being lifted. If, however, a tiny blip, like making an 'h' enunciation, is impinged upon the airstream by the throat muscles, and these blips are exactly synchronised with the finger movements, those unwanted sounds can be eliminated. It is a technique very well worth acquiring for using with other slurs, although difficult upward slurs across register breaks are best smoothed out (or 'faked') with more positive articulations such as 'y' and 'r' (see *PRS*, p. 85 and *PB*, Exx. 44 & 45).

Breath vibrato

As the recorder operates at a generally low breath input, and as little resistance to the passage of air is offered by its sound-mechanism, most players find that there is insufficient pressure pushing back down on to the diaphragm for it to be easily able to induce constant rapid fluctuations in the column of air rising from the lungs. Diaphragm vibrato can be felt by placing your hand on the triangle formed under the bases of the rib-cages. Recorder breath vibrato is therefore usually controlled by the throat muscles, as deep and far back as possible, almost as if, in imagination, the impulses *had* originated from the diaphragm. The action may be represented by the syllables 'hu-hu-hu-hu-hu' aspirated deep in the throat without any interruption in the actual flow of air. The effect is most easily obtained on a sopranino or descant with high breath input and pressure. If, as may be the case with small recorders playing high notes loudly, there is enough resistance to breath input, you may actually be able to generate a throbbing effect from the diaphragm, but, when the breath pressure is too low for the air-column to be controllable in this manner, still feel that the throat muscles impinge upon the whole column of air, not just the airstream passing through the mouth.

Start with a 'long wave-length' (slow 'hu-hu's') and increase the frequency until you get a 'short wave-length' of oscillations – this is the so-called 'natural vibrato' that some beginners produce without realising it (they find it all the harder to play a plain note without vibrato – see p. 93). Once the knack is acquired – and it is deceptively easy – you will soon produce a comfortable short wave-length vibrato. Practise also the other extreme – slow vibrato (long wave-length); aim at keeping the oscillations absolutely steady and even, at about six to a second without getting any quicker, continuing to use a high breath pressure to aid control. Attempt, too, something between this slow vibrato and more normal rapid vibrato (call this 'medium wave-length'). The following diagram may clarify matters; note that the 'long wave-length' vibrato is generally played with wider amplitude than the 'short wave-length' vibrato:

long wave-length: ⌇⌇⌇⌇⌇

medium wave-length: ⌇⌇⌇⌇⌇⌇

short wave-length: ⌇⌇⌇⌇⌇⌇⌇⌇

no vibrato: ——————————

Apply the three vibrato wave-lengths to your hymn-tune practice. Play each of them at three different levels of breath input and breath pressure – high, medium and low, disregarding any changes in the pitch of the hymn tune this may cause. Counting the plain note, this gives twelve ways of playing the same hymn tune. Try to develop support from the diaphragm for the work of the deep throat muscles, as if you were initiating the action from the very source of the airstream. You may then feel you are producing and communicating a richer sound. Recorder vibrato is difficult to describe as it is as much a psychological process as a physical one, but this ambivalence will become more meaningful as you master the technique and understand its unique qualities. The production and use of vibrato of all kinds will be considered in greater depth, especially in relation to its effect on tone-quality, in Chapter VIII.

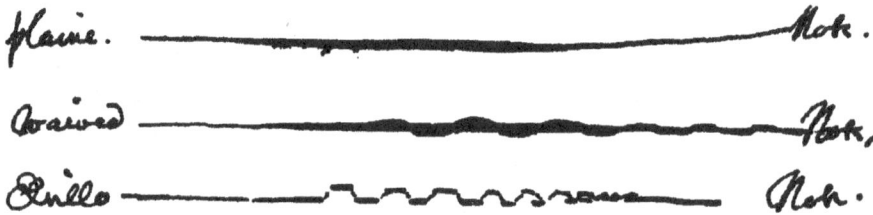

Roger North's diagrams of note-formations in his 'Notes of Me'
(c. 1695), from Plate II of *Roger North on Music* (ed. John Wilson,
London, 1959). North was a viol player and his concept of the 'plaine
Note' derives from the sound produced by the outcurved baroque
bow, held underhand, which accounts for the slow articulation at the
start of each note, and its long attenuation at the end. A recorder note
is quicker-speaking and more even. The 'waived Note' represents
finger-vibrato, the *flattement* as described by Hotteterre (1707) – see
pp. 94–5). And see also *PRS*, p. 76.

III

* TONGUING (ARTICULATION)

The last chapter described only the process of making the middle part of the note. This deals with the beginning and ending of a note on a recorder—how to 'give it breath with your mouth', and to take it away.

The consonant to aim at for normal tonguing is a whispered 'dh', obtained by placing the tongue in the position to say 'd' but then at the last moment changing it to 'h'. Try this with the second syllable of the word 'London' in mind, quietly whispered to yourself, and with the 'er' vowel sound held on for a second or more. It is a very soft sound, almost imperceptibly a consonant. Yet, within limits, it can vary in strength (compare the 'dh' sounds made in 'dhaa', 'dher', and 'dhee').

Strong tonguing is easy to do – in fact those very words 'to do' are instances of it. Both 'd' and 't', like 'dh', may be played with different degrees of 'explosion', so extending the usual range of tonguings. Light tonguing, softer than 'dh', is harder to master, but its acquisition is imperative for playing the lowest notes of the recorder and any notes requiring cross-fingerings ('forked' fingerings), e.g. low Bb, Eb, high C♯, etc. The more fingers that are below the hole left open, the lighter the tonguing required. Try, for example, the notes produced by the fingering 0 – 23 4567, arriving at it by descending from E 0 –23 –––– and adding one finger at a time; with the faintest tonguing imaginable, the note should be somewhere near Bb, while a slightly more definite tonguing should give F♯'. Observe that the note produced seems to depend as much on the tonguing as on the breath input used. Now, taking off a half-hole at a time and using the very light tonguing, play a series of notes that will be in the vicinity of Bb, C, C♯, and D. Once struck, play them as loudly as you can without causing them to break upwards. In the slightly stronger tonguing you should get a similar range of less than semitones from F♯' to A': once struck, play them as softly as you can. This illustrates the important principle that strength of tonguing in articulating a note does not necessarily vary with the breath input accorded to the note itself. Practise jumping from one 'register' to the other in quick succession over these five pairs of notes: do this so that each note speaks clearly and immediately. This function of the tongue is known as the 'selection' of a required pitch.

To appreciate gradations of tonguing from light to strong try the following exercise. Starting with a good lungful of air, play, without vibrato, the note G', keeping the tongue still. Gradually move the tongue backward and forward without quite letting it touch the protruding ridge in the gum (or front palate) above the front teeth: this introduces 'tongue-vibrato' into the note (see p. 95) and may be termed 'y' tonguing. Now bring the tongue movements forward so that the tip of the tongue just grazes the very angle of the teeth-ridge, having the effect of impeding but not quite stopping the flow of breath: this is the whispered 'r' position of tonguing, the lightest possible tonguing (for 'y' is a sort of

---

* Readers may find it useful to refer to *PRS*, pp. 77–80, where the material in this chapter is summarised.

non-tonguing or 'half-tonguing'). The 'r' is not the English palatal fricative nor the French glottal 'r', but more like the Scottish 'r' as in 'baron'; in American pronunciation that word could be changed to 'badden', which emphasises that the movement is a single tongue-stroke. By gently pressing the tongue slightly forward at the same point of contact on the teeth-ridge you will come into the 'l' tonguing position in which the initial flow of air is actually stopped centrally but is only slightly impeded at the sides of the tongue. Next go to the whispered 'dh' position, which may be regarded as normal single tonguing. The 'dh' position is the same as for 'r', except that instead of grazing against the teeth-ridge and impeding the airflow the tongue touches the teeth-ridge and just (but only just) cuts off the gentle flow of air momentarily, with the greatest possible delicacy. 'd' itself is more deliberate, being a sufficiently firm contact of the tongue upon the teeth-ridge to build up a slight pressure of air immediately before the release of the tongue to enunciate the note. In the 't' position the tongue is more rounded, less flat, and thus touches at its tip between the teeth-ridge and the top of the front teeth. Note that in no tonguing position does the tongue actually need to touch the teeth although, as we shall see later, it does do so in French-style tonguing of 't - r'. 't' allows for a greater pressure of the tongue and consequently a greater build-up of air pressure before the moment of release, i.e. it is in character the most plosive of tonguings. Yet, like all tonguings, it has a wide range from a Gallic spit to its softness in a quietly-whispered 'butter'.

Practise this range of graduated teeth-ridge tonguings, in both directions, on a repeated G', attempting to maintain constant volume. It requires determination to avoid a crescendo or decrescendo, but try it at different breath inputs, i.e. a constant *mf* throughout the exercise, then a constant *f*, then a constant *p*. If 'er' is used as the vowel sound for the flow of breath after tonguing, the exercise may be expressed thus (forwards or backwards): 'ter–der–dher–ler–rer–yer–er', each syllable except the last being repeated three or four times as part of a gradation throughout.

It would be a convenience in recorder playing if this exercise could be done with very short strokes of the tongue whatever vowel sound is used. But the tongue has to travel in order to get from grazing the teeth-ridge to the 'or' position where it least impedes the airflow, that is to say, at the bottom of the mouth with the tip touching or near to the soft palate under the lower gums. It is quite a long traverse back from here to the upper teeth-ridge; but it should be made very rapidly and slowed only on the point of graze or contact (like a car braking suddenly to avoid a collision). As we have already noted, the 'or' position gives the largest mouth cavity with the cheeks relaxed, and the most cavernous opening for air to travel through on its way to the recorder windway. This seems to favour low notes giving them their richest quality. When you play high notes, or when you play softly, you will, in imitation of a singer and to maintain control of breath, use a less hollow and a more shaped and narrow wind-passage through the mouth. This enables you to use a smaller transverse in the tongue stroke (see also p. 70). You will notice that the preceding vowel sound changes the angle at which the tongue approaches the teeth-ridge to articulate the next tonguing consonant. This causes slight changes in the character of that articulation (see p. 91).

The position of the lips is related to the tongue positions, to the the shape of the beak of the recorder, and to the necessity of opening the mouth wide to allow the diaphragm to draw in quick deep breaths. In earlier editions of this book I used 'oo' and 'aa' as 'normal' mouthing vowels after a tonguing: I have now chosen 'er'. No vowel in fact is quite right in relation to the lips. 'oo' is more forward in trajectory, but one does not round one's lips in putting the recorder to the mouth. 'oo' brings the cheeks in, whereas they should normally be slack, as should the lower jaw, in readiness for opening far enough to draw in a quick deep breath. 'aa' indicates this labial relaxation, but the lips are too wide apart to surround the mouthpiece. 'er' better indicates normal lip position on the recorder, and feels most relaxed. And it lies close to the teeth-ridge.

The lips should be slack enough to be moulded into shape by the recorder's mouthpiece, but then firm enough to make the contact absolutely airtight. The beak of the instrument should be just far enough into the mouth to make it impossible for the lips to close behind the windway, i.e. to enunciate 'p', without forcing the recorder forward. If it goes in further, the lips will not be able to form themselves gently as if they were in the same shape as the windway opening. Do not seem to be swallowing the mouthpiece. Except for certain tone productions and very quiet playing (see p. 91), the teeth should be apart so as in no way to affect the flow of the column of air from the lungs to the windway. If the teeth impinge upon this flow of air they may form eddies which could affect tone-quality. Their distance apart may narrow slightly from 'or' to 'ee', but not so as to disturb the seal of the lower lip upon the mouthpiece. Latitudinally there is movement at the ends of the lips between 'aa' and 'ee' as the lips widen. This makes the lips slightly tighter on the mouthpiece for high notes, slightly more forward for low notes. A recorder player seems to smile at high notes, and become more serious for mellow low notes.

If these lip positions are kept firmly in mind, and the lips, as it were, held set in one of them, it is possible to practise tonguings without the recorder. You can thus practise one of the most important aspects of recorder technique at any time (in private). Keep the lips still, and whisper – do not say or voice – your tonguing syllables or mnemonics. Use exactly the same flow of breath as you would in actual recorder playing. When you practise tonguing, you can hear much more clearly what you are doing if you put ear-plugs in your ears (or wear a sound protector).

Certain notes on the recorder require very careful tonguing. One of these is C♯', or, even more pertinently, G♯' on the tenor. This is a particularly slow-speaking note and unless it is tongued very gently will either cough before speaking or will strike a tone and a half too high. Passages where this note has to be repeated rapidly need cautious treatment, and it is wise not to break the flow of air after the first tonguing, saying, as it were, 'dher–yer–yer–yer–er' instead of 'dher–dher–dher–dher'. The same is true of repeated F″s. Special tonguings are needed for the highest notes of the recorder (see Chapter VI). A trick to soften tonguing, particularly when breath pressures are high (e.g. in a series of high notes), is to breathe out momentarily through the nose at the same time as tonguing. This is a useful anti-panic device when a high F″ is looming up, though the solution to this note is relaxed thumbing.

A player should be able to start a note without tonguing, aspirating 'h' from the throat (see p. 28).

RECORDER TECHNIQUE

Attack and rhythm: portamento and staccato

Any musical note may be thought of as having extremes of attack, length, and loudness. Between each of these extremes (e.g. volume from *ppp* to *fff*) lies a wide vocabulary of different ways of treating a note, each suited to a particular context. Tonguing on a recorder constitutes articulation or attack; it is equivalent to the start of a bow stroke on a stringed instrument. Tonguing combines with variation in the length and volume of notes to create rhythm (for the role of note-length in this process, see p. 82 and *PRS*, pp. 36–7 and 53). In a bar of four crotchets in common time all on the same note, rhythm is primarily established by the degree of attack accorded to each note. The attack on the first note is more definite, and it is played longer and louder than any of the remaining three: a secondary emphasis is placed on the third note, while the last is the slackest, shortest and quietest of the four. On the note G′ practise bars containing one note-value in 4/4 time, 3/4, 6/8, and slow 2/4 ('One – and – two – and'), and by using variations in tonguing, length of note, and volume, establish rhythms. Try this at different speeds, and in different styles between legato and staccato, from *ff* to *pp*. Then attempt to do the same thing with tonguing only, using notes of equal length and loudness. If, *using tonguing only*, and playing only the note G′, you can communicate to a friend the difference between a 4/4 bar and a 2/4 bar at the same speed (in quavers), or between a 6/8 bar and two 3/4 bars at the same speed, you have acquired considerable subtlety in tonguing control. Gradation of attack such as that which differentiates

 from

by means only of tonguing, illustrates nuances of technique in the service of interpretation (*PB*, Exx. 9 and 10).

Tonguing is not only the main ingredient in establishing rhythm, but it also controls rhythmic subtleties such as playing a note slightly before or after the established beat rather than exactly on the beat. Used with discretion, this device can, as every conductor knows, increase the expressive impact of music. A note in a slow movement (e.g. a Siciliano), fractionally delayed in its articulation, can cause a *frisson* of pleasure to the listener: if it happens too often, it becomes a nagging mannerism. A note played fractionally before its beat can, if used with discretion, give an impetus and excitement which mechanical slavery to the beat would never create.

Long notes barely separated by light tonguing constitute 'portamento', the word deriving from the fact that one note is all but carried over, or slurred, to the next (see *PB*, p. 40). The musical indication is

although portamento tonguing may be used for playing some other legato passages: in one with a series of notes of equal written length, such as the example quoted, after the first note the normal 'dher' tonguing becomes 'lher'. The tongue itself should be made to feel soft and flabby in portamento tonguing, only just grazing the upper part of the mouth for each note. An extreme portamento effect can be achieved by using the compound tonguing 'ly', but fingering must be quick or the notes will trip over each other. Portamento is an important technique to acquire not only for its interpretative applications (*PB*, Exx. 11 and 12) but also because the ability to tongue with an infinitesimal interruption of sound helps you to master and control forms of tonguing where the flow of breath is momentarily impeded but never actually stopped. The grazing effect referred to above is executed so lightly that the airstream is continuous; it may be referred to as 'half-tonguing'. It is invaluable in suggesting a slur over notes that would (for lack of an acceptable alternative fingering) be extremely difficult to slur properly without 'clicks'. An instance where this form of deceit (but see *PB*, p. 44) might be used is the following bar from No. 8 of 'Fifteen Solos' (Schott):

Only the most brilliant players could play this slur perfectly without any suggestion of sound other than its three notes, and without stressing the top D'. With a touch of half-tonguing between the notes the player can eliminate 'clicks' and deceive most listeners into hearing a slur, particularly if he plays the remaining three notes of the phrase fairly staccato. This technique is referred to again on pp. 43–44, 75 and 112, in *PB* under 'Slurring', and frequently in *PRS* (see index under 'slurs – semi-articulated or tongued slurs').

Staccato may be considered the converse of portamento, since it consists of short notes played with strong to medium tonguing. One of its developments is 'echo tonguing'. This is the recorder's equivalent of the harp pedal on the harpsichord and is used for echo effects in passage-work. Echo tonguing is produced by pressing the tongue firmly on and below the teeth-ridge (in the 't' position) and releasing it momentarily and only enough to allow a little air to pass to produce a short and stifled note. The impression to the player is that his tongue is almost drowning the sound of the instrument by the noise of its activity (see *PB*, Ex. 55).

Tonguing in terms of duration of articulation (speed of speaking)

Up to this point we have considered tonguing in terms of 'strong' and 'light'. We have characterised 't' as a strong tonguing and 'r' as a light tonguing. But we have noted that each tonguing is susceptible to a wide range of strengths depending on tongue pressure and the extent of build-up of airflow immediately before the tongue is drawn back to articulate the unimpeded flow of breath which makes the body of the note. Thus in whispering 'London' the stressed first syllable requires the 'l' consonant to be stronger than 'd'. Nevertheless 'd' is inherently more plosive than 'l'. Put another way, however hard you try, you can never make 'l' so strong that it is stronger than the strongest 'd', nor make 'd' so light that it is lighter than the lightest 'l'. Thus at each extreme of tonguing there is a forcefully spat 't' and a barely enunciated 'y'.

But for a full understanding of the art of tonguing one needs to consider another dimension. This is in terms of how long (in microseconds) it takes to enunciate the tonguing. 't' may then be described as sudden, precise, sharp, quickly articulated. 't' is always precise and quick-speaking, whether it is said strongly or lightly. 'd', because in normal speech it is voiced and a little space of time is needed for the larynx to give voice to it, takes longer to articulate than 't', even when it is whispered. 'l' and 'r', both voiced in normal speech, take longer to enunciate than 'd'. They are slow-speaking tonguings, whatever their strength or lightness. 'y' is so slow to articulate that its status as a consonant is at issue: it is a semi-vowel. The slow-speaking tonguings are less precise, making them difficult to use in upper-register selection for the neat artictulation of high notes. One writer refers to them as 'unctuous'.

We must now look at other tonguings used as components of double-tonguing, that is to say, the alternation of two tonguing consonants, the second taken on the rebound, as it were, from the first. These were sometimes referred to as 'direct' and 'reverse' tonguings. Thus 'd' or 't' could be alternated with 'r', i.e. a quick-speaking tonguing may provide the impetus for a slow-speaking tonguing on the rebound. For passages of gently undulating smoothness, 'l' was the direct tonguing followed by 'r', both slow-speaking tonguings. Writers from the sixteenth to the eighteenth century exhorted recorder players to practise their 'diri liri's', for double-tonguing with 'r' was, and perhaps should still be, even more important in recorder playing than single tonguing. Even nineteenth-century flute tutors advocated 'territory' as a mnemonic.

Reverse tonguing is an especially appropriate description of the palatal tonguings 'k', 'g', and 'gh', which are produced by the tongue against the back of the roof of the hard palate in the position it reaches at the end of the releasing or withdrawing stroke from the teeth-ridge tonguing. They alternate with 't', 'd', and 'dh' respectively. This alternation between a forward and backward tonguing helps the player to feel the rebound of double-tonguing, and provides a tonguing differentiation sufficiently marked to achieve a feeling of control over fast semiquavers which is greater than can ever result from single tonguing. Yet in terms of which is of greater duration of articulation, 'k', 'g', and 'gh' are exact counterparts of 't', 'd', and 'dh'. They are slightly less plosive, but are each as quick-speaking as their partners. 'k' is the most precise; 'g' is slightly less so because it is voiced in normal speech; and the aspirated and less plosive 'gh' is only a more whispered 'g'. They enable groups or passages of short notes to be played at a higher velocity of double-tonguing than is physically possible with single tonguing. In the twentieth century, when the prime function of double-tonguing to achieve control and expressiveness was largely lost sight of, 't-k' and 'd-g' pairings became the only form of double-tonguing, in their pyrotechnical role.

To complete this parade of tonguing consonants (ignoring Ganassi's 'head-breath', or 'p' tonguing), there is the mainly eighteenth-century 'dl', and its associate 'tl', slow-speaking reverse tonguings paired with 'd', 't', or 'l' as in 'tiddle-diddle-liddle-diddle' or 'tittle-tattle'. They are similar to 'l' in that airflow is released at each side of the tongue, but they must be linked with 't', 'd', or 'l' for their completion: they can therefore only be used for groups of equal-value notes at a fairly quick speed. Because they are reverse strokes *par excellence*, they will, when mastered, smooth up passage-work in a highly gratifying way, but as they are relatively slow-speaking, they cannot cope with passages of great velocity, nor with high notes. 't', 'dl', and 'l' together make an easy-swinging triple-tonguing, useful in jigs, pronounced as a three-syllable 'tiddly' or 'diddly'.

It must be stated that it is possible to play the recorder well by using the full range of strengths of tonguing available with single tonguing on 'dh' and 'd', and having recourse to double-tonguing 'd-g' only for passages of great rapidity. Even in the baroque period some players, it seems, advocated this approach. But the overwhelming historical evidence supports the use of a wide range of double-tonguings in flute and recorder playing.

Tonguing as described by 16th- and 18th-century writers

Many recorder players on first reading Ganassi's *Fontegara* (1535) are staggered to discover that so complex and refined a technique was used in recorder playing (at least in Italy) at this date. It is reasonable to suppose that highly developed techniques had existed for many decades previously. This is especially true of tonguing. Most of *Fontegara* is devoted to the art of improvised ornamentation and in Hildmarie Peter's translation there are only five pages of technical instruction, a fingering chart, and a chart of trills. Ganassi deals with tonguing in thirty lines, but they are rich in information.

The most important point is that all Ganassi's articulations are in double-tonguing. He divides these into three basic sections, being hard and sharp, intermediate (= normal), and gentle and soft. The hard and sharp group has 't' or 'd' as its first component, 'k' as its second. Remembering that all Italian consonants are articulated much less strongly than English consonants, this will equate with our modern 'd-g', i.e. a pairing of quick-speaking tonguings. Ganassi places vowels after his consonants to indicate the gradations of tonguing quality available on each consonant, and, I suspect, to stress his principal point that the recorder should imitate the human voice (see also pp. 86 and 91). Ganassi's intermediate group has the slow-speaking 'r' as its reverse stroke, and 't', 'd', or 'k' (all quick-speaking) as its direct stroke. The soft tonguings, which almost 'melt into one' (i.e. become nearly a slur), are all based on 'l-r' i.e. two slow-speaking tonguings; but as Ganassi says, all this shows only 'a few of the possibilities'.

That Ganassi's advice represents standard Renaissance practice is confirmed by the injunctions of other writers (e.g. Agricola, 1529) to practise 'diri-diri's. It would seem, therefore, that Renaissance players cultivated light, slow-speaking legato tonguings; to play Renaissance divisions portamento (on a Renaissance type of recorder) sounds infinitely more right than using a staccato level of attack, especially as the latter detracts from beauty of phrasing. It also suggests that 'chiff', needing sharp tonguings, was more of a special effect, perhaps used in dance music. The need for double-tongued legato ('dhaa-rer-lhaa-rer' or 'dhoo-ri-lhoo-ri') is all the more important in Renaissance music as players were expected to play fast *passaggi* of semiquavers or quicker notes without slurring. Slurring was probably a last resort for extremely rapid tremolos; perhaps it was even judged as an admission of poor technique. Slurring was used in the seventeenth century, but at first only sparingly over pairs of descending notes.

Seventeenth-century Italian references to wind-instrument tonguing do not vary significantly from Ganassi's precepts. The more detailed accounts of Freillon-Poncein

(1700), Hotteterre (1707), and Quantz (1752) on flute tonguing give a good idea of the art in the eighteenth century. All three writers give musical examples with a tonguing scheme set out in full under the notes. Freillon-Poncein makes it clear that soft tonguings (Ganassi's intermediate) remain in the ascendancy, even though the recorder had changed in construction and voicing. His main concern, as ours must always be, is in the application of the more precise 't' and the more unctuous 'r' to various phrasing contexts, with particular reference to inequality in the French style. Although Corrette (1750) advocated single-tonguing technique, Quantz's advice (1752) is based on double-tonguing with 'r', but with 't' or 'd' as the direct stroke in different contexts. He is very careful to characterise the different uses of 't' and 'd'. Passages of single and double-tonguing are much more freely mixed, with single tonguing on successions of slower notes. Quantz says (in Reilly's translation, cited in Appendix 2): '"Tiri" is indispensable for dotted notes; it expresses them in a much sharper and livelier fashion than is possible with any other kind of tonguing.' Quantz's examples, illustrating a variety of contexts, deserve close study (they are set out in Veilhan's *The Baroque Recorder*), remembering to scale down the 't's and 'd's to French consonant levels, and to recorder, rather than flute, articulation. It is Quantz who first mentions 'did'll did'll' for double-tonguing rapid semiquavers, a technique he derived, he says, from earlier players (it was not his invention – see my article 'Quantz dediddled' in *The Recorder Magazine*, Summer 2000, pp. 54–5).

Quantz advocates the use of a variety of tonguings to avoid uniformity of attack and to 'give each note its proper expression'. For, he says, 'the tongue is the means by which we…animate the expression of the passions in pieces of every sort, whatever they may be: sublime or melancholy, gay or pleasing'. It is tonguing, therefore, which differentiates one player from another; '…these differences rest upon the correct or incorrect use of the tongue'.

A knowledge of historic tonguings, complex though they may seem, will in my view enable you to understand the kinds of sounds the composer himself had in mind, and to communicate them to an audience. Although you are playing to a present-day audience, most of them, I imagine, will want to hear early music played in the style of its time, rather than in some form of interpretation modified to suit today's tastes. It needs also to be realised that no two recorder players using exactly the same historic articulations on identical recorders will produce exactly the same sounds, as their oral profiles and ways of speaking are not precisely the same. So each recorder player produces a different sound, an individual expression of his own personality which overlays, re-animates and enhances his expression of the thoughts, manners and intentions of the composer.

Tonguing in relation to speech

Even were it not for the advocacy of tonguing variety by contemporary theorists from the periods of most concern to recorder players, the nature of the recorder itself would lead players to adopt the same approach to tonguing. Unlike any other wind instrument, the recorder requires a level of breath pressure which is little more than that used in normal speech. It places no strain upon the lungs, nor upon the lips. One can almost 'talk into' a recorder. As Hamlet puts it, ' 'tis as easy as lying'. Because of the moderate flow of breath used in recorder playing, the instrument is extremely responsive to the articulations used in say, making a speech, or reading poetry aloud. Ganassi says that with some players it is possible 'to perceive, as it were, words to their music'. Recorder players are failing to take advantage of the special sensitivity of their instrument to subtleties of articulation if they do not use a wide range of tonguings drawn from the articulations of speech, especially those of poetry. This is particularly important in Renaissance music where the subtle relationships between the speech rhythms and the on-going pulse (even though the latter is weakened by polyphony) are paramount.

The relationship of recorder playing to poetry is even more instructive if consideration is given to poetry in different languages. For example, French, unlike English, is spoken without tonic stress, each syllable in a long word having much the same weight. French poetry cannot therefore be based on syllabic stress. Its gentle rhythm derives from contrasting length of syllables. In articulating French music, the duration of a tonguing is therefore more significant than tonguing stress. The slower-speaking tonguing 'r' may thus become more dominating than the quick-speaking 't', both enunciated at the same strength (it must always be remembered, however, that all tonguings must be done quickly and neatly – 'l' and 'r' are only relatively slower-speaking than 'd' and 't'). Thus in French music, 'r' may come on a down-beat, provided it is preceded by an off-beat 't' or 'd'. 't' is seen as weak in this context because it is quick-speaking. Inequality in French music (i.e. the lengthening of the first quaver in a pair and the shortening of the second) emphasises the role of the slower-speaking 'r' which takes the on-beat longer quaver, creating the basic iambic rhythm of eighteenth-century French music, 't – r', t – r'. The 't' is articulated forward on the upper teeth, and the tongue then rolls backwards and upwards to the 'r' position. Trochaic rhythms have their place in French music for contrast, where a more lengthened 'd' takes the down-beat and the 'r' the up-beat, but this has the effect of reducing the inequality in the pair of quavers. This rhythm is often indicated in French music by means of a slur sign over pairs of quavers (which are not actually slurred). French was the language of *politesse* across Northern Europe and the recorder player needs to comprehend this mode of tonguing in interpreting much seventeenth- and eighteenth-century music.

The slow-speaking 'r', articulated with plenty of stress, may be used with 'd' to set up a forward-swinging chaconne rhythm. The strong 'r' becomes almost 'th', but this is a lisped 'th' formed with the tongue upon the teeth-ridge, not on the teeth. A firmer rhythm, e.g. in a sarabande with its strongly stressed second beat, may be achieved by (exceptionally) bringing the tongue forward to enunciate 'th', as in 'the', against the upper front teeth. This rhythm may be represented 'De ther, tiDe ther', etc.

Acquiring the art of double-tonguing

It is best to begin with 't-k', the most precise and mechanical of double-tonguings, but the least expressive. It should be practised with quite a strong flow of breath on the note G'. Initially the vowel sound used should be 'i', where the tongue is fairly high in the mouth and the traverse to and between the tonguing positions is short. To start, therefore, play

loudly, staccato, fairly quickly, a repeating phrase ♩ ♪, saying to yourself 'ticky-tee'.

RECORDER TECHNIQUE

It is especially important not to proceed further until the tonguing is absolutely regular and balanced. Too much haste at this point will cause problems of synchronising tongue and fingers at a later stage.

Next slacken the tonguing on the same exercise to 'dugger daa'. This is a little slower-speaking, and the tongue movement greater and more deliberate.

Now practise the same exercise with four semiquavers and a quaver, then six, then eight semiquavers, still on a loud G'. You should now be finding, however, that you can double-tongue at lower breath pressures, and less staccato. Move on to repeated upper C's, then, as you gain control at lower breath inputs, to lower C and other notes between.

You have now reached the point when you should try double-tonguing on two alternating adjacent notes, E to D. Be sure to synchronise the finger movement exactly with the tonguing. Try other pairs of two adjacent notes in the centre of the recorder's range which involve a single finger movement, up or down. Do not yet go below C or above C'.

Now double-tongue ♩♩♩♩ ♪ from G' to C, all the time maintaining a clockwork regularity. The patterns to attempt next are C to G', D to A', and A' to D. Having mastered these, you may now venture into other semiquaver and passage-work groupings, including whole scales, gaining confidence, speed, and smoothness. Apply your new ability to pieces you have played before, perhaps badly, with single tonguing.

You will notice how double-tonguing helps in fast passages, e.g. in Telemann's trio sonatas in G minor and D minor (PB, Ex.14). Double-tonguing has the excellent secondary effect of evening up wayward rhythms, due to the pairing of the notes and the placing of an accent on the 'dh' note. It is invaluable in playing four isolated semiquavers nicely in time as well as pairs of semiquavers which might otherwise get rushed. Double-tonguing can smooth out a three-semiquaver entry to a phrase, which should be pronounced 'gher–dher–ghi(–Dhoo)' with an accent on the 'dher' (PB, Ex.15): the pattern is often met with in overtures in the French style, where the groups of three demisemiquavers are articulated 'g–d–g–'. In most contexts in eighteenth-century music the time-value of a dotted note is longer than it is in modern music; conversely, the short note following a dotted note is played shorter than it is written (as useful concept is that the short note takes up one ninth of the beat in which it occurs). With the single-tonguing 'd-Dhoo' this very short note tends to be muffled, but the double-tonguing 'g-Dhoo' gives a clearer and tauter enunciation, and encourages a forward impetus.

You will now have reached the critical point in acquiring the art of double-tonguing, in which compound articulation must be thought of not only as a way of playing fast notes neatly, but also as a means of expression.

The starting point is to slow down the 'd-g' tonguing, playing legato and fairly softly.

Keep it absolutely even and practise ♩♩♩♩ ♪ first on repeated Cs, then on lower repeated notes, then on moderato passages involving groups of low notes: use the syllables 'dhoo-gher-dhaa-gher'. As you get used to this tonguing at the slower speed, you will begin to find it somewhat monotonous. So substitute the slower-speaking, softer 'r' for 'gh', to provide contrast: 'dhoo-rer-dhaa-re'. Play your groupings more slowly, more legato, lightening the tonguings all the time. Finally substitute 'laa' or 'loo' for the second 'dhaa': 'laa' is close to 'dhaa' but is a little slower-speaking and softer. Your tongue will assume a kind of rolling gait within your mouth. Make sure that the gentle stress pattern of this tonguing accords with the weighting of four crotchets in a four-four bar (see p. 34). In fact you will find that the exercise of conveying this rhythm to a listener by means of tonguing only is decidedly easier with double-tonguing. This tonguing takes practice (which may be without the recorder) to achieve a regular, clean, and even articulation. Do not allow the 'r's to become too sluggish.

Play and practise 'd-r-l-r' tonguing, on a repeated low-register note at first and quite slowly, with across-the-bar phrasing – 'd r-l-r-d r-l-r-d'. This is the standard pattern of continuous quavers in Renaissance music.

Up to now, all your 'd-r-l-r' practice should have been on low notes which respond more readily to the slow-speaking tonguings. Venture into the middle and upper ranges of the recorder, but never use this tonguing on high notes because it is too imprecise (see Chapter VI). Play it gradually faster and a little louder, but never allow the tonguing to relapse back into single tonguing (as it may threaten to). You will need to use 'i' as your vowel, entailing a shorter tongue traverse, but never lose the rolling feel of tonguing. At last we have arrived at the standard Renaissance 'diri diri' or 'diri liri' tonguing. Try applying it with a tenor recorder to the Van Eyck Variations. Again you will need much practice (abundantly supplied by Van Eyck) to master a soft legato 'd-r-l-r' at speed. Remember that in Renaissance and baroque music you should only have recourse to the easier and more mechanical 'd-g' tonguings when absolutely necessary. Very fast Renaissance ornamentation is best taken 'dh-y-y-y-y-y-y-y' (on 'i') with extremely rapid and short tongue movements – avoid slurring if possible (see p. 102). In the lower register the Renaissance 'diri liri' must be smoothed out to 'doo-ri-loo-yi'.

The next phase of understanding double-tonguings should be devoted to the use of 'r' in French music. It should be practised first on strings of dotted or unequal quavers with the short off-beat note as a light 't' or 'd' (not the more aspirated 'dh' as that is too slow-speaking) and the longer down-beat note as 'r' taken neatly and lightly. Remember that 'r' must always be preceded by 't' or 'd' so it cannot be used for the first note of a phrase. 'r' was not generally used for the last note of a section, nor for a note bearing ornamentation. The best exercises are Freillon-Poncein's *Préludes* (ed. Lasocki, Faber). Study the tonguings shown at *PRS*, p. 68 for a French sonata movement. Avoid stress, even at the beginning of the bar: the melodic or harmonic structure of the music will give sufficient emphasis of itself.

To be able to double-tongue 'd-dl' is a valuable but not absolutely essential requirement. Follow the same procedures as for 'd-g'. Ideally, let Quantz be your teacher (Reilly translation, pp. 79-85). 'd-dl' is especially valuable on pairs of semiquavers, or on an unslurred turned eight-semiquaver trill, as it is faster than tonguings with 'r', without being as abrupt as tonguings with 'g' or 'k'. With practice, it will work on high notes, though it is an extreme test of any double-tonguing to be able to use it for rapid upward leaps, for this requires a sufficiently precise reverse stroke to achieve clarity in crossing from the low to the high register while keeping rhythmic emphasis upon the low notes. 'd-dl' is extremely valuable in phrasing semiquaver scale runs, especially rising scales,

when the phrasing usually is off the beat. Try a rising scale ♫♫ ♫♫♫ ♪

with the mnemonic 'to tootle do, de durdle Dee' (i.e. Quantz's tonguings plus vowel forms to take account of the upward movement) and you may become convinced of the value of this form of tonguing. At high speed a slight side-to-side movement of the tongue across the teeth-ridge gives an additional sense of control in the 'd-dl-l-dl' tonguing.

Much of the skill of recorder playing lies in accurate synchronisation of tongue strokes, especially in double-tonguing, with finger movements – this is the key to virtuosity. It is tempting to give more room for the finger movements by using quick-speaking double-tonguings and short notes (staccato). This may give an impression of dazzling neatness but gives less opportunity for good phrasing. The strings of semiquavers in Renaissance variations or baroque passage-work need shapeliness of phrasing just as much as an Adagio song-tune: indeed they call for more thought about phrasing because phrasing patterns are less obvious. Phrasing is best achieved with a mixture of legato and staccato to give light and shade to passage-work. The acquisition of a good 'diri-liri' as the essential basis of legato double-tonguing is therefore of the highest importance.

Unfortunately, in a very long passage of double-tonguing (e.g. the second movement of Bach's C major Flute Sonata) the tongue will become tired long before the fingers, thereby causing it to lose co-ordination with the fingers. Much practice of double-tonguing, with or without the recorder, will help to remedy this, but fatigue can be alleviated if you switch from one type of double-tonguing to another. This also affords variety of attack to the music. The Bach movement I have mentioned can be 'coloured' by changes of tonguing from one section to another, tonguing serving alongside changes in volume and good phrasing of the semiquavers to draw out the full quality of the music.

Sometimes the balancing of a phrase and the avoidance of being tongue-tied can be better achieved in fast passages by using a strongly articulated 'l' as the launching pad for a series of 'd-g' tonguings. This is especially true with long passages of triple-tonguing (see below). It is the *contrast* between the slower-speaking 'l' and the quick-speaking 'd-g's that provides the sense of control: this is the whole basis of the effect of double-tonguing in evening up passages which, played with single tonguing, would trip you up. Most tonguing consonants can be used as the 'reverse' element in double-tonguing if they are taken lightly 'on the rebound' with no fresh impulse of breath, e.g. 'Teddy', 'Ditty'. The relationship between tonguing and breath impulses from the lungs is fundamental to musical expression; it is this technique which underlies the shaping of a phrase, and the balance of groups of notes within a phrase.

Triple- and other tonguings

Triple-tonguing

Triple-tonguing is a necessity for triplets of high velocity, as in the first movement of Vivaldi's *Tempesta di Mare* concerto, Op.10 No.1 (*PB*, Ex. 16). At this speed only the fast-speaking 'k' and 'g' are of use. According to the phrase shape, use either 'd–g–d, d–g–d' or 'd–g–d, g–d–g'. Mnemonics, however silly, help control (e.g. 'do good to gaudy girl), and enable you to maintain a particular tonguing pattern in long fast passages without becoming tongue-tied. These triple-tonguings, aspirated with 'dg' and 'gh', or the more expressive 'diddly', are also of value in slower moving triplets or jigs, to even up and enliven phrasing.

Flutter-tonguing

Flutter-tonguing consists of trilling the tongue against the roof of the mouth in the manner of an extended rolled 'r': a fairly high breath pressure is usually needed to get it going. It can also be done by vibrating the tongue against the back of the palate (uvular vibrato). It is used in Benjamin Britten's *Noyes Fludde* to imitate the cooing of the dove.

'Y' tonguing

Although there is no historical evidence for what may be called 'y' tonguing, it is a versatile device for those who wish to take advantage of it. Strong and light 'y' tonguings serve different purposes.

The strong version of 'y' may be represented as in an emphatic 'Oh, yes'. The forward thrust of the tongue is halted at its sides by the upper molars, so that the tongue is just prevented from grazing the teeth-ridge, although it comes very close indeed to doing so. This impedes the flow of air sufficiently to give an impression of separated notes. Try a forceful regularly repeated 'd–y–y–y' on a high note such as C', slowly at first to get the muscular feel of this tonguing. When you have a regularly repeated 'y' tonguing under control on a high note, work down to lower notes, with as much deliberation but less force. Some instruments (especially basses, which abhor strong tonguings), may articulate better in the low register with 'y' rather than even a soft 'dh'. 'y' is unsuitable for articulating a note in the high register because it is far too slow-speaking. Scale practice with 'y' is salutary in that it evens out irregularities that may be perpetrated in slurred scales. 'd–y–y–y' is useful for enunciating and balancing scalic four-semiquaver sequence patterns in baroque music. A good practice piece is the last movement of Vivaldi's *Cardellino* concerto, Op. 10 No. 3. This includes repeated groups of unslurred semiquavers on B'-C♯'-D'-E': many recorders will slur from D' to E' without crossing the register break by lifting 2, and with 'y' tonguing this fingering may still work yet give the semblance of unslurred semiquavers.

The light version of 'y' may be represented by the unemphatic 'y' in the phrase 'Do you take tea?' The tongue is now only lightly touching the molars and is a tiny bit further back from the teeth-ridge, though close enough to constrict the flow of air sufficiently to differentiate the phrase from 'Do take tea'. This is the lightest possible of all tonguings, and it can convey the impression of a slur if done artfully enough. It then becomes a 'half-tonguing' (see p. 35) and shares with 'l' and 'r' the capability of constricting the airstream without interrupting its flow. Though light, it has to be precise, and in perfect synchronisation with finger and thumb movements; it should never become flabby. The regular, slight (but definite) movement of the tongue to and from the light 'y' position will even up difficult slurs, such as fast chromatic runs. It helps, as a 'touch of tonguing' ('doo-yee'), in slurs across register breaks, as the constriction made by 'y' causes the increased air velocity needed for the upper register. Try its effect in Exx. 32–44 of the *Practice Book*.

A strong 'y' may be found useful in separating the eight notes of a very fast turned trill in Renaissance ornamentation at the end of a 'groppo', and a light 'ye' in controlling slurred baroque trills. Try (at speed) the trills on p. 105, first separately articulated with strong 'y's – 'D-y-y-y-y-y-y-y D', then with light 'y' half-tonguing controlling the balance of a slurred (baroque) trill, and then slurred without 'y's.

Ending a note

Ordinarily, there are no difficulties. The return of the tongue into the correct 'dh' position effortlessly and efficiently both stops one note and prepares for the next, during which tiny stoppage of airflow all finger movements take place.

Difficulties arise when there is no next note. They mount still more if the last note of a phrase, or worse still of a whole piece, happens to be a long note. If this last long note is marked *ff* a player may swoop up an exuberant semitone in a final burst of defiance to the composer, and if it is marked *pp* he may expire almost a semitone flat with appalling pathos. Control must be retained until the very end of a piece of music – and a second or two more. The actual stopping of the note may be done in the normal way of putting the tongue back to the 'dh' position with great speed and delicacy; the effect is of the final 'n' in the elongated whispered last syllable of 'London'. If the note is very quiet and therefore hard to control, the tongue may come forward into the 'lh' position while the note is still being played, the stop being made by a quick forward pressure of the tongue. Reference is made elsewhere in this book to the use of breath delivery constrictions which increase breath pressure for very low breath inputs, as a means of controlling steadiness of intonation on long quiet notes. A more outlandish way of ending the final note of a piece is to cut off the air with the lips, plucking the recorder from the mouth at the same time. The lips should close firmly and instantaneously behind the instrument. This method can be surprisingly effective, both aurally and visually.

The imperceptibility of good tonguing

It is a great irony in recorder playing that, except for special effects such as echo tonguing or flutter-tonguing, the more you acquire skill in using the whole range of single and double-tonguings described in this chapter, the less apparent it will be, as a technique, to the uninitiated listener. You should practise double-tonguings until they are as neat, regular, and as even as single tonguings. What you and your audience will notice is that your performance is more varied, more lively, above all more expressive. Ultimately, tonguing technique should be imperceptible, as it becomes totally subservient to good phrasing and imaginative interpretation. If a recorder player's performance does not hold your attention, it is probably his tonguing technique that is at fault.

IV

INTONATION

A note is in tune when it bears a perfect relation to the notes preceding and following it (melody) and to other notes being played at the same time (harmony). A person can only achieve an understanding of the relationship of one note to another by listening to music in such a way that he hears all the separate strands of a piece of music (preferably by concentrating on the middle voice and remaining aware of the treble and bass) and is at the same time conscious of the construction of each chord. A recorder player can only keep in tune, therefore, if as well as playing his own part he listens to everyone else's. If his part is too hard or the structure of the music too complex for him to do this, he should at least listen to one other part, and that should be either the bass or the part next below. Intonation is always improved in a consort if the players sit in the order of their parts. Only by listening carefully along and through a piece of music as a whole can such justness of intonation be achieved as the narrowing of the semitone between a leading note and its tonic, or the flattening of minor and sharpening of major thirds and sixths. It is important that a note or a chord should be imagined in the mind's ear before it is played; no true musician will embark upon playing a note without knowing what it is. This chapter, therefore, describes the means at a recorder player's disposal of communicating the exact note he has in mind.

Whatever beginners might learn, the thumb and first three fingers of the left hand on the treble recorder do not necessarily produce a definite note C. If the instrument is 'in tune' and warm, and if the player delivers a medium amount of breath input, he will, however, produce one of the many notes that are conveniently represented by a mark on the second space down on a stave with a treble clef, rather than one that would be better represented by the same mark with a sharp or a flat in front of it. The player has the power to cover the whole range of notes that are expressed by this C, starting from the territory uneasily shared with B right up to the foothills of C♯. He has the freedom of the singer or the violinist, and is not confined, like the pianist, to pressing a key and accepting a note at a pre-tuned pitch.

The experiments in breath input advocated in Chapter II will have shown that on the note G' the range of intonation is, on most recorders, a whole tone or slightly more. The intonation range of notes above or below G' is rather less, but even on top F" or bottom F most recorders will range over a semitone. The fact that recorder intonation is so sensitive to changes in levels of breath input is both an advantage and a disadvantage. It is an advantage in so far as small alterations in breath input will move the pitch of a note slightly without a noticeable effect on the volume of sound produced. This enables the player to make minor pitch corrections of a note either to keep in tune with other players or to overcome imperfections natural to his own instrument. A treble player might, for example, find that his F' was a little flat and would correct it by blowing harder. One comes to make these modifications automatically when the idiosyncrasies of a particular recorder are known – indeed they must be made on every recorder for it is neither possible nor desirable that a recorder should be constructed absolutely in tune throughout its chromatic register with an unchanging amount of breath input.

This admirable flexibility of intonation reaches its limits when a change in the amount of breath delivered made in order to raise slightly, or to lower slightly, the pitch of a note gets to the point where the concomitant increase or decrease in volume becomes noticeable enough to affect the role of the note in the shaping of a phrase. It might be too loud or too soft for its musical context. If the lower octave C on one's recorder is a trifle flat, correcting its intonation by blowing a little harder might within limits be acceptable if the music is in the key of C major. The resultant slight prominence of the note due to a barely perceptible increase in volume might be justified by the context and phrasing. But if the key is C♯ major, that same note (but now designated as B♯) would be the unstressed leading note before the tonic of the key. Normal fingering by increase of breath input to correct intonation would not sound right, especially as C♯, a cross-fingering, tends to be both weak and sharp. That leading note will need to be re-fingered – the solution may be 0 12– 4567. To give another example it is obviously musically undesirable that a player with a very flat F' should blurt it out loud (but in tune) every time he comes to it.

Conversely, as we shall see in more detail in Chapter VII, the sensitivity of intonation to varying amounts of breath input causes problems when stronger variations in volume are called for by the composer or by the style of the music than those with which your instrument can cope without noticeably going out of tune. True echo effects, for example, are delightful, but not if the 'echo' is a semitone flat. Baroque-voiced instruments have the flexibility to cope with a rather wider range of dynamics before going out of tune, but if the instrument is badly tuned by its maker in the first place this stability of intonation in itself causes problems.

Shading and shade-fingering

The chief technique for flattening a note is called 'shading'. To shade a note means to lower the 'unused' fingers over the open holes until the note is flattened to the extent desired. As an experiment play the note E on the treble loudly and lower the second finger of the left hand over its hole until the stream of air coming from the hole can be felt on the ball of the finger. Now, lowering the finger slowly, press the column of air down into the hole until the finger is just grazing the edges of the hole. Very gradually press the finger home to complete your slide down from E to D. Shading with the uppermost unused finger is extremely critical as a tiny movement affects the note's pitch, and it is less nerve-racking to impinge upon the lesser columns of air emerging from holes lower down: the whole process of shading E with the third finger of the left hand cannot lower it as much as a semitone, and the first finger of the right hand has less than a quartertone effect. It is perhaps best to shade with all the fingers at one's disposal. Try playing E and moving the unused fingers up and down to produce a controlled, slow, wavering effect reminiscent of American steam railway engine whistles. In this exercise the fingers of the right hand may actually cover their holes, but the two left-hand shading fingers have to be moved with more care and should never be low enough to touch the instrument. Another method of shading is to place the shading finger on the instrument but at the side of its hole, from where it may roll over towards the hole as required. This method is particularly useful when only one finger is available to do the shading; an example is bottom G which is sometimes a little sharp and can be flattened by placing the little finger, politely bent, on the brink of its half-hole. Middle G' is another note that is often sharp, and although it can be shaded from above, the easiest way to flatten this note, as well as F' and alternative E, is to swivel the left wrist back so that the first finger of the left hand leans against the side of the instrument, with the finger almost straight and jutting out diagonally above the hole in such a position that bending its top joint causes extra flattening. The other fingers lie low, and the little finger may actually be on its hole covering both half-holes. Another method is to arch the finger across its open hole to touch, or nearly touch, the edge of the far side of the hole.

Shading may be achieved by completely covering holes left open, provided that the hole taking the shade-fingering is low down on the instrument in relation to the position of the fingers making the note itself. The most useful fingers for this method of shading are the little finger and the third finger of the right hand, for the degrees of flattening they control are made finer by their double holes. Little-finger shading is the most delicate of all: shading a note such as E or F' with the little finger scarcely lowers the pitch, but the little finger comes into its own not only on lower notes such as A or C but in the upper octave where the effects of shading are accentuated (compare the flattening effect of adding the little finger to the ordinary A' fingering with the same movement an octave down). Another form of shading is the covering of a hole below an ordinary 'forked' fingering. Many recorders, for example, produce a sharp C# with the usual fingering (0 12– 45––), and the third finger of the right hand has to cover its half-hole or both half-holes to bring the note into tune. Alternatively, if the sharpness is slight, little-finger shading may be applied. Another method is to lower the third finger of the left hand into the airstream emerging from the open hole beneath it to produce the same flattening effect; control may be gained by resting the little finger of the left hand against the side of the recorder. The choice of method depends on which comes easiest to the player, though it is generally advisable for full shade-fingerings to be applied to notes that are consistently out of tune, while the other methods of shading are used for controlling intonation in passages where dynamic range and expressiveness are called for, and for corrections resulting from intonation exigencies of ensemble or consort playing, or the use of remote keys. Shading is vital when whole passages need to be played loudly, in order to avoid sharpening (see Chapter VII).

It comes as a shock to realise that this technique is as old as Ganassi – 'An instrument can imitate the human voice by varying the pressure of the breath and shading the tone by means of suitable fingering.' (*Fontegara*, Chapter I).

Slide-fingering

Sharpening a note without increasing breath input may be achieved by 'slide-fingering'. This simply means pulling the lowest of the fingers forming the a note to one side to expose some or all of the hole it covered. It is easy to do this on a note that is normally a forked fingering, such as B♭ or E♭ : it is simple, too, with some of the thumbed notes near the top of the upper register, for if the thumb-hole aperture is widened, the note is slightly sharpened – but care must be taken not to overdo this, otherwise the octaving effect of the pinched hole is spoilt and the note breaks downwards with an ugly crack. Intense concentration is needed, however, if a plain-fingered note such as C is sharpened by slide-fingering the third finger of the left hand, for a hair's breadth moving of that finger from its hole will send the pitch of the note up; perfect synchronisation of change in breath input with the finger movement is required to keep the intonation of the note steady. Control is enhanced if the operating finger is pressed firmly on to the instrument so that every edge of the hole except the fraction being released is felt as the finger is pulled slightly sideways, using the elasticity of the flesh of the finger-pad to create the minute aperture. Alternatively, the finger may be moved upwards, that is, lifted so as to rest lightly on the hole rather than properly cover it, but this method, even more than that of slide-fingering proper, is hard to control and also adversely affects tone-quality – the good round sound of the plain-fingered note is weakened as the pitch rises. To make matters worse, in slide-fingering a plain-fingered note such as C, tone deterioration happens quite suddenly the moment the finger begins to cause leaking of air from the hole. Slide-fingering plain notes is therefore a device to which one must have recourse only when absolutely necessary. On the other hand, slide-fingering forked notes is a vital technique for achieving flexibility in recorder playing.

Half-holing techniques, referred to by Ganassi, were apparently commonly used in sixteenth- and seventeenth-century recorder playing. Ganassi writes that holes 'should be half closed a little more or less according to the demands of pure intonation...Remember that you can sound every softly by slightly uncovering a finger hole and using less breath...You should half-close the holes somewhat more or less as your ear requires and as you feel to be right.' Blankenburgh in 1654 even goes as far in his fingering chart as to prefer half-holing to cross-fingering for normal sharps and flats, indicating whether a hole is to be rather more than half closed, or rather less than half closed. This may be a legacy from transverse flute fingering (Renaissance and early baroque flutes had no keys) as cross-fingering has a more subduing effect on flute tone than it does on that of the recorder. On a wide-bore recorder the tonal change on slide-fingering C is a little less marked and sudden than it is on a baroque recorder, and half-holing techniques, in which a really skilled player can achieve a very fine control over intonation, can be used more readily. The larger finger-holes of Renaissance recorders facilitate the use of this technique. See the illustration on p. 68.

It is of course in the converse of making a note sharper by slide-fingering with steady breath input that the use of slide-fingering for dynamic control resides. If you play a note on normal fingering at *mf* and then wish to decrescendo to *pp*, it will stay in tune only if slide-fingered (see Chapter VII, where fingering techniques are considered in relation to dynamics).

One form of slide-fingering that works well on upper octave notes without affecting thumbing is to slide-finger with the first finger of the left hand. Do this by pivoting the first finger very slightly off the far side of its hole, while still keeping the finger on the recorder ('leaking-finger' technique). This has effect down to Bb', which as a forked fingering is easy to slide-finger with 6. By using alternative A' Ø 123 4–67 one can slide-finger 7 and thus complete the repertoire of *pp* notes in the upper octave. A problem with slide-fingerings is that, to a greater or less degree, in slightly sharpening the note in question they cause change to the breathy undertone that is present as a 'shadow' to the main note on most recorders and is a constituent of its tone-quality. The undertone is likely to be more in evidence on the upper notes of the second octave, and thumb or first-finger slide-fingering of high notes can cause poor tone-quality in the transition from *mf* to *pp*. You must see how it works on your own recorder.

Below A' the two-finger forking of F♯, E♭, C♯, and B all lend themselves to slide-fingering, and there are forked alternatives for the plain-fingered notes to open up slide-fingering possibilities, at least down to G (see next chapter). The half-holed low notes A♭ and F♯ slide-finger without problem. Leaking-finger techniques can be tried on notes in the lower octave, normally using the finger first above the lowest finger down. This just about works with F, but G is so rich in tone that any leak affects it too suddenly.

Leaking-finger techniques can be applied to the bottom octave by using the thumb. Try this at low breath input from F' down the scale, checking intonation with normal fingerings at normal breath input, or with an electronic tuner. The thumb-nail needs to be in about a one-eighth aperture position for the F' to be in tune, depending of course on the amount of breath used. As you go down the scale, tighten the thumbing more and more so that for the lower notes you are pressing the thumb-nail quite forcibly against the edge of its hole. The thumb-nail needs to be cut to the right length, i.e. quite short; exerting lateral pressure with the right-hand little finger upon the side of the recorder helps to hold the instrument steady in the process. As you go down the scale push this little finger more firmly against the recorder by turning the wrist inwards. Breath input needs to decrease markedly as you reach the lowest notes, and the thumb-nail pressed very hard and tight. Breath input for the last three notes has to fade down to almost nothing – it is extremely difficult to control evenness of breath at this very low level. I find I use this technique considerably in playing music of all periods. It works particularly well for echo effects in the lower octave (*PB*, Ex. 53).

Quiet notes in the lower register can also be produced by using a variant of thumb-leaking. This is achieved by lightly placing the tip of the thumb-nail not within the circumference of the thumb-hole but directly on to the rim of the thumb-hole, or slightly outside it, and then allowing a 'hair-leak' to occur at the thumb-hole rim (this can be sensed by the skin of the thumb as a tiny vibration). One has to find the exact point where the note plays softly, is in tune, and has a good enough tone-quality for soft playing. This should be done for each of the notes of the lower octave, the amount of leak seeming to approach infinity as one gets down to bottom F. Another way of achieving these minute thumb-leaks is to drag the thumb slightly sideways from its normal closed position, using the resilience of the surface of the skin to make the leak.

Re-fingering

Some notes may be played sharper or flatter by re-fingering them – in other words using one of the alternative fingerings that are dealt with in detail in the next chapter. To illustrate the possibilities and complexities of intonation control, let us consider the note F'. Its normal fingering (i.e. thumb and second finger of the left hand) is often a trifle flat. It is easy to make it flatter either by shading with the first or third fingers (or both) of the left hand or by using any of the twelve feasible shade-fingerings available in the right hand. It is not, however, an easy note to sharpen, for slide-fingerings in this position are rather critical. But there are plenty of alternative fingerings for F', with and without the thumb. Here are some of them:

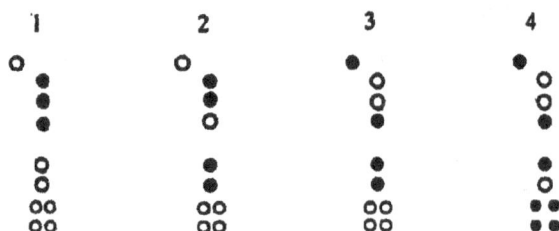

1	2	3	4

1 and 3 are the important alternatives. 1 varies considerably from one instrument to another, but generally gives either the same pitch as the normal fingering or is slightly sharper. It can, of course, be flattened by shading either with the thumb (too critical to be safe) or the first finger of the right hand, or by shade-fingering, the most useful being with the second finger of the right hand. As it is a forked fingering it is amenable to sharpening by slide-fingering. If 1 is flat, however, the variant of it as shown in 2 can be used, and this, being a double fork, is extremely easy to sharpen further by slide-fingering if necessary. 3 may be a little flat, but, because it is what one may call a 'wide fork' (there being two middle holes left open), it is less critical to slide-fingering and one, or even both, of the right-hand fingers may be taken off without sending it up to F♯'. 4 bears the same relation to 3 as 2 does to 1 and is therefore a little sharper than 3. With experimentation you will find at least thirty fingerings (excluding half-holes) that produce some version of the note F'. Most of the middle notes of the recorder behave similarly. Even though low and high notes offer less opportunity for variations of fingering, intonation control of some kind is obtainable with every note on the recorder. A thoroughly bad recorder, therefore, can be played perfectly in tune, though the result would not justify mastering the difficulties.

Tuning: devices and gadgets

There is no point in knowing how to play in tune if one's instrument is basically out of tune with the other instruments in an ensemble. The first requirement of a consort is that all the recorders should be warm. The motion of sound waves becomes more rapid in warm air, and the resultant rise in pitch is not compensated for by the expansion of the instrument as it gets warmer with the player's breath. A cold recorder, therefore, plays flat. If a consort starts with cold instruments there is not much point in tuning until you have 'warmed up'.

As it is easier to flatten a note than to sharpen it, the obvious rule for a recorder consort is to tune to the flattest instrument, warmed up and at medium breath input. If you know that your F' or D is generally on the flat side with the fingering you normally use for it, and you then find it is flatter than the other recorders you are playing with, you must either re-finger your flat notes, sharpen your instrument or persuade the other players to flatten theirs.

Flattening a recorder is easily done by 'pulling out', that is, adjusting the main joint so that it is not quite home and the instrument is thereby lengthened. A quarter of an inch is the utmost practicable limit of pulling out a treble recorder as the effect is more marked on the notes of the upper octave than the lower and more pulling out causes poor intonation. If bottom F tends to be sharp, try the effect on it and on other low notes of pulling out the foot-joint by no more than a quarter of an inch (otherwise your little finger may not reach its holes). The flattening effect of plasticine 'wings' is a little more evenly distributed, and the device can be used to tune a recorder made in one piece (e.g. a sopranino). The wings are vertical extensions by about an inch of the side walls of the 'window' of the recorder with pieces of plasticine rolled and flattened and pressed on each side of the window. The 'wheelbarrow' sound-projecting device (see p. 83) has the same flattening effect. Both devices make tone more 'plummy'. This method of tuning is used with metal organ-pipes which have two strips of metal standing out on either side of the mouth and at right angles to the lip: if bent inwards they lower the pitch and if bent outwards they raise it.

A recorder may be sharpened evenly throughout its range, with only a slight coarsening of tone-quality, by the use of tuning holes (see Kottick, *Tone and Intonation on the Recorder,* pp. 21–2). One or two small holes of a sixteenth of an inch diameter may be bored in the sides of the instrument at about a half to one inch lower down the instrument than the labium edge (more for bass, less for descant). Normally these holes are kept closed with wax (candle wax is easy to apply and remove) or with a wooden stopper, but if it is desired to raise the pitch of the instrument one or both of the holes may be opened. Amateur carpentry on recorders may, however, cause damage, so such modifications are best carried out by an instrument repairer.

If your recorder is slightly out of tune with itself, it may be quite an easy matter to re-tune it. Recorders may in fact slightly change in tuning as they age, irrespective of how well they are maintained. Again I refer readers to Kottick (pp. 22–7) for a clear account of what can be done with the minimum of risk by a player with no pretensions to carpentry, and of how to re-tune in order to remedy various faults. However, a good ear and a second opinion are strongly recommended.

Beats and difference-tones

Recorder players are lucky in that the 'pure-tone' quality of their instrument provides them with the assistance of audible 'beats' and 'difference-tones' to check intonation. Beats, which are most noticeable in two-part playing on high instruments, are caused when two recorders are not quite in unison: the beats become faster as the notes get more out of tune, and when the two notes are a minor third apart the frequency of the beats has become great enough to form an actual note, or difference-tone, technically 'heterodyne', which should be in harmony with the notes producing it. Two descant players can therefore play a trio by creating their own bass part in difference-tones, but they need to play most consummately in tune – and there is no reason why they should not.

A brilliant example of actually putting this phenomenon into effect may be found in Howard Harrison's *The Most Amazing Duet Book Ever* (Boosey and Hawkes, London, 1985) where (p. 27) two flutes (or treble recorders) play an arrangement of 'The Coventry

RECORDER TECHNIQUE

Carol' which creates its own bass in difference tones, which, however, vary in their prominence. Here, with permission of Boosey & Hawkes, is the second duet, arranged for two descant recorders; if when you play this you can hear the carol beneath perfectly in tune, you and your fellow duettist will have achieved unsurpassable control of recorder intonation.

V

ALTERNATIVE FINGERINGS

If the question were put 'what is most important in recorder technique – breath control, articulation, or fingering (including thumbing)?', one would prefer not to answer because all are so important, but if forced, the answer would have to be 'fingering'. Because the fixed windway and edge minimises control by the mouth and lips, a recorder player depends far more than other woodwind players on fingering devices to achieve good intonation, wide dynamics, and variety of tone. They are also needed to overcome the weakness of many recorders in making extraneous sounds ('clicks') when slurring across register breaks at G' to A', and D' to E♭'. As recorder semitones are generally cross-fingered, unlike those of fully keyed woodwind instruments, normal fingering on the recorder is rather complex, and attention needs to be given to means of facilitating passages involving contrary finger movements.

Daniel Waitzman, in *The Art of Playing the Recorder* (p. 79), challenges the idea of 'normal' fingerings – 'The concept of "standard" fingerings is of doubtful value for all woodwinds; it is of virtually no value on the recorder, an instrument with a very rich vocabulary of fingerings. On the recorder more than any other woodwind, selection of fingerings influences volume, timbre, and other qualities generally subsumed under the heading of "expressivity". Although there are no "standard" fingerings in the broadest sense of the term, there do exist fingerings which are more or less standard for a given musical-technical situation. The selection of the proper combination of fingerings to achieve the desired result constitutes the grammar of recorder fingering; it is this, rather than the mere unorganised knowledge of scores of different fingerings, that represents a true understanding of fingering on the recorder.' 'Normal' fingerings, will, however, on a well-tuned treble recorder be used perhaps nine times out of ten in playing Renaissance, baroque, and much twentieth-century music (see for example the number of instances where alternative fingerings are marked in the *Practice Book*), although they may be fine-tuned by shading and leaking. It is the ability to use the alternative fingering in the right place that distinguishes the experienced from the inexperienced player.

The physical mechanics of moving fingers and thumb on and off their holes, including subtleties of thumbing, are dealt with elsewhere in this book (e.g. pp. 110–12) and in *Introduction to the Recorder*. Many examples in the *Practice Book* are designed to develop good fingering (Exx. 18–49). This chapter is therefore devoted to a consideration of alternative fingerings and their use.

For a recorder player proceeding beyond the elementary stage, the discovery of the existence of alternative fingerings opens up wide vistas of new possibilities of the instrument: fast passages that tangled the learner's clumsy fingers suddenly become easy; ugly slurs full of 'clicks' and 'in-between notes' become neat and smooth. New alternatives are discovered that make awkward bars child's play. But then the player becomes more critical. Tonal inequalities in his alternative-fingered notes begin to make themselves heard, faults in intonation become apparent. He finds that the new facility in fingering which the use of alternatives has given him makes it quite easy to play previously hard passages with ordinary fingerings, which anyhow are more reliable both for sight-reading and under the strain of performance. And eventually he hits upon the paradox that alternative fingerings make the recorder harder to play, not easier. He uses them more sparingly, but to far greater effect.

The diagrams on p. 50 for F' fingerings illustrate the principle of finding alternatives. Most notes of the F major scale are 'plain-fingered', in other words, working from the thumb down you have a number of holes all covered followed by the remainder of the holes all left open. F, G, A, C, D, and E are plain-fingered, while Bb and F' are forked fingerings. Nearly every plain note has a forked alternative, but not necessarily perfectly in tune with it. Thus E can be played with the thumb and the first finger, or with the thumb and the second and third fingers; this latter is the best known of all alternative fingerings. Some of these forked alternatives can be 'double-forked' by lifting the lowest finger of the forked fingering and putting down fingers below it. Many forked fingerings can be widened by leaving two holes open and counteracting the sharpening by covering more holes lower down. An ordinary forked fingering can be flattened so much by adding fingers below that a note, a semitone, a tone, and possibly even a tone and a half below the original can be made to sound, so giving alternatives for other notes. Alternative fingerings produce notes that vary to a greater or less degree in intonation and tone-quality from notes produced by normal fingerings. Generally speaking, the more forked a note the poorer its tone-quality and its capacity to react to stronger tonguings: even carefully controlled vibrato cannot disguise its tonal weakness. Forked fingerings over an open thumb-hole tend to coarseness.

The tonal differences between a plain note and an alternative are seldom so slight that they can be ignored. In the following uses of alternatives, therefore, these variations in tone-quality have either to be overlooked or exploited (see Chapter VIII).

1. Trills

In trills and other rapid decorations the notes pass by so quickly that weaknesses in tone-quality are less likely to be apparent. Neatness and shapeliness are the main factors. Good execution at speed can best be achieved by utilising the minimum finger movements in passing from one note to another, and the employment of an alternative fingering can sometimes make the difference between moving five fingers or more and moving only one to change a note. Ideally all trills should be with one finger. This, then, is the most important use of alternative fingerings – indeed, they are often called 'trill-fingerings'. Sometimes the tonal inequality of the two notes of a trill adds interest and brilliance but care must be taken not to allow a preponderating note to spoil the pattern and fluency of a trill. Because a trill-fingering is generally forked, it is usually easy to add the turn at the end of the trill by putting down fingers below the fork: with normal fingerings some trills with turns are difficult to manage. The forked fingering of a trill often makes the final turn, which would otherwise threaten to be a mess, very simple to play, usually by adding two fingers below as in the F' to E trill (adding one finger) with a D turn (adding two more). It is frequently unwise to begin, and, even worse, to end a trill in an alternative fingering position, for once the repercussions have ceased, the possible poor quality of the note shows through. Quick thought matched by quick finger movements is necessary to get from the normal fingering of the appoggiatura on to the alternative for the trill itself, and then off it for the closing note. If you work all through the 'Three Blind Mice and baroque trills' exercises in Appendix 1 of this book you will become familiar with nearly all the trill fingerings used in recorder-playing.

2. Slurs

Quick slurs often demand alternative fingerings for the same reason that trills do. Try the effect, for example, of slurring G'–A'–Bb' quickly with ordinary fingering and then with the usual alternatives for G' (all on except thumb) and A' (lift second right): one is inevitably clumsy and full of 'clicks', the other is – or should be – neat. But this fingering is less useful in a slow, quiet movement as the coarse quality of the G' followed by the much thinner A' spoils the evenness of the flow, and the quiet thumbed G' should then be used. Somewhere between adagio and allegro, varying according to the player's skill in tonguing and his instrument's voicing and tone-quality, lies a point where the danger of perpetrating a 'click' matters more than disadvantages of unequal tone, for in all slurs, and in particular wide slurs, the player must above all aim at a smooth transition – that is the composer's intention in marking a slur. Eliminating 'clicks' over slurs is one of the chief objectives of recorder technique. The key to success lies in employing a judicious mixture of alternative fingerings and breath input techniques, in particular, according to context, 'y' half-tonguing or 'h' articulation.

3. Runs

Slurred runs in quick music can often be played more neatly with alternative fingerings. Moreover, a run which threatens to be uneven because of a difficult finger change immediately before an unaccented note can be made fluent and shapely by using an alternative fingering which throws the greatest finger movement on to an accented note. A good example is the D major scale played in the usual pattern of quaver, six semiquavers, crotchet (PB, Ex. 42). The accented note in this run is G': with normal fingering the greatest finger movement is from G' to A', which throws an accent on the A' and makes a 'click', but if the G' alternative is used the unavoidable five-finger movement is from F#' to G', where the accent is needed. Incidentally, the C#' at the end of this slur can be played with the second finger of the right hand instead of the first so that a one-finger movement (lifting of third left) is substituted for the normal three-finger movement. Economy in finger movement is the main purpose in using alternative fingerings in fast music.

4. Passage-work

The playing of broken chords and other semiquaver passages in allegros is simplified by alternative fingerings. Particularly useful are fingerings such as F' with three left and no thumb (illustrated on p. 50), and G' with third left and first right only, as they can form a pivot around which other notes may be grouped. For instance, the common semiquaver groups A'–F'–C–F' and G'–Eb–Bb–Eb are difficult to play rapidly with ordinary fingering, but with the alternatives mentioned they become easy because the fingers forming the alternative F' and E remain still for the whole group of notes, enabling movements higher and lower on the instrument to pivot round them with a sort of rocking motion: the finger(s) forming the 'fulcrum' should be held down firmly. This rocking effect is the secret of well-balanced passage-work. Intelligent fingering prepares the way to good interpretation.

5. Intonation Control

This use of alternative fingerings was dealt with in Chapter IV. A player should experiment with his instrument to find to what extent he may use alternative fingerings for intonation control without unduly affecting tone-quality.

6. Decrescendos

All alternative fingerings are forked fingerings; in the last chapter it was pointed out that forked fingerings are amenable to sharpening by slide-fingering. Conversely, such slide-fingerings may be used to keep intonation constant under a variable breath input, so allowing a note to swell or die away. The latter effect is difficult to manage on plain-fingered notes and an alternative must generally be used, but once again with the proviso that it does not unduly change the tone-colour, or, if it does, that such a change is justified.

7. Tone-quality changes

The different timbre of alternative-fingered notes may be exploited to add to the range of expression of the recorder (see Chapter VIII).

8. Keeping within the register

There are fingerings both with and without the partly closed thumb-hole for A', Ab', and G' (and also F#' but the thumbed alternative is rather stifled). The timbre of the thumbed notes matches that of the upper register, while the open notes have the fuller tone of the lower register. In playing a slurred adagio phrase that goes up or down to one of these notes it is as well to use the fingering that is least likely to make the note predominate by sounding different in quality. In fast music these notes are valuable to effect a smooth transition between the registers as the thumb may be brought into position while they are being played (as, for example, in the common G'–A'–B' slur – *PB*, Ex. 39).

In the following survey of alternative fingerings allowance must be made for differences between instruments: an alternative that works on one instrument will not necessarily do so on others. Readers of this book who have had little or no experience of using 'non-standard fingerings' (as they are often called) may find this survey rather perplexing. If so, I suggest they turn to Appendix 1 which, though chiefly about baroque trills, introduces alternative fingerings more in order of their frequency of use than in list form from the recorder's lowest note to its highest. This has the added advantage that you will study these fingerings in a musical context rather than considering each note in isolation; and you will learn how to do trills at the same time. My survey in Chapters V and VI can then be used to follow up this study and for later reference.

Alternative fingerings in the lower register

E: Officially the lowest note of the treble recorder is F. But a sharpish low E can be faked by lowering the instrument against the upper leg so that the bottom opening of the instrument is sufficiently shaded to flatten F by a semitone; the note should be played with little or no tonguing or it will sound F'. This, with care, can be surprisingly convincing, so long as nobody notices. It is difficult to approach from F, but much easier from F♯, G or notes above, as the bell-covering can be put into place while the preceding notes are being played.

F: There are no alternatives for F (but see p. 49). In order to play it pianissimo, gingerly slide-finger 7 over the bottom half-hole. F easily goes flat with lowering of breath input. For an F that might sound louder, shade the bell as for E, and use light, slow 'l' or 'r' tonguing.

With some recorders, especially the larger ones, bottom F (or C, as the case may be) may be sharp; this can be remedied by pulling out the foot joint – but not so far that it becomes difficult to reach the holes or key(s).

More on keyless tenor recorders than on trebles, the bottom note may not sound because of leaks in finger-hole coverage, and it is sometimes quite difficult to locate the culprit. First, make sure that the foot of the instrument is turned to its optimum position following the procedure described on p. 22, and readjusting until both the percussive notes ring clearly at each bang down of the little finger. Now try playing the bottom note again. If it still does not play properly, first check finger 4 which may have slipped downwards. The last possible culprit to try is 6; or perhaps 4 and 6 are both leaking. When you have got things right, do some bottom note practice, as at *PB*, Ex. 23. Remember that you can leave 7 in position when the preceding note is B♮ or above; and it is already in position with B♭.

F♯: G♭: No alternatives, other than very tight squeeze-thumbing for a *pp* version available on all lower register notes. The 'bending finger' and 'wrist swivel' methods of covering half-holes are described and illustrated in *Introduction to the Recorder*, pp. 43–4. If your music is in a sharp key, with no F♮s, stay in a slight wrist swivel position so that the little finger does not need to be bent to cover its half-hole. F♯ can be made more powerful by bell shading, which brings in a strengthening harmonic. It can all too easily be overblown, so use a big, low-pressure breath input, in the 'or' tongue position.

G: A rich-sounding note, slightly sharp on some recorders. If so, prefer reduction of breath input to shading, as shading is of necessity very critical and coarsens tone-quality. In the trill A♭ to G, G may be played 0 123 45⌀7*, with the half-holing 6 well arched and without swivelling the right hand round to the half-hole position; trill with 7 (asterisked). It is important to make sure you cover both half-holes with 7. You may find that clenching the thumbs and all the other fingers on the recorder (especially 6 on its half-hole), provided all the holes are properly covered, makes this trill easier to play, although generally in fingering, fingers and thumb should just rest on their holes without applying any pressure.

A♭: G♯: 0 123 45-7 with 6 heavily shaded may be used as the only alternative to half-holing. If normal A♭ is weak in tone-quality, first ensure that its half-hole is completely covered without impeding the air emerging from the neighbouring half-hole. If it is still weak, as may well be the case with some recorders, adjust your breath input using the 'or' tongue position until a small element of its first harmonic – the A♭' an octave above – merges into the sound. This, and a little touch of vibrato to cream it up, will endow it with the richness and penetrative power that may be required by the musical context. The same process can also be made to work with a weak bottom F♯, though a strengthening of that note is less often wanted.

When playing normal A♭ in a key where that note is part of the key signature, bring the right wrist to the full swivel position and (probably) keep it there. You may wish to look back at *Intro* to remind yourself of half-holing technique for the low notes, and to practise movement of the wrist between its three positions, i.e. for F (normal position), F♯ (half swivel) and G♯ (full swivel). The slur starting in the second bar of *PB*, Ex. 27 requires the use of all three positions – a good exercise for your right wrist. (Another one is the third of Alan Davis's *Fifteen Studies* (Schott, ED 11480)).

A: An alternative which provides one way of trilling B♭ to A is 0 123 4̸567, with 5 trilling in a well-arched position on to the near half of its hole. Placing the little finger of the left hand on the side of the instrument will give extra control over finger movements of the right hand.

B♭: A♯: Sharper (or softer) versions are 0 123 4-6̸7̸, or 0 123 4-6-, 0 123 4-6̸7̸ and 0 123 4-6̸-. The latter is useful for the B♭ to A♭ trill, trilling with 5.

A very slight lifting of 5 from the normal A fingering will give a poor B♭, virtually a semitone sharpening of A by slide-fingering. The right hand should be raised so that 5 is in an arched position and the curve of the fingertip just touches the far side of the hole, leaving the near side open. Although the tone-quality of this note is weak and stifled, it provides another way of doing fast trills from B♭ to A. The trilling finger continues to touch or nearly touch the recorder during this trill, seeming to move on the elasticity of the fleshy finger-pad. Although the movement is small, it should be controlled and regular, otherwise poor intonation and blurring result. The recorder needs to be held firmly to negotiate this trill, so it is helpful to steady the instrument by putting the little finger of the left hand underneath it, pressing upwards. Both this and the B to A trill (see below) tend to sharpness as it is difficult to keep the finger movement narrow enough. Unless the trill has to be played very rapidly it is better to do a B♭ to A trill with normal fingerings, despite the difficult contrary finger movements in the right hand: it is not necessary to keep 7 down for the trill itself.

In extremely rapid figurations you can get away with 0 123 4--- for B♭, although it is very sharp. But there may not be time to get 6 and 7 down and then back up again.

In a trill with C, try using just 4, not three fingers together. The flattening of the B♭ is so slight that it will not be noticed at speed.

B: If normal B is sharp, 7̸ should be added, or even all 7.

As normal B is a two-finger cross-fingering low on the instrument, it tends to be weak on larger recorders, and has to be given as full a tone as possible with the right tonguing and breath input, and perhaps (depending on the context) a touch of vibrato.

The very sharp alternative 0 123 –5-- may be used on the common B to A trill. Such sharpening makes a trill more brilliant, but it is a trick that can become a vice (though Ganassi advocated it). B to A trills can be more accurately negotiated with 4 moving in the same way as 5 does for the B♭ to A trill. It is preferable, however, to play this trill with normal fingerings, despite the contrary motion.

B to A♯ trills are done with 4 trilling on half its hole.

The poor-quality alternative 0 12∌ 4567 may be used for the turn after a D to C♯ trill. Reference is made on p. 97 to a very powerful B alternative.

On some large bass instruments with a key for finger 4, 0 123 4––– gives the best B.

C: 0 12– 4567 is a rather thin-toned alternative which nevertheless is valuable in soft passages or for echoes. It also does service in the rare C♯ to B♯ trill – it occurs in a Bach flute sonata – and as a D♭ to C trill in a Boismortier trio (PB, Ex. 58). A clear-toned alternative available on some recorders is 01–3 4567, which may be sharper or flatter, so needing shading with 2, or slide-fingering with 7, but it can only be obtained and held on with very low breath input and articulation without the tongue.

0 1–3 4567 may be used for the turn after an E♭ to D trill, but it is almost as awkward as using ordinary fingering.

C♯: D♭: It is debatable whether the normal fingering for this note is 0 12– 45––, 0 12– 456–, or even 0 12– 45∌–. Some recorders have a C♯ key.

A C♯ to B trill is taken 0 123* –56–, with 3 trilling low, or as 0 12– 456*7* with 3 shading slightly – too much activates a harmonic (PB, Ex. 26). Both are sharpish and need to be played with a drop in breath input.

For the C♯ turn after an E to D♯ trill 0 1–3 456∌ may be used, and for a D♭ turn after an F' to E♭ trill 0 –23 456–: both these alternatives are rather poor in quality for other uses.

D: The most important alternative fingering to be dealt with so far is 0 1–3 45∌–, the 'one-and-a-half-below' alternative for D. This is used primarily in the E♭ to D trill and slur. The trill can be done just with 5. It has a thin and remote quality that contrasts strongly with the powerful ordinary D, and as it is heavily forked it is amenable to slide-fingering and therefore to decrescendo effect. This alternative is a little on the sharp side, but as D is flat on some instruments by ordinary fingering, the one-and-a-half-below fingering is invaluable for getting it in tune when a compensatory increase in breath input would be undesirable.

The value of this fingering in the downward slur from E♭ may be demonstrated by playing the slur with the ordinary and then the alternative fingering: the transition from the subdued tone-quality of the forked E♭ to the firm ordinary D is ugly compared with the gentle sighing effect of the slur to the alternative D.

On some recorders the one-and-a-half-below D is too sharp to use, and the alternative must be fingered 0 1–3 456–. This makes the C turn after an E♭ to D trill easier, using 7, but with a reduction of breath input.

Another useful D alternative is 0 –23 45––. It is too heavily forked to be of good quality; its tone resembles that of the one-and-a-half-below but is weaker and less stable. It comes into its own in trills and fast slurs over the notes F'–E–D, where the well-known 0 –23 –––– alternative is used for E. Whenever the notes F'–E–D–E are encountered in fast music, this fingering should be employed.

The D alternative – 123 45∌– is of poor quality, so is only serviceable as a turn after an F♯' to E trill – 123* 4–∌–. 0 ––3 4567 is only a tonguing exercise.

E♭: D♯: As the normal fingering of E♭ is forked, it offers all sorts of variants: adding fingers below (seven variants) flattens it, while double-forking, e.g. 0 1–3 ––67, generally sharpens it. Because the ordinary fingering has a tendency to sharpness on some instruments the most useful of this large group of alternatives is the flattening 0 1–3 4–6–. This is often the best fingering with Renaissance recorders.

A second group of nine possible alternatives is based on the important fingering 0 –23 4–––. This note has a reasonable tone-quality, though inferior to the ordinary fingering. It affords the best way of managing the common F' to E♭ slur and trill (0 –23* 4–––), and the trill is easily turned by adding a finger (5) to give a D fingering already mentioned. Unfortunately the basic fingering of this group of alternatives is sometimes sharp and it must be flattened by adding a finger below such as 0 –23 4–6– (the F' to E trill still works with 3). The trill can, however, be played with an F' alternative followed by an E♭ alternative, e.g. – 1*23 45––, or –123 4*5*––, although this method may be criticised on the grounds that the upper note of a trill should, wherever possible, be a normal fingering, both to give the best tonal results and to make the trill easier to negotiate in the stress of performance. As it is quite impossible to trill neatly from F' to E♭ with normal fingerings for both notes, the execution of this trill and its turn in different contexts is a problem that every serious recorder player has to solve for himself.

The fingerings – 123 45–– and – –23 456– (which has little or no use) complete the pattern of alternatives for E♭. The first group consists of forked flattenings of the note E; the second group are flattenings of F'; the third is a flattening of the normal F♯', and the last of G'. The more remote the original note is, the heavier the forking has to be, and, in consequence, the poorer in quality the alternative and the more difficult to tongue with any degree of attack.

The E♭ to D♭ trill, which occurs in keys with four or more flats, is a problem. It cannot be resolved with an E♭ alternative, and in any case it is better to avoid starting trills on alternative fingerings. So it must begin with normal E♭. Adding 56 gives a D and not a D♭, so more flattening is needed. Adding all 7 to this either takes us into the next register or, with low breath input, produces a wheezy sharp C♮, which however might possibly be serviceable for a turn, although difficult to manage. Half-holing 7 does give D♭, but this is likely to be too sharp and may also still be on the edge of the register break. All that is left is to shade 2, but again this tends to activate the register break. The only solution is to combine some half-holing of 7 with some shading of 2, preferably done with an unbent finger. The trill can then be accomplished with 5 on its own, i.e. 0 1ƶ3 45*6ƶ.

On some Renaissance and bass recorders, E♭ is fingered 0 1–3 –––– (i.e. normal baroque fingering without 4), or 0 1–3 –5––.

E: The alternative 0 –23 –––– is so well known that it has been taken for the normal fingering of E. The plain-fingered 0 1–– –––– gives a richer note, however, and the fingering is easier to manipulate, particularly in the treble's basic key of G major. The alternative, which is not perfectly in tune on all instruments, is most useful in F' to E slurs and trills (with a 0 –23 45–– D turn), and it also reduces the number of finger movements in slurs from the upper octave such as C' to E. It may also be preferable to the main fingering in the common G' to E slur, but this, together with its use with C, is a matter of personal choice.

The flattening of F♯', already a forked fingering, gives – 123 4––– as a fairly poor-quality alternative E: it may be sharp but can easily be flattened by further forking (with

60

further tonal damage). This alternative is of use for an F♯' to E trill as follows:
– 123* 4–6–, and as the turn after a G'–F♯' trill (PB, Ex. 59).
The two usual E fingerings, the plain fingering and the 0 –23 –––– alternative, seem to meet all exigencies, for they are both amenable to intonation shifts on the principles set out in Chapter IV. The plain fingering can be flattened by wide forks such as 0 1–– 4–––, and the alternative may be flattened in the same way with 5, or sharpened with fingerings such as 0 –2– 45∅–.

The upper notes of the recorder's lower octave, from C upwards, are increasingly amenable to thumb-leaking for soft notes, although the thumb-nail has to be positioned very accurately to maintain good intonation (see p. 49).

F': F' alternatives have already been discussed in some detail (p. 50); if they were all counted it would not be surprising to find that there were more than a hundred possible fingerings for F' (allowing half-hole variants and tonally useless alternatives).
The main alternative is – 123 ––––. Although the tuning of this note varies quite a bit from one recorder to another, it generally tends to sharpness whereas the normal fingering tends to flatness: it is therefore very useful for dynamic purposes, particularly as it is amenable to further sharpening. It is invaluable in passage-work moving from the lower to the upper octave across F' as it allows time for the thumb to move into place (PB, Ex. 29): play rapidly C'–F'–C–F' with both ordinary and alternative fingerings to prove the value of the alternative (see also p. 55). This fingering should always be used to play E♯' partly because it is tonally weaker than the tonic F♯', and partly because it makes the F♯' to E♯' trill easy to negotiate with –123 45–– as the D♯ turn.
The other important alternative, with a surprisingly good tone-quality, is
0 ––3 4––– (sharpish) or 0 ––3 45–– (flattish), with 0 ––3 4–6– as a variant, and they can all be flattened, e.g. with 7. The latter fingering provides a further F' to E♭ trill, using 1.
F' may be played ∅ 1–– 45––, ∅ 1–– 4–––, or ∅ 1–– –––– according to the amount of thumb opening. The first of these poor-quality alternatives has obvious uses in quick jumps or slurs from top F"; octave jumps from E' to E can be managed, but less well, in much the same way. They all form part of the recorder's repertoire of soft fingerings.
A useless F' alternative is 0 ––– 456∅: but it is interesting because, contrary to expectations, sliding the little finger across on to both its half-holes does not always flatten the note but may cause it to 'break' upwards to between F♯' and G', a phenomenon otherwise peculiar to the upper octave.

Alternative fingerings in the upper register

The exact position of the thumb makes or mars the production of good notes with alternative fingers in the upper octave. To describe the movement of the thumb in its octaving function it is preferable to use the word 'thumbing', rather than 'pinching', although the latter appears in eighteenth-century tutors. This is partly to discourage the taut and unrelaxed positioning of the thumb implied in the word 'pinching' (some players press so hard against the side of the thumb-hole that they actually bend their thumb-nail), and partly to facilitate the employment of the method of octaving which involves drawing the thumb slightly to one side from the closed position and opening a crevice between the flesh of the thumb and the rim of its hole instead of between the thumb-nail and the rim as in 'pinching'. This method of octaving requires the minimum of movement from the position in which the thumb-hole is closed, so long as the thumb is always kept fairly upright (see *Intro*, illustrations on pp. 32, 33, and 22). The thumb movement need be no more that a pivot on the soft flesh of the thumb, a smaller movement than 'pinching'. Compare the ease with which rapid C to C' jumps can be managed by pivot thumbing with the awkwardness of alternatively pinching and closing the thumb-hole. Note that in pivot thumbing the thumb-nail may still be touching the recorder, as it may in the fully closed position, but it touches just outside, not inside, the thumb-hole rim. The disadvantage of this method is that it is less easy to make the minute measurements of thumbing necessary for the perfect production of high notes (see Chapter VI) than it is with the thumb-nail; octave slurs from D to D' will demonstrate this. The ideal is a combination of the two methods, the thumb-nail being brought into use for greater precision or when accurate thumbing is called for on high notes (*PB*, Ex. 35), for the *ppp* bottom octave, or for other purposes.

Widening the thumb aperture in the upper octave sometimes causes sharpening. With the thumbed F♯' (see below) the sharpening is considerable; with A', however, there is no such effect (a useful phenomenon), nor is there any until C♯', where the sharpening is limited by the note breaking downwards when the aperture becomes too wide. Within the bounds of safety, however, thumb sharpening can be used as a form of intonation control for C♯' and notes above it. Much better intonation control for C' and above can be exercised by slide-fingering 1 (see p. 48).

Widening the thumb aperture also causes the breathy undertone which is present in some degree with all thumbed notes to become more prominent, raising its quite perceptible pitch at the same time by as much as a tone and a half. This sharpening of the undertone has sometimes been confused with the much slighter (if any) sharpening of the main note – what actually happens can be tested with an electronic tuner. Too wide a thumbing aperture produces a kind of multiphonic, not a particularly pleasant one even if the two notes harmonise. Great care must therefore be taken in controlling the tone-quality of thumbed notes.

F♯': G♭': The normal fingering – 12– – – – – is a forked flattening of G': it can itself be flattened by further forking, e.g. – 12– 45– –, although with too many fingers added it may go down to F' or, surprisingly, break up to A♭' (e.g. – 12– 456⫫).
The note may be sharpened (for it often offends by flatness) by double-forking, e.g. – 1–3 4– – –, or – 1–3 –5–7: there are many variations.
The fork may be widened to give either sharper or flatter alternatives such as – –23 – – – – (sharper),or – –23 4–6(7) (flatter). The even wider fork – – –3 456– is a curiosity because it seems uncertain as to whether it wants to play F♯' or A♭'; its efforts at both can be poor, although on most instruments A♭' is quite good.
F♯' played 0 – – – – – – – is probably too powerful in tone-quality for normal use, but 0 1*– – – – – – gives a heroic F♯' to E trill on a D major cadence. Virdung (1511) and other Renaissance writers, however, give it as normal fingering for F♯', for it is more even in quality with its neighbours on a Renaissance wide-bore recorder. Baroque F♯' tends to be flat on Renaissance recorders: other possible fingerings are – 1–3 – – – –, – 1–3 4– – –, or – 1–3 –5– –. Variants of these can be used as soft fingering alternatives with an open G' fingering for G'–F♯' trill.

F$\sharp$' is the first note we have got to which responds to thumbing, though its tone-quality, too, sounds 'pinched'; the thumb aperture should be small: $\emptyset$ 123 4567. It can be used for an F$\sharp$' turn after an A' to G' trill resolving upwards, in fast slurs with high notes, or fast slurred runs (with G' as $\emptyset$ 123 456–) in the upper register where F$\sharp$' is the lowest note; its use in an arpeggiated slur is shown in *PB*, Ex.38, bar 4.

G': Like all notes in the middle of the recorder's compass, G' can claim a vast number of fingerings, particularly as – ––– –––– gives a G' (very sharp and coarse). One finger on anywhere gives G' although – 1–– –––– is rather flat, and most combinations of two or three fingers also produce it – a veritable *embarras de richesse*. The most useful one of this huge group of alternatives is – ––3 4––– which is handy for the common E$\flat$ to G' slur as it makes it a two- instead of a four-finger movement. If normal G' is flat (e.g. with a Renaissance recorder), it can be played with 3 instead of 2. This also very useful as a soft G' fingering, as its tone-quality varies only slightly from normal G', like most of the fingerings in this group, which are referred to as 'open G'' fingerings.

By far the most important G' alternative, and the second in importance of all alternatives, is – 123 4567, referred to as the 'closed G'' fingering. It is powerful and sometimes rather coarse in tone-quality and must therefore be treated gently. Moreover, it tends to vary in accuracy of intonation from one recorder to another, and must be tested against normal open G'; it may be the case that on some recorders it is too out of tune to be really usable. But if it is flat it can easily be sharpened by slide-fingering 7 or 1, which also makes it slightly less strident. While its strong tone-quality can be put to great effect in certain musical contexts, the chief value of closed G' lies in its crucial position at the register-break crossing, and in its use in the A' to G' trill. This is generally fingered – 123 45*67. Occasionally 6 has to be used rather than 5 for this common trill, although – 123 456*7*, and $\emptyset$ 123 456*$\not{7}$(*), are possibilities, the latter, which is the 'thumbed G'' discussed later, being useful when – 123 4–67 gives a sharp A'. When this trill, as it often does, commences with an A' appogiatura, the A' should be thumbed, for with an open thumb-hole it is coarse in quality and sometimes difficult to articulate; the thumb should be moved immediately the trill begins or the G' will be very flat. If the trill finishes with an F' or F$\sharp$' turn, the G' before the turn should be the normal fingering, and so, generally, should the G' after the turn. The semiquaver phrase (slurred) A'–G'–A'–G'–A'–G'–F'–G', with the first two G's being closed alternatives and the last two ordinary, should be practised to perfection (see p. 128).

On most recorders the upward slur from open G' to A' tends to 'click' with normal fingering, and it is well to become accustomed to use the –123 4567 G' alternative for this slur in most contexts. The only objection to its use is in slow music where the coarseness of the G' alternative may become noticeable and spoil a phrase by tonal ugliness or false accentuation: the solution, then, is to tongue on normal fingerings with such subtlety that an impression of slurring is given. The use of the G' alternative should be almost a reflex action for G'–A'–B' and G'–A'–B$\flat$' slurs, fingered – 123 4567, – 123 45––, $\emptyset$ 123 –5––, and – 123 4567, – 123 4–67, $\emptyset$ 123 4–6– respectively, in each case the thumb being moved into its octaving position during the playing of the A'. In slurred D major runs or scales (which are frequent in recorder music) the G' alternative should always be used in the upward slur, firstly because it facilitates fingering, the first finger of the left hand being able to stay down, secondly because the dangers of 'clicking' between F♯' and closed G' are far less than between ordinary G' and A', and thirdly because the finger movement favours the shape of the run (see under 'Runs', p. 55). In F' to closed G' slurs the likelihood of 'clicks' is greater than in F♯' to closed G' slurs, and fingering in an F'–G'–A' slur is therefore a matter of choice, dependent upon the musical demands of the context, upon personal preference, and upon how reluctant and 'clickish' your recorder is when crossing the break – some recorders are able to cross the break with elegant smoothness in which case normal fingerings may be used instead of the clumsier alternative G'. Rapid F'–G'–A' slurs can easily be negotiated by using an open thumb-hole alternative for F', e.g. – 123 ––––, followed by – 123 4567 and – 123 45––. In slurs down from A' to G' use the ordinary G' and not the alternative fingering (unless the slur goes down and then up again).

The third important group of G' fingerings is the thumbed G' ∅ 123 456⁊, which has a reedy, slightly stifled quality. Again its intonation varies markedly from one instrument to another, but good tuning can be achieved at most volumes (but not loud as it easily breaks upward to D') by widening the thumb aperture or by slide-fingering 7 or 1. It is beautifully clear as a soft G' fingering, even down to *ppp*. Moreover, because it is so easy to tune, it will trill with A' by using only 6. This is the better A'–G' trill in quieter music, the trill with closed G' being used for louder music. A thumbed G' variant is ∅ 123 45∅7, which is awkward, but ideal for trills with A' in the quieter range. Some recorders will actually play an accurate thumbed G' without ⁊, a considerable advantage, but one likely to be offset by fingering problems elsewhere. But, with close thumbing, this makes a good G' at low breath input. Thumbed G' is also useful for the mordent A'–G'–A', in a G' turn after a B' to A' trill, and in certain slurs and jumps to high notes where neatness at speed can only be managed if the thumb stays still. With or without ⁊ it may need to be used for most A'–G' trills if your closed G' is sharp.

A♭': G♯': This note has two fingerings, analogous to the closed G' alternative and to the thumbed version, each with comparable tone-qualities. The ordinary fingering is generally given as – –23 456–, or the same with the first finger down (flatter and coarser). It will strike on most instruments without the second finger down (i.e. – ––3 456–).

The sharpest alternative is – ––3 456 (or ∅) –, and it is also the coarsest. Even this, however, on some instruments is not as sharp as it should be, and an accurate A♭' can only be achieved by octaving the lower register fingering ∅ 123 45∅–, which then becomes the normal fingering. This note is true but comparatively subdued, its tonal kinship being with E♭' rather than G'. It is easily flattened (little finger shading) or sharpened by slide-fingering, rolling ∅ back very cautiously.

Players who are able to use both the thumbed and the open A♭'s are happily faced with the opportunity to exercise their musicianship by suiting the fingering to the context. The easy sharpening of the thumbed A♭' makes it more suitable for use in quiet passages; while the open A♭' is used where strength or an accent is required. Jumps to the lower register are more easily managed with the thumbed fingering, particularly if the pivot method is used, but here again the context may require the more powerful note.

The A♭' to G trill is a crux in recorder playing. Here are ten possibilities to try, not all of them of value:

(i)	–	1 2 3	4*5 6 7	(Ab' rather flat).
(ii)	–	1*2 3	4*5 6 7	(accurate but rather difficult).
(iii)	–	1 2 3	4 5 6 7*	(Ab' rather flat).
(iv)	–	1*2 3	4 5 6 7*	(accurate but very difficult).
(v)	Ø	1 2 3	4 5 Ø 7*	(G rather sharp).
(vi)	–	– 2*3*	4 5 6 –	(like the remainder, 'clickish').
(vii)	–	– – 3*	4 5 6 –	
(viii)	–	– 2 3*	4*5 6 –	(gives an F' turn with the thumb).
(ix)	–	– – 3*	4*5 6 –	
(x)	–	– – 3	4 5 6*–	(G rather flat).

A choice of evils lies before the recorder player: the first might be favoured for very fast trills and the second or fourth where intonation becomes a consideration, while the ninth can have a pleasing bright neatness admirable in some contexts, despite the clicks (see p. 97).

The difficult G#' to F#' trill may be fingered – –23 4*56–, – 1́23 4*5*6–, or – 123* 4*56–, all being decidedly 'clickish'. Alternatively it can be played without 'clicks' with the extremely awkward fingering Ø* 123 4567*.

A': By a very short head, the best fingering for A' is the normal Ø 123 45––, but – 123 45–– and – –23 45–– are identical in intonation and only slightly less good in tone-quality (compare the windy undertone produced by each). They are similar enough in quality that, except in slow music, the thumb may be brought into the octaving position during the playing of the note. This characteristic is taken advantage of in the G'–A'–B' and G'–A'–Bb' slur fingerings already referred to, and it should be exploited whenever occasion demands so that the thumb can be carefully placed in the correct octaving position for the following notes (this is yet another good reason for always reading a few notes ahead of the note you are actually playing). Generally speaking, the proximity of G's and F#'s calls for an open A', while higher notes and lower octave notes suggest the normal fingering for A', particularly if pivot thumbing is used for jumps from the low octave.

In the G'–A'–Bb' slur fingering the note A' is produced by the fingering – (or Ø) 123 4–67. This is a weaker fingering as it needs light tonguing and is coarse in quality with the thumb off. It tends to sharpness (again varying from one instrument to another) but this does at least increase its value as a soft fingering. It is useful in the Bb' to A' trill, although one needs a supple little finger to keep it going long. A sharp Bb' to A' trill is Ø 123 45*––, but it can be brought into tune by trilling with 5 very low. Trilling with 7 is preferable in most contexts.

Another crux in recorder technique is how to negotiate the common slur F' to A'. The only answer is to use normal fingering, pivot thumbing, and carefully concealed tonguing. At first the proposition – 123 –––– to – 123 45–– looks attractive, but in fact it is very 'clickish' and this fingering only comes into its own when applied, trumpet-like, to the slurred fanfare C'–A'–F'–C– A–C–F'–A'–C', or, without upward slurring, to passage-work (see above under the note F'). A slight increase in breath input at the moment of the slur up to A' helps considerably, but it is agility of fingering and thumbing that counts most.

Bb': A#': This note needs to be played with careful control of breath input as on some recorders it tends to blurt. It may be slightly sharpened by slide-fingering, to which, as a forked fingering, it responds well. Ø 123 4–Ø7 gives a slightly sharp Bb' that is useful before the trill with Ab' Ø 123 45*Ø–. This is a more accurate trill than the coarse and

65

sharp – 123 45*6– fingering, which can, however, be mollified by a touch of thumbing. Ø 123 4––7 gives a sharp (or soft) B♭'.

A slur or trill from B' to A♯' is taken Ø 123 –5∅*– with 4 going down for the turn. This A♯' fingering is tongueable but sharpish. The right hand should adopt the wrist pivot half-hole position for this alternative.

B': As with all forked fingerings, intonation control is easy to manage, sharpening by slide-fingering 5 or 1, flattening with a touch of ∅.

An alternative worth mentioning is Ø 12– 45–– which can be used as a mordent or turn after C♯'. In using it breath input must drop slightly or it will strike E', for which it is, of course, the normal fingering. And then there is the extraordinary curved finger half-holing of 4, described on p. 97.

C': When buying a recorder, one of the things that should be tested is the accuracy of the note C', for it is a dictator among the notes of a recorder as it lacks a range of alternative fingerings. For sharpening, thumb slide-fingering does nothing, but it is effective with 1. Flattening is of course straightforward, either by ordinary or by little-finger shading. The effect of the flattening Ø 123 ––6– is just about slight enough to make a one-finger movement of the C' to B♭' trill: Ø 123 4*–6–.

Mordents or trill turns after C♯' may be fingered Ø 12– 4–6–, but this C' (or B♯') cannot be tongued with security. Adding first 5, then 3, starts a slur down in C♯ major.

C♯': D♭': This note requires at least two-thirds coverage of the thumb-hole, preferably an aperture equivalent to one-tenth or less of the area of the thumb-hole (though optimum thumbing apertures for high notes will vary from one recorder to another – the fractions given in this book are only guidelines). Rapid repetitions require light, precise tonguing and close thumbing (but see p. 33). There is enough latitude of thumb movement to effect some sharpening (which is often needed as C♯' is flat on many recorders), but as this note often tries to clear its throat before speaking it is wise to begin with close thumbing and the moment the note speaks to slip the thumb across to sharpen it – it should all be done so quickly that nobody notices. It is amenable to some slide-fingering with 1, and shading with ∅.

A useful C♯' alternative in slurs (it is very difficult to tongue) is Ø 12– –5––. This is handy for the common A'–B'–C♯'–D' slur (or its reverse) as well as for the tricky B♯'–C♯'–D♯' upward slur; it needs tight thumbing to negotiate the C♯' and the register break between it and D♯'. As is to be expected of a wider fork, this fingering for C♯' is slightly sharper than the normal fingering.

Ø 123 4567 is a sharp C♯' fingering useable only in slurs down from E' and D♯'. It is impossible to slur from D♯' to the slow-speaking normal C♯' without a 'click', so trills between these notes (or E♭' to D♭') should be done with this fingering, trilling with 3 and 7 together, or, sometimes better, with 2.

If you try to articulate this Ø 123 4567 fingering for C♯', you may get it, but you might get F♯' for which it is the thumbed fingering. As we have seen, there are articulation difficulties with the other fingerings, and with close thumbing C♯' is often flat – compare it with your D♯' a tone above. There is a strong case, therefore, for cultivating C♯' as a half-holing of 3. The amount of half-holing needs to be very accurate and this requires a lot of practice and some boldness in a performance situation. It resolves the articulation and intonation problems, and the tone-quality is gentler than, but as good as, the normal fingering. Adding 5 below it gives C', and adding 4 and 6 gives B♮'.

We have now, however, reached another turning point in the mechanics of the recorder, for contrary to expectations, adding a finger below C♯' results in an upward break instead of flattening. This phenomenon is the basis of high note fingerings described in the next chapter. It does, however, give the C♯' fingering ∅ 123 –567. On Renaissance wide-bore recorders and with some basses, normal C♯' can be so difficult to tongue that it is too unreliable for general use, whereas ∅ 123 –567 gives a sweet and responsive C♯'.

Extended alternative fingerings

Lest it be thought that the foregoing is a complete review of alternative fingerings up to C♯' I would refer the reader to Michael Vetter's book *Il flauto dolce ed acerbo* (instructions and exercises for players of new recorder music) (Moeck, 4009). This lists several hundred fingerings for standard pitches of the open register, i.e. with no bell-key or the bell-key open, for chords, and for notes incorporating white noise ('rustling noises of air and harmonics'), and then repeats the process for the fully closed register, and for the covered register, i.e. with the bell covered but not airtight. Other lists include thumbed harmonics in the lower octave (p. 60), and similar very thin sounds in the upper octave. Even so, Vetter does not attempt to list the multitude of fingerings needed for playing microtone compositions.

To take an example, reference is made on p. 57 to playing bottom F *ppp* and in tune by slide-fingering 7. In practice this can be achieved by slide-fingering, or rather just leaking, *any* finger or the thumb, and each thin quiet note produced has a slightly different quality. A contemporary composer may wish to use a particular sound, probably electronically amplified, in which case he will indicate the desired fingering.

Another review of fingerings, much shorter and more critical, appears on pp. 81–106 of Daniel Waitzman's *The Art of Playing the Recorder*. This includes bell-key fingerings, but is nevertheless a useful commentary for players of keyless treble recorders. The treble recorder, more easily than recorders of other sizes, can be shaded or even covered by lowering it upon the upper leg (see pp. 57 and 74). If it is fully closed (airtight) with all fingers and thumb on, the treble recorder produces a cavernous low B♭. With other fingerings the closed, covered, or shaded bell produces a wide range of interesting notes, increasing the recorder's tonal range for use in contemporary music. There is then, however, the problem of taking account, while playing, of all the different fingerings required by the composer and indicated in the score, or of learning the piece by heart with the special fingerings.

To attempt to play avant-garde music certainly increases one's knowledge of the recorder's ultimate capacities. Berio's *Gesti*, for example, dissociates fingering from articulation so that a percussive noise (based on a Telemann duet) is produced by the fingers alone while the breath articulation is itself not synchronised with the fingering. Such a piece needs to be prefaced by an explanation of the signs used in the score – although it might be said this is no more than was the case with eighteenth-century French music. Whether players will wish to master this vast vocabulary of fingerings will depend on their adventurousness, their open-mindedness and their judgment as to whether the reward in musical satisfaction is worth the considerable effort of so greatly extending their technique (see p. 139–140).

This double-pipe player, frescoed around 1330 by Simone Martini in St Martin's chapel in the lower church of St Francis at Assisi, is probably playing a two-note chord to accompany a melody plucked on a small lute (mandora). The two held notes need to be exactly in tune, and to achieve this the player has half-holed, or slide-fingered, the first finger of his right hand. This image predates unambiguous evidence for the existence of the recorder by some fifty to sixty years, but our instrument may have come into being at any time during the last half of the fourteenth century (see *Companion,* Ch. 1). Methods of fingering its predecessors would have been taken over by players of the recorder, and half-holing is still used today by skilled players of six-holed duct-flutes in various parts of the world. Ganassi confirms that recorder players were expected to use these techniques in 16th-century Venice. A less close detail of Simone Martini's musicians illustrates my 'Short History of Partial Venting' in *The Recorder Magazine* for June, 1995; fine control of partial venting is needed to produce accurate and beautiful high notes on recorders.

VI

HIGH NOTES

Readers who have followed this book recorder in hand should now shut windows and warn neighbours, for it is probable that in introducing oneself to the highest notes on the recorder some rather loud and unpleasant noises might be perpetrated before they become softer and sweeter through familiarity and a growing command of tonguing and thumbing.

Tonguing and thumbing – these are the clues to success in the highest register. Look back to Chapter III and practise again some of the exercises suggested there until you are sure you have learned the knack of altering the strength of articulation in the tonguing without changing the breath input on the note itself. To obtain high notes cleanly, use the precise tonguing 't'. It is precision of tonguing that matters, i.e. the speed and pointedness of the tongue stroke on to the teeth-ridge, not its strength (i.e. how firmly the tongue is pressed on to the teeth-ridge and air-pressure built up before the note starts). Nevertheless high notes will respond to variations in the strength of tonguing. Practice D' with 't' tonguing, varying from a strong 't' down to the lightest 't' at which the note will strike. You will find that it responds better to the lighter tonguings: the strong tonguing will give a less clean articulation, for the D' will be mingled with elements of the next harmonic, A". If you tongue more strongly, you will in fact strike A" or thereabouts. It is a very common fault when embarking upon the intermediate stage of recorder playing to tongue high notes too strongly. Having felt the range of tonguings within which D' can adequately be articulated, construct for yourself a gradation of light, medium, and strong tonguings for D'. Now on each of these play the note in turn *f*, *mp*, and *pp* (i.e. nine variants) keeping within the range at which the note, once struck, can be played with an acceptable tone-quality at different volumes (ignore intonation changes for the time being).

You should next see what happens when you articulate repeated D's with double-tonguing. If you try 'diri-diri's, you will have difficulty in getting the note to start cleanly with 'r'. This is too imprecise an attack for high notes. 'l' is not much better. High notes will respond to 'k', within the double-tonguing 'tee-kee, tee-kee', although they come more easily on the 't' stroke. Quite apart from fingering problems, this is why fast passage-work at the extreme of the recorder's compass is so difficult, unless the voicing and construction of your recorder especially favours high notes. Generally, try and manage high notes with single-tonguings (PB, Ex. 46), except in high velocity scales and passage-work where a very deliberate 't–k' might be preferable. The shortness of tongue movement using 'tee's' and 'dee's' helps.

Consider next the position of the tongue in the mouth between the tonguing strokes. It should be high, in order to make your column of breath flow through the mouth at a higher pressure, but using no more air than for lower notes. This point is explained more fully on p. 27. The vital thing to keep in mind is that as you go higher on the recorder you change from 'er' for the middle notes to 'ee' for the high notes. You 'smile your way up' to the high notes.

While the narrowing of the airstream passage resulting from the 'ee' position is adequate for most high notes, some notes may still be difficult to articulate cleanly, especially when they are played softly. There is a still higher tongue position, which may help to solve such problems. This is 'ü' as in German or French, a vowel sound given by Hotteterre for flautists. To find this position anchor the sides of the tongue firmly against the upper molars, and stretch the lips so hard that the insides of the cheeks push between the back teeth. Arch the tongue upwards close to the dome of the hard palate, leaving a narrow passage across the top of the tongue and past its tip which is just enough to allow the airstream to get through, but not so constricting as to create turbulence which will insinuate a breathy sound into the tone-quality of the note. In this position the tip of the tongue is ideally placed for a very short traverse to a very quick-speaking 't' articulation. While it is indubitably effective in producing good high notes, this grimacing position strains the facial muscles and is hardly conducive to relaxed recorder playing.

Now turn your attention to the thumb, still practising on the note D'. As 'pinched' thumbing is more reliable than 'pivot' thumbing for high notes, first cut the nail fairly short. Place the thumb into its hole, and, in as relaxed a manner as possible, move the thumb about the hole, gently feeling its edges. Try pivoting on the thumb-nail so that the fleshy side of the thumb is lifted slightly away from the far side of the thumb-hole. This produces 'double-thumbing' where the thumbing aperture is divided between the upper and lower area of the thumb-hole. It has the effect of moving the 'speaker' aperture lower down the body of the instrument, where it seems to respond more readily to the higher breath pressures used for high notes. You may well find that double-thumbing helps you to play all high notes more confidently. It is important, however, never to allow the thumb to tense up in the process of discovering the optimum double-thumbing apertures for each note. All the while in playing high notes the thumb should be absolutely relaxed, and should touch its hole so lightly that, if someone gave it a gentle flick while you are playing, it would be pushed away. Of course, if the thumb-hole is damaged or worn down by harsh thumbing it should be re-bushed, for it is not easy to produce good high notes with a worn thumb-hole.

Apart from controlled tonguing and sensitive and relaxed thumbing there is another prerequisite to the successful playing of high notes. Drops of moisture in the tone-producing areas have a pernicious effect on high notes, and as air is pushed more rapidly through the windway in producing high notes, conditions are conducive to wetness. It is therefore essential that for playing a piece containing high notes the recorder should start clean, warm, and dry.

In fingering all notes of the recorder, and particularly high notes, all the fingers, and indeed the whole hand, should be relaxed. Each finger should rest firmly but gently on its hole, lightly enough for an infinitesimal movement to be sufficient to make the difference between closing and just not quite closing the hole.

Let us now proceed to the fingerings for each note.

D': This is not always an easy note to produce. Its normal fingering, Ø 12- ----
requires no more than medium tonguing, otherwise it will overblow. It is often flat, but may be sharpened by widening the thumb aperture immediately after striking, although

this makes it sound more breathy. D' will only strike with a fairly small aperture – never less than eight-tenths closed, but on the other hand too close thumbing will make the note harsh and tight pinching therefore spoils it. It is probably better to slide-finger 1 for soft D's, which will then need 'tü' articulation. Shade with 7 for loud D's.

The main alternative for D' is ∅ 12ƶ 4567, especially useful for trills after E' and E♭', with 3 variously shading or half-holing to control intonation. The trill with E♭' can be done with 7 or 6, and with E' both together, or, surprisingly, with 2 doing the trilling (*PB* Ex. 60). The alternative D' is very useful for turns after trills involving E'. A more subdued variant is to half-hole 7 and leak 3. With some instruments this may provide more satisfactory trill configurations.

In the previous chapter we saw how a wide-bore recorder's reluctance to speak C♯' with ∅ 12– 4––– could be overcome by using ∅ 123 –567. Similarly, as the end of the compass of a wide-bore recorder is reached, problems may be encountered in getting D' to speak. The apparently perverse fingering ∅ 12– 4567 may in fact be the solution. Some Renaissance recorders, however, are happier with only one added finger, e.g. ∅ 12– –––7. In this respect recorders react in the same way as reed-cap instruments – they seem to like 'stabilising' right-hand fingers added for notes made with left-hand fingers. The same may apply to bass recorders, although a bass recorder tends to be a law unto itself in fingering high notes. D' may tongue adequately on an F-bass recorder with normal fingering, but you may find that it becomes more responsive to a range of tonguings if stabilising fingers are added. The same may apply to C♯', and even to C'.

E♭': D♯': The normal fingering, ∅ 12– 456–, gives a clear and lovely note on most instruments, even on basses and wide-bore instruments that are capricious on D' and C♯'. The thumbing is not critical – the note can be induced to strike with only three-tenths of the thumb-hole closed: the optimum thumbing is nine-tenths shut. For pianissimo playing the third finger of the right hand may be brought back to its half-hole: the note can be flattened by moving the little finger across to its half-hole. These could be your normal fingerings if you need to correct the tuning.

E♭' has a number of alternatives such as ∅ 12– –56–, ∅ 12– ––6ƶ, ∅ 12– ––67 and ∅ 12– –––7, which vary in tone-quality and intonation. On some instruments, the first of these may be better than the 'normal' fingering with 4 down.

E' is another easy high note with ∅ 12– 45–– as its standard fingering. It responds best to firm, precise tonguing, and strikes at seven-tenths thumbing, the optimum being just over eight-tenths, a slightly wider aperture than the best for D'.

An alternative available on some instruments for slurs after D', and trills E' to D' (using normal fingering for the first E') is ∅ 1–– ––––. Despite its undeniable usefulness, on other recorders it may be found not to work reliably; if it is risky, avoid it, as the trill may start but then collapse, with dreadful effect, as it is continued. With this fingering it is usually necessary for the thumbing to be as close and tight as possible, for the trilling finger (2) to trill low, and for the breath input to be no more than medium, otherwise – strange phenomenon! – the fingering may give F″ instead of E'. A fast D'–E'–F″ slur is best played with this fingering for E' as the 'click' between E' and F″ is much less than the 'click' across the powerful register break between D' and E' with normal fingerings. E' is sharp on some instruments and may then need 7 to be in tune.

E' can be obtained with good tone and quick tonguing response by flattening F″ with 67́
or 67. Over-tonguing must be avoided or the fingering may strike G″. This fingering can
easily be sharpened or flattened so it is useful for obtaining dynamic gradations. Daniel
Waitzman also advocates it for slurred leaps from below (try from B'). With a very wide
thumbing aperture it is possible to do octave slurs with lower register E, using breath
pressure control by tongue movements.

On basses and Renaissance instruments the starting point for E' is always the 'two left,
two right' normal fingering, although the two right-hand covered holes could easily be 56
instead of 45. If E' is flat, leaking 1 or 2 may be the solution, or even taking 2 off
altogether, although it is disconcerting to have to finger normal F″ to play E'.

F″ needs considerable care. Its normal fingering is Ø 1-- 45-- and the optimum
thumbing is nine-tenths. With this thumbing F″ may be played fairly softly. More than
nine-tenths thumbing makes a harsh F″, so it is a fallacy that for top F″ the tightest
possible thumbing should be used. With less than seven-tenths thumbing, F″ will not
articulate. Experiment with F″s of different volume (although *mp* is about as soft as one
can safely go), and gradually the note will present fewer terrors – and it is fear of the note
that causes unrelaxed thumbing, over-tonguing, and disaster.

You may find that F″ is easier to articulate, more stable, and even perhaps clearer in tone-
quality, if you shade finger-hole 3 very slightly, but not enough perceptibly to flatten the
note. This shading, which may also be of value with other high notes, may be done by
keeping the third finger of the left hand straight and resting it beside hole 3 with the bony
part of the finger below its pad touching the side of the recorder. It helps if the little finger
of the left hand gives lateral support. Some players, myself included, keep the little finger
permanently in this position against the side of the body of the recorder, though it may
need to be lifted away for trilling with 3. It is shown in this position in some
representations of the recorder in works of art, including Savoldo's picture on the cover
of this book, and in Picart's engraving on p. 114.

F″ is often flat, but fortunately after articulation it is amenable (more so than E') to
sharpening by slightly widening the thumb aperture. It can also be sharpened by
cautious slide-fingering of 1, or by fingering with 5 leaking. If it is sharp, add 6. This is in
fact a more stable F″ and tongues more easily.

Repetitions of F″ are difficult because the note is very slow-speaking. Double-thumbing
with little (or even no) aperture on the thumb-nail side may be found to help, as will the
shading with 3 referred to above (and see also p. 33).

Always remember to 'smile at' top F″ for it responds best to a thin high-pressure airstream. Whisper 'tü' into the instrument, and with accurate relaxed thumbing it should
not fail you. Provided the tonguing remains precise, it is surprising how lightly one can
then tongue, and still strike the note.

On some instruments, F″ is not an easy note to sustain with good tone-quality, as the
undertone can be threatening. Thumbing has to be very accurate and breath pressure
very steady, maintaining 'eee', or the tone-quality will diminish. If its quality is generally
not good, breath vibrato may help to sweeten it.

If breath pressure on normal F″ is reduced by lowering the tongue to the 'er' position,
there is a fair chance that a perfectly acceptable middle F' will be produced, useful for
grace-note octave slurs. It needs a touch of tonguing on the journey back up to F″.

Wide-bore instruments are likely to have no F″, except by rather unsatisfactory slurring up from E′, or by using a bell-covered fingering (see below).

Basses may produce F″ with normal fingering, but, as always, it is worth experimenting to find the best fingering. This may turn out to be the first finger of the left hand plus almost any grouping of fingers in the right. Or it may be a flattening of normal G″, such as Ø 123 4567 with 6 leaking. You might try experimenting by lowering the position of the speaker hole, even further down the bore than 'double-thumbing' brings about, by covering the thumb-hole completely, or almost closing it with the pinched thumb, and using a leaking 1 as the speaker hole. This device can improve the intonation and tone-quality of some high notes. But it is no easy matter when playing a group of notes to make the thumb/first finger change, and to get the first finger leaking by just the right amount. It takes a great deal of practice. It may be worth it if it produces a sweet-toned, accurate, and quiet top F″ instead of an unreliable and coarse loud note.

F♯″: G♭″: This, it is said, is the recorder's 'missing note'; one maker told me 'we don't do treble recorders with high F sharp'. Nevertheless, this note was occasionally used by Telemann, and Edmund Rubbra, in his deeply-moving *Meditazioni sopra 'Coeurs désolés'* for treble recorder and harpsichord, puts a held F♯″ in a climactic position. Carl Dolmetsch advised composers writing for him that there was no need for them to avoid high F♯″, but he may have used a lip key (see p. 84) to obtain it. Robert Schollum's serial Sonatina (1966) uses F♯″ six times, and *PRS* (pp. 156–9) gives five different fingerings designed to suit different contexts in that piece. But all of them pose problems.

Of the five different treble recorders I have used as my test-bed for this book (see p. 77) only two will produce without bell covering an F♯″ that is reasonably secure to articulate and is also in tune. In both cases, however, there is a price to pay. One, a narrow-bore baroque model, produces a breathy F♯″ with Ø 1-- 4---, but with 1 and 4 leaking slightly. Leaking for this and other high notes is best done by lifting the fingers slightly off the far sides of their holes. And it needs the shading of 3 described above to stabilise its articulation. This is in effect a sharpening of F″. But the F♯″ only works because on this recorder F″, E′ and E♭′ are all sharp and need flattening with ∅ and/or by leaning the shading 3 further across its hole. Double-thumbing is advisable, perhaps essential.

This fingering can be slurred up to from E′ or F″, but the second fingering in *PRS* is better when F″ is within a slur. It is extremely difficult to tongue it directly. This is Ø 1-- 45--, another sharpening of F″. The amount of opening of 1 can be controlled by rolling back the whole left hand. This is the fingering suggested for the fast slurs from D′ at the end of Herbert Murrill's Sonata (*PRS*, p. 93). It tends to be even more on the flat side than my first suggested fingering. Its tone-quality is poor, and it is really only useful for short notes, as it tends to break down when held.

My other recorder which plays F♯″ is a Renaissance type with a so-called 'Ganassi bore' i.e. one which is likely to respond best to the fingerings given in Ganassi's *Fontegara*. The fingering is Ø 123 4567, the third in *PRS*. With the correct tonguing it gives an F♯″ which is perfectly in tune and of excellent tone-quality. It is the maximum flattening of G″, but on most recorders even this is not quite flat enough, unless played very softly with tight thumbing. It nevertheless might do service in a fast downwards G major scale, especially if you play the G″ slightly sharp, but at slower speeds its sharp intonation will be all too obvious, as will the register-break click as it goes down to E′. My Renaissance-type recorder plays that perfect F♯" with a heavy penalty – its F", E' and E♭' are all flat. While it is easy enough to sharpen E♭' and E' by slide-fingering 1, such a sharpening works much less well with F", as the note then tends to break down an octave.

The only completely satisfactory answer to the F♯" problem is to cover the bell opening. In a seated position, lower the end of the recorder gently down on to your thigh. As the coverage need not be airtight, it does not matter what the material of your clothing is. There is no need to press hard or stab down. Hold the recorder at an angle downwards close to the body so that your chin presses on to the bottom of the curve of the beak. The downward move is then done with the head and by the thumb and the first or second finger of the right hand. All the other fingers and left thumb could then be lifted from their holes, and the lips could be parted. In this position there is no risk of knocking the front teeth. If you lean slightly forward and put the recorder an inch or so away from your leg while playing the notes or phrases before a bell-covering is required, the final quick movement is so short that it may hardly be noticed. The return from bell covering to normal playing also needs to be done as a quick short movement. You will find, however, that in slurs from C' and D', and wide slurs from or to the lower register from A through to G', there is no need to make hurried movements, as these notes will play reasonably satisfactorily, though with a changed tone-quality, while the bell remains covered. A treble recorder is just the right length for bell coverage; it is not practicable with smaller instruments but, a little awkwardly, bell covering can be used by players of tenor recorders and, more easily, of voice-flutes. As we shall now see, bell covering will enable you to play a number of clear-toned and accurate notes in the lower part of the third octave. It is normally indicated by adding 'X' after a fingering.

The problem is that a recorder player cannot cover the bell inconspicuously if he plays standing up. One is expected to stand up in performing a sonata to an audience (see p. 120), and certainly for performing a concerto. Standing up is better than sitting for good breathing. At least one professional player puts his foot on a stool to raise his leg while playing, but this looks bizarre. One can have a foot section with a bell-key fitted, which changes fingerings and affects tone-quality, or use a recorder constructed as a bell-keyed instrument, perhaps resolving some fingering problems but still producing a different tone-quality from the one which a player may want. But with the recorder's undemanding breath pressures, to play sitting down is physically not particularly disadvantageous, and this is how chamber-music players (including wind ensembles) perform. If bell covering is required, it should be accepted that the player needs to sit down.

The main bell-covered notes are F", F♯", G", A" and B♭". Above that there may possibly be a noisy C♯", and experimentation could reveal others. The lower bell-covered notes are gratifyingly amenable to variations of fingering for intonational or dynamic adjustments. Up to A", they are responsive to a surprising variety of tonguings and tonguing strengths without articulating other notes, and to different levels of breath input. They come most easily, however, with a fairly strong 't' or 'd' articulation at a fairly high breath pressure: very strong tonguing is needed for the two highest. Generally they like tight thumbing, which produces beautifully clear tone-quality. Memorising the complex fingerings, however, is a problem, as they seem to have no logic – some raise their non-bell-covered partner by a semitone, others make it go a semitone lower. This peculiarity causes the unfortunate gap at A♭" – it would be useful to be able to stay in the covered register chromatically from F" to B♭". But A♭" is one of the easiest notes to play in the open register.

Although Telemann uses F♯", A" and C", baroque composers usually do not employ the range of notes that come within the covered register, and their value for treble recorder players is therefore in compositions of the last half-century. Bell covering does, however, enable skilled recorder players, especially tenor and voice-flute players, to indulge in widespread piracy of the repertoire of the transverse flute and the oboe, up to and beyond the end of the eighteenth century (see p. 142). Renaissance alto recorders were normally in G, and some quite high notes are used in the florid divisions of Italian composers around 1600. My Ganassi-bore recorder will play up to A♭", as well as a high B♮", with normal fingerings, and it can be made to produce B♭" in the open register, leaving A" as the only note requiring bell covering as its normal A" is impossibly flat. As this example illustrates, with these high notes each recorder has its own peculiarities which need to be discovered by experimentation. When you have found the best fingerings it is advisable to write them down on a card to keep with the instrument, and then start the long process of trying to get to know them so well that they can be used in a performance situation without any anxiety. The basic fingerings given below are therefore to be regarded only as a good starting point for this process.

Reverting to F♯"/G♭", this note, oddly, has two quite different basic fingerings in the covered register. Bell covering causes normal F" to go up by roughly a semitone, and normal G" to go down by a semitone. Usually the former gives a slightly flatter F♯", which can easily be raised by slide-fingering 1. If Ø 1–3 4–67X is too sharp, it can as easily be adjusted by shading 2 or 5, thereby offering a choice of tone-qualities. Full closure of 5 flattens it down to the basic covered-register fingering for F" which leaves 2, along with 7, to do any necessary adjustments; it is often easier to articulate than normal F", and also superior in tone-quality. But other F"s are obtainable, for example by bell-covering normal E', or with Ø 1–– –56–X. One of these may even sound better. These bell-covered F"s are available on my Renaissance recorder, but some need sharpening by slide-fingering 1; they are much more reliable and in tune than this instrument's normal F". How such variants are used depends, as always, on the judgment of the player as to what particular groupings of fingerings will interpret a musical phrase most economically and neatly in terms of fingering movements, and most fluently and expressively in terms of the music itself (see e.g. *PRS*, pp. 158–9).

G": The normal fingering is Ø 1–3 4–6–, a ' double fork'. It comes easily with about three-quarters thumbing, and is an assertive note both in terms of tone-quality and in its unwillingness to slur down to F" without a horrendous register-break click. The upward slurs to it need so much tonguing assistance that the 'faking' is hard to conceal. Unwittingly, J.S. Bach provided the ideal practice in 'Sheep may safely graze' which has the slur E♭'–F"–G", not just once, but twice, the second one being an echo of the first. This, especially the echo, needs an aspirated half-tonguing such as 'dee–ree–lee' and, despite a hopefully unnoticed flatness, the use of 7 to help get at the G". On some instruments adding half or all 7 gives the best intonation for this note. Experimentation will reveal where on your recorder it is best to slide-finger for playing G" softly without the undertone spoiling it. There are a number of variants to help you with this process, and in the end you may be rewarded by being able to play a sweet-sounding soft high G".

The covered-register G" is fingered Ø 1–3 –––X or Ø –23 –––X. Adding right-hand fingers will provide you with trills to F♯" and F". You can even turn the latter trill with 2, but this covered register E' is generally too sharp to use in other circumstances.

G♯": A♭": Normal fingering is Ø –23 –56– with about nine-tenths thumbing though, as for G", the thumbing is not particularly critical. Variants are without 2, or without 56, but there are several others including Ø 1–3 –––(7).
This note seems to have no covered-register fingering, an unfortunate omission.

A": The basic open-register fingering is Ø –2– ––––, but on many recorders it is depressingly flat; slide-fingering 2 by opening the lower arc of its hole may bring it into tune, but it is a risky process.
The absolutely safe covered-register basic fingering is Ø –23 –56–X, a partner of G♯". It is in tune and of good tone-quality. A sharper variant is Ø –23 45––X, but this may need high breath pressure.

A♯": B♭": A loud and sharp B♭" plays in the open register with all fingers down, tight thumbing, and either 3 or 6 leaking. It needs strong tonguing or it will sound G", C♯' or D'. The much better covered-register B♭" is Ø 12– 45––, the partner of the B♮" fingering below. A slur or trill to A" can then be taken by adding 67 and shading 3.

B": The fingering for this note is the same as the fingering for E', but it is not difficult to differentiate its articulation by using a stronger tonguing, with tight thumbing. On many instruments it does not have to be played very loudly after articulation. A good clear sharp alternative is Ø 12– 4–6–.

C": The same applies to this note, fingered Ø 1–– 4–––. The infamous passage in the last movement of a Telemann C major recorder sonata should be played with deliberation rather than force. It works rather well with strong 'k' tonguing.

C♯": Ø 12– 4567X, with 6 leaking, and very powerful articulation – you have to get the articulation just right in order to select this harmonic. Probably its only value is in demonstrating that a recorder can play chromatically across two octaves and a sixth.

D": Only my Renaissance-type recorder failed to produce this note with Ø 1–3 –5––. Two of my five recorders played it quite prettily. You will need it (as A") if you play the J.S. Bach solo flute sonata on a tenor recorder in its original key of A minor.

A bass recorder may without offence to the ear be able to play a complete third octave up to F‴, depending on its bore and voicing. Carl Dolmetsch kindly gave me the fingerings he used for the upper third octave, which are as follows:

C♯"	Ø 1–– 4–––
D"	Ø 1–3 –56–
E♭"	Ø ––– –56–
E"	Ø –2– 4567
F‴	Ø –2– –56–

Reverting to the lower third octave, my Stieber great bass (in C) plays C#″ with
Ø 123 4–67, D″ with Ø 1–3 4–6– (normal fingering but quality is improved with 1
leaking for this and all higher notes), E♭″ Ø 12– ––6–, E″ Ø 123 –567 with 3 leaking,
F″ Ø 12– 45–7 and F#″ Ø 12– 4––– with 2 leaking. Experience with other bass
recorders suggests that fingerings such as these are reasonable starting-points from which
to discover third-octave notes on basses generally. There are higher notes, but those
mentioned, if played accurately, would be good enough for serious musical purposes if
one could manage to remember their fingerings in time. To play successfully in this third
octave demands mastery of shading and leaking-finger techniques, or of other methods
of partly covering the finger-holes by the required amounts.

Finding very high notes on recorders is an amusing game to play, but to use these notes
in earnest is a different matter. The last two pages of Daniel Waitzman's book take the
treble recorder up to B♭‴ in the fourth octave, but the author adds, however, that these
notes are 'almost impossible to obtain'. Four and a half centuries earlier, Sylvestro
Ganassi's Chapter 4, 'The art of producing seven more notes on the recorder', makes
equally fascinating reading.

The following treble recorders comprised my 'test-bed' –

> Dolmetsch (No. 2598)
>
> Yamaha, plastic
>
> Albert Lockwood (narrow bore)
>
> Albert Lockwood, low pitch (a′ = 415)
>
> Hopf, Renaissance model

The opening movement of Telemann's D minor recorder sonata, shown in facsimile from the original print, contains three double echoes (see *PB*, Ex.54 and p. 48), which need to be contained within a milieu of expressive dynamics (see p. 79). Even though the two fine *Essercizii Musici* recorder sonatas are as late as 1739–40, Telemann still uses the French violin clef (note the position of the B♭ in the key-signature), which avoids high ledger lines.

VII

VOLUME (DYNAMICS)

Chapter I of this book was concerned with becoming acquainted with recorders of different kinds, Chapters II and III with getting to know more intimately the playing characteristics of your own recorders – how they respond when you articulate and give them breath, and Chapter IV with how to play your recorder in tune within the limited range of a moderate amount of breath input. At that point, fingering, the most important element of recorder technique, became a prime consideration, and the following two chapters considered fingerings in detail. This and the next chapter examine how fingerings play their part as the ultimate control mechanisms in recorder expressivity. To be truly expressive, an instrument has to be able to apply to the music it plays a variety of dynamic and tonal colours and contrasts – to quote Ganassi from 1535, 'just as a gifted painter can reproduce all the creations of nature in varied colours.'

The volume of a recorder varies with its voicing, its bore, and possibly also the material of which it is made (see Chapter I). Moreover, different-sized recorders have different loudnesses – sopranino and descant recorders sound louder than trebles, tenors, and basses. But even the lower instruments can be made to penetrate if they are played with a full round tone which gives the impression of loudness because of its clarity and its individuality: a tenor sounding well at its optimum breath input, at which all the breath put into it is translated into tone, sounds louder than if it is blown harder to give a more forceful but less pure note when some of the breath input is wasted on unwanted undertones and harmonics and in fluffiness ('white noise').

Generally speaking, however, the simple rule for a recorder player to make a louder sound is to put more air into the instrument. As we have seen in Chapter II, it is the greater *amount* of air that does this, not its *velocity* (cf. amps and volts in electricity, or a broad slow-flowing deep river then rushing through a gorge). Thus high notes can be played softly with a thin high-velocity air-stream, and low notes loudly with big slow-moving exhalation.

In *Playing Recorder Sonatas* a distinction is made between 'expressive dynamics' and 'structural dynamics' (p. 37 and Ch. 3.). The former relates to the undulations of a phrase or a group of phrases which make up the equivalent of a quatrain in lyric poetry (see under 'phrasing' in Chapter XI). It is often the case that as a melody rises it gets slightly louder, and as it falls to the repose of a cadence it gets slightly softer. This comes naturally in playing a recorder as its higher notes tend to be louder than its lower notes. Such undulations in phrasing, where the climax may well be at the highest note of the phrase, are so expected that the ear of the listener may not perceive any resultant slight increase in pitch. Conversely, of course, particular care must be exercised in the dynamic shaping of those less common phrases where the climax is at a low note, which will then need to be nourished with a rich airstream with the tongue in the 'or' position. Once the general level of sound is established, the shaping of expressive dynamics, other than echo effects, can often be quite satisfactorily managed by breath input variations alone.

In this respect a player is further assisted when practising this small deceit upon his audience – even upon other members of his ensemble – by chord progressions in the music. In Chapter II it was suggested that fluctuations in breath input should not allow a note to exceed a range of ten cents (i.e. a tenth of a semitone), as the majority of listeners cannot perceive a pitch difference of this small magnitude. In practice, however, if a player is carrying his audience with him, he can risk increasing his dynamic and therefore intonational latitude some way beyond this. If a melody, or a chord progression, requires a particular note, and if it is played convincingly in the process of expressive communication, an audience will expect and hear that note even if, on its own, the needle of an electronic tuner might show it to be anything up to around twenty cents out of tune. In fact, many listerers may not identify even a difference of twenty cents as a change in pitch – it is only a fifth of a semitone. A recorder player should therefore use volume variations fearlessly to express the melody he is playing: he must listen that he does not go obviously out of tune, for if he gets worried about slight fluctuations in intonation, his audience will do so too, and both his attention and theirs will stray from the music itself and its meaning.

Although what may be regarded as this rather cavalier approach to control of intonation within limited dynamic variations may serve a recorder player adequately in much ensemble music, it will not do for music which has expressive dynamic markings. Most twentieth-century pieces have crescendo and decrescendo signs, or, even more challenging, *a niente*, where a note dies away at the end of a composition. Vivaldi's structural dynamics require sections to be played *pp* or *ff*, with many levels between. A player must therefore be free to blow at any breath input he wishes, so long as good tone is maintained. In doing so he makes for himself an intonation problem, and must apply one of the intonation control techniques mentioned in Chapter IV. In a *ff* passage, therefore, every note is shaded, no finger rising more than a quarter of an inch from the instrument, with the lowest fingers actually covering their holes for most notes. In a *pp* passage the unused fingers are lifted clear of the instrument (but see p. 111), and most of the plain-fingered notes will be played with alternative fingerings, while notes normally forked will have the lowest component of the fork slid to one side or lifted altogether. It is excellent practice to play each note on the instrument *ff*, *mf*, and *pp* without changing pitch. The note C, for example, is heavily shaded for playing with maximum breath input, and, as it is not amenable to slide-fingering, re-fingered for minimum breath input, thus:

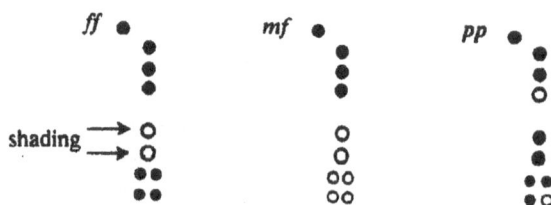

The quality of the refingered *pp* C is not so good as normal C, but this weakness is masked by the low level of volume.

An even more valuable exercise is to do a gradual crescendo from *pp* or *ff* on each note of the recorder. A good note to start on is G'; begin it with no fingers on at all, then as breath input increases lower the second finger of the left hand to get normal fingering at *mp*, next begin to shade with the first finger, and finally add the little finger and the third finger of the right hand to their holes, with a bit of extra shading with the third finger of the left if the note has not by then broken: alternatively all the shading can be done by the first finger of the left hand if it is moved with extreme care. Similarly practise a decrescendo from *ff* to *niente*. When such dynamics are called for in recorder music it is best to get at once on to a forked fingering with its greater intonation control, and even the common diminuendo sign is a warning to begin the note with some shading. A difficult effect to learn is the sudden diminuendo following a rinforzando; only careful practice can synchronise the finger movement with the drop in breath input. Extremes of volume variation should be mastered if a player is to feel confident in applying the more normal fluctuations which need to be used to give even the simplest phrase its rise and fall. He should feel that each note is a being possessed of plasticity in pitch and intensity.

Although it is something of a trick to impress upon a sceptic that the recorder does possess a wide dynamic range, it is also a valuable exercise to play a two-octave F major scale at your recorder's extreme limits of loudness and softness. For bottom F played loudly you may need to shade the bell; also for bottom G, though you can now bring in a little-finger half-hole shading, still shading the bell. For A, take the little finger across to shade both half-holes, and shade 6 as well. For Bb, 5 will need to exert heavy shading by arching across its hole, even touching the far side. C will have 6⁄ down and 4 and 5 shading. By the time you reach F' you will have 567 down, with shading on 3 and 4 and a little on 1. G' could be closed G' with thumb shading. A' will be shaded with ⁄ down, and Bb ' with 7 down and 5 shading. Do not take 7 on to both half-holes in the upper octave as this may cause register change, but shade heavily with the others. Top F" will have ⁄ down, and 2 shading. Be careful not to overshade, however, as even with increased breath input there comes a point where a note gets no louder, and further shading defeats its own purpose.

For the *ppp* scale the bottom octave should be controlled by leaking at the thumbnail (see p. 49). G' will need to be a thumbed upper-register fingering, e.g. Ø 123 456–, A' Ø 123 4–6⁄, and Bb' Ø 123 4–⁄–. From C' upwards control is exercised by slide-fingering 1. All your skill will be needed to get F" to strike softly; follow all the precepts for playing top F" given on p. 72 with infinite care, including that touch of shading with 3. Leak 1 very slightly. And it may also help if the tiny needle of airstream (a precise but whispered 'tü') is directed slightly on to the roof of the windway channel. Although extreme dynamic variation is the main object of this exercise, if you can also manage to produce a good clear tone-quality and accurate intonation across the two octaves, so much the better.

When, by practising the exercises I have suggested, you have become familiar with the reactions and capabilities of your recorder in dynamic control by gradations of fingering, you will then need to apply your skill to the music you play. There are many examples in

PRS, including (pp. 49–50) a note-by-note fingering schedule for playing the *Grave* of Telemann's D minor sonata from *Essercizii Musici* at a *pp* level throughout, 'sotto voce' as a prayer. There is an excellent article by Peter Wells in the Spring 2001 issue of *The Recorder Magazine*, pp. 8–11, on 'Fingering for expressive purposes in the music of the baroque', with fingering suggestions given for an excerpt from a Sarabande by Hotteterre. But, as is so often the case, the ideal is to study with an experienced teacher who uses the recorder's full dynamic range in performance situations.

I would put learning to play the recorder expressively as the main objective of a player developing his abilities from 'intermediate to advanced.' Mastery of the fingering techniques required to realise the dynamic potentialities of the recorder is at the heart of this process.

Other aspects of dynamic control

Even though finger movements are the main factor in volume/intonation control on the recorder (unlike on most other wind instruments where the lips can compensate for changes), methods of blowing – quite apart from variation in the amount of air input – can give the impression of volume variations. A note can be given prominence, for example, by playing it with vibrato, and, when a note is being played loudly, vibrato has the double effect of enriching its tone-quality and of preventing it from crossing the break upwards.

An effect of variation in dynamics can be achieved by altering the attack accorded to a note (i.e. tonguing), and by changing the duration (or length) of a note or of a series of notes. This method is used within its limits to shape a phrase, the more prominent notes being played with stronger tonguing and held on longer; or it can be used on a larger scale when whole passages are to be contrasted for the purposes of structure or variety by using what Thurston Dart called 'terraced' dynamics (see Appendix 2). When extremes of loudness and softness are sought, however, care must be taken not to injure rhythm, which is itself established mainly by tonguing and comparative durations of notes (see p. 34). If, for example, three crotchets on the same note in a minuet bar are played with equally strong tonguing and are equally long (each note almost being slurred on to the next) the effect is of forceful, continuous sound, and so of loudness, but the bar does not constitute a unit of rhythm as no one note is stressed more than another. Slight reductions in the attack on the second and third notes and in their duration (the third note being fractionally shorter and less strongly tongued than the second) provide the differentiation between the three notes necessary to define rhythm, while maintaining conditions in which nearly all the bar is filled with sound. The dynamic effect of 'filling a bar with sound' by note-duration is particularly useful in non-slurred scale passages in the recorder's low register in baroque and rococo sonatas; using portamento tonguing (pp. 34–5) and high breath input enhances the loudness of such passages, even on the lowest notes. At the other extreme, if an effect of quietness is required, the first note may be played with light tonguing and a length equal, perhaps, to a quarter of the duration of the beat, while the second and third notes are played even shorter and slacker, the last just being touched as a pin-point of sound: silence far exceeds sound in such a bar yet the forward thrust of rhythm is still apparent. Recorder players must exploit such methods of obtaining gradations in volume as the natural dynamic range of their instrument is less than that of most other instruments. Practise shaping phrases by using no other means than varying the length and placing of notes, keeping the same breath input and the same tonguing throughout. Then add in breath input variation and changes in tonguing to make the same phrases, and groups of phrases, even more effective and delectable. The possible volume variations in a bar where there are notes off the beats are legion, although in fast passages it is often sufficient to alter volume only at the on-beat notes, or even the first note of the bar. Experiment with a passage-work echo by shortening only the first of four semiquavers to get some volume reduction: then for greater contrast shorten all the notes in the echo, possibly keeping strong tonguing to achieve the dampened effect mentioned in Chapter III (p. 35). Try this on *PB*, Ex. 55.

When a number of people play together, small volume variations can be magnified into big ones, and the method of obtaining dynamics by altering the length of notes becomes more useful still, particularly as varying the amount of breath input outside narrow limits will only add to the intonation problems that already exist in consort playing. Composers of multi-part consorts, such as Gabrieli and Gibbons, build in their own dynamic variety by restricting sections of a piece to two or three parts. Changed dynamics in repeats can easily be managed by having fewer players to a part – perhaps only one to a part, which would facilitate ornamenting the repeated sections. When a recorder is playing with strings or keyboard, the wider volume range of these other instruments can, by sensitive playing, assist the less richly endowed recorder. Subtle changes in speed and mood in consort playing can give the impression of more volume; if the music is exciting and intense it sounds louder, if it is calm and relaxed it sounds softer.

The recorder player should make the most of his instrument by choosing a position where the acoustics of the room will favour him most, e.g. in a corner which reflects sound. He should not put a screen immediately between himself and his audience in the shape of a sound-absorbing sonata copy perched high on a music stand.

A player may 'pull out' to tune flat if he wants to perform a whole piece at a high volume level; or tune sharp for playing softly. Some players even adjust their overall tuning between movements of a sonata.

Volume devices

Muting. It is possible to mute a recorder for quiet practice by covering all but the uppermost part of the window with a piece of felt held in place with an elastic band. Another method is to put a piece of paper half in the voicing end of the windway, but this is a messy business when the paper gets wet and it is best never to touch this sensitive part of a recorder with anything at all.

Sound enhancement. Volume can be enhanced by fitting projections above the walls of the window. This can be done by using plasticine 'wings' (see p. 51), or with a special plastic attachment shaped like a wheelbarrow without a bottom which clips over the window (obtainable from Dolmetsch). The effect of these devices is that the pitch of the recorder is flattened, so encouraging compensatory higher breath inputs, and also that the 'breaking' point of notes, particularly those in the lower octave, is reached at a considerably higher breath input. All this makes it possible to play the recorder louder, but not without making tone rather rasping.

Bell key. This is an open-standing key operated by the little finger of the right hand to close the hole in the foot at the outlet of the bore. The technique for playing the bell-keyed treble recorder is fully described by Daniel Waitzman in *The Art of Playing the Recorder*. Ideally a recorder with a bell key is bored, voiced, and tuned with the bell key in mind. Its compass is greater, and an abundance of fingerings is available to conquer register breaks, afford variety of tone, and improve dynamic resources. Overall, however, the tone-quality of the recorder is less open (even a little stifled) and less focused.

'Echo' key. This consists of a tuning hole (see p. 51), bored so that its opening is in the base of the beak of the recorder, and covered with a closed-standing key operated with the chin (a slight lifting of the player's head does the trick). When this hole is open, the pitch of the instrument is sharpened, or, conversely, it becomes possible to play much more quietly without flattening. In terms of pitch, the 'echo' key causes a sharpening of about a quarter-tone. As, with care, this key can be positioned between open and shut, it affords excellent volume and intonation control, making shading techniques look primitive. But then perhaps the recorder itself is somewhat of a primitive instrument. It was said of a certain harpsichord maker who continually brought out improved instruments, that if he had gone on long enough he would have re-invented the piano.

'Improved' recorders

In his book *Woodwind Instruments and their History*, Anthony Baines writes, 'Should the treble recorder prove too soft for a modern festival orchestra, then let somebody remodel it to be louder, as has been done with every other woodwind instrument in the course of the last one hundred and fifty years' (p.75). It is not difficult for a recorder maker to build a recorder which is louder if he designs it to require a greater input of breath by increasing the cross-sectional area of the windway exit and/or bore profile, or widening the angles of the chamfers. This, however, could result in a less refined tone-quality, and unreliable high notes, even reduced compass. Moreover, a recorder which needs more breath input causes the player to have to inhale more frequently, perhaps at places where the phrasing of the music might be compromised. Except for concertos, and for sonatas with piano, loud-volume descant recorders are of no particular value as the descant's high pitch makes it sufficiently assertive. Loud trebles are advantageous for soloists, but less so for consort players; some makers produce both 'solo' and 'consort' models. Tenor recorders need to have plenty of volume to hold their own, even in consort music, but with open voicing and wide bores they become very demanding, perhaps too much so, on a player's breath input capabilities. This is even more the case with bass instruments. So in consort music, even with only one descant, the lower parts may need to be doubled to achieve balance.

Tenor recorders may sound louder if they are constructed to overblow to harmonics which are in tune with their fundamentals rather than slightly sharp, although this can produce less than ideal tunings and tone-qualities with some notes. This design principle is implemented in the Maarten Helder recorder.

Especially during recent decades, much thought and experimentation has been given to increasing the recorder's volume by mechanical devices and by electronic technology. Based on the inspired designs of Maarten Helder, it is now possible to purchase – at a price – a recorder of tenor size which plays loud and sonorous notes yet has a usable range of over three octaves; moreover, it incorporates an adjustable windway providing different levels of resistance to breath pressure, and a *piano* key operated by the lowest knuckle of finger 1 which gives dynamic range without recourse to the complex and difficult fingerings referred to earlier in this chapter. Some professional players regard it as the recorder of the twenty-first century. As well as contemporary music, they are able with the instrument's beautiful third octave to perform nineteenth- and twentieth-century music written for transverse flute, making it sound almost as good as when played on the flute itself.

The volume of a recorder will of course be increased if it is played into a microphone. Electronic improvements to the instrument itself started by simply fitting a sound amplification system on to a bell-keyed recorder, but now extend to digital sampling. The result enables the improved recorder to participate in the range of sounds used in various contemporary kinds of music-making (see Appendix 3).

It remains the case, however, that most professionals play music from different periods on the types of recorders that were used at those times. To many players the appeal of the recorder lies in its simplicity; like a violin, it is simple in concept although difficult both to make and to play well. Improvements seem to 'dehumanise' the instrument. The recorder is the only major woodwind instrument not to have succumbed to mechanisation. It is, moreover, a very intimate instrument: the player's fingers are, with recorders down to the tenor, all in contact with the bare wood of which it is made, without the intervention of a mass of keywork, and, except for high notes, the player's lips take the mouthpiece without muscular strain or facial distortion. Giving the recorder breath is a more natural action than for any other wind instrument. Whatever its technical demands may be, particularly in managing a full dynamic range (even though this may only be from *ppp* to *mf*), the recorder is in essence still a simple 'flute douce'.

The frontispiece to Ganassi's *Fontegara* (Venice, 1535) tells us a great deal about recorder playing. Although the book is a recorder tutor, Ganassi has chosen to show a singer as the leader of the group, keeping time with his left hand. And the players are surrounded by other instruments – viols, a lute, and an alto and tenor cornett. Like other writers after him, Ganassi expected the expressivity of the recorder to come as close as possible to that of vocal music; his opening paragraph tells us to endeavour to learn from and imitate the human voice.

Two of the three players here play right-hand lowermost, while the third plays left-hand lowermost. But the paired little-finger holes of Renaissance recorders, one of which was blocked with wax, allowed for this.

VIII

TONE

Musical terminology can be misleading. A 'tone' can simply mean 'a note'. Or it may refer to an interval – tone or semitone. It is used for modes of plainchant. But here it refers to 'tone-quality', the characteristics or timbre of a musical sound.

Recorder players, perhaps more so than players of other instruments, usually possess several recorders. I imagine that most readers of this book will have a descant (soprano) and a treble (alto) recorder and probably a tenor as well. As each of these instruments has its own particular tonal qualities, an element of choice in tone-quality already presents itself. Play lower octave E first on a descant and then on a treble, with both instruments being of the same general design and material. Subject to their voicings and bore profiles also being similar, the treble is likely to have a weightier tone-quality, the descant a more penetrating one. Then try E' on the tenor, i.e. the same note. The acoustic configuration differs yet again; the treble E with only a finger and the thumb covering their holes will tend to sound more open than the descant's E, with five fingers down, and on the tenor we are into the instrument's second register. Nevertheless, the tenor E' will be richer but less commanding than that of either the treble or descant; it may share the velvety quality of tenor sound so abundant in its lower octave.

The composer's stipulation, or the range of music, will generally determine which instrument you play. But not always. If the music is an arrangement, or no particular instrument is designated, and if the compass allows (as it always will for descant and tenor), you may yourself be the judge of which instrument to choose. To increase this element of choice it is important that treble players learn to play 'an octave up' or 'Tr $^{8'}$, with their middle F' on the lowest space of the stave (see PB, Ex. 63). Some consort pieces within descant compass sound better with Tr ^{8} - so long as they do not go up to high E' or F'', especially if the tessitura gets into the squeakier upper regions of the descant. Much undesignated French baroque music is within range of either the treble, tenor or descant. Which is going to sound best for the style and 'affekt' (see PRS, pp. 4–5) of the music? We know that French baroque musicians changed instruments to suit each piece. A Gigue may be played on a descant, a Sarabande on a tenor.

Furthermore, even with instruments of the same size and kind, there is a choice of tone-quality. Some baroque-design trebles are made as 'concert' instruments, ideal for playing, for example, eighteenth-century Italian-style sonatas. Others have more modest qualities, giving their best in ensemble playing. The kind of treble which Arnold Dolmetsch designed, with its open and powerful tone-quality, to perform music with piano accompaniment (harpsichords being rare in his day) is just right for mid-twentieth-century compositions. I was, so to speak, 'brought up' on Dolmetsch recorders of that time (they have greatly changed since), and when I first played a Bressan baroque treble at the Grosvenor Museum in Chester I felt I had been transported into a new sound-world. Low-pitch baroque-design recorders sound enticingly different from those at a'= 440.

RECORDER TECHNIQUE

Many players now possess recorders based on Renaissance models. Here again is another sound-world. But Renaissance recorders themselves are made in a variety of tone-qualities. At a week-end course at the Bate Collection in Oxford (which has an original Renaissance bass in good playing condition, possibly made by a member of the Bassano family), we heard two quartets of recorders brought by two separate makers; the sounds were very different, but equally beautiful.

If you go to a good recorder shop, such as those in Bradford or Bristol, you may well be asked 'what kind of music do you want to play?' You need to think carefully about this, and get advice, before purchasing your main, or perhaps only, treble recorder.

Fortunately, although the range of tone-qualities is limited, more so than, for example, that of a violin, French horn or guitar, a single recorder is by no means incapable of producing some tonal variety. But it is a limited range, like the volume range, and recorder players should therefore be all the more determined to study their instruments and the techniques of playing them in order to produce a greater variety of good sounds.

Achievement of optimum tone-quality

A recorder player should know enough about the construction of recorders and the types of tone-quality associated with different shapes of bore (see Chapter I) to judge what tone-quality the maker of his particular instrument had in mind for it to produce. A recorder with a sharply tapered bore cannot be made to lose its reedy quality for the purer, clearer sound of a more cylindrically bored instrument. He should, moreover, not mistake poverty of tone due to some fault caused by bad construction or poor maintenance of the instrument for an inherent characteristic. A breathy or edgy tone may well be the result of an instrument being in need of revoicing or re-bushing, although recorders have on occasion been sent back to the maker for revoicing when all they have needed is a good clean. It is all too easy to overlook a speck of dirt just inside the windway exit that can spoil purity of tone.

The finish of the recorder bore should be such that it encourages the gradual formation of a thin and even film of moisture during play. If this forms too profusely it makes droplets which run down the thumb-hole into the thumb-nail in a most uncomfortable way, or, even worse, block the windway. The recorder should therefore be warmed by a *dry* heat, preferably in the hands or a pocket or against a hot-water bottle at body temperature – more may damage the instrument (fires or radiators are generally too vigorous for recorder warming). A recorder gives its best tone not when it is absolutely dry but when any unevenness in the resonance of the bore of the instrument is smoothed over by a thin film of moisture. To quote Bacon, 'a pipe a little moistened on the inside, but yet so as there be no drops left, maketh a more solemn sound, than if the pipe were dry, but yet with a sweet degree of sibilation or purling. The cause is, for that all things porous being superficially wet, and, as it were, between dry and wet, become a little more smooth, and if the body that createth the sound be clean and smooth, it maketh it sweeter.' (*Natural History*, cent. III § 229–30, adapted.)

The best made and best kept recorder, played in a dry, warm room, needs skill and understanding before it will produce perfect tone throughout its range. The player must become aware which notes are weakest and, by concentrated experimentation and listening, should determine the exact breath input required for the best possible sound of each note. Then should follow slow scales and pieces to accustom him to these tiny fluctuations of breath input until they become reflexes conditioned by each particular instrument that is played upon. This takes us back to the exercises suggested in Chapter II, but, developing our expertise, we are now bringing the process an important stage further by concentrating our examination of each note primarily upon achievement of its optimum tone-quality. You will have found that some notes are capable of producing stronger tone than others (e.g. G, G', and F'), that certain notes are by nature coarse (e.g. Ab' without thumb) and some sweet (e.g. Eb'), and that cross-fingered notes are poorer and fluffier proportionately to the extent of the cross-fingering. In fact, before long you will feel that every note has its own personality. Nevertheless, a recorder player needs to cultivate equality of tone, as a prominent note in the wrong position can ruin a phrase. He must, therefore, be prepared to reduce breath input on a strong-toned note, or even re-finger it, so that it plays below its best tone and gives its neighbours the chance to be as or more important.

The optimum tone-quality for a note on its own is therefore far from being its best tone-quality when it becomes part of a musical phrase. In a particular context a 'degraded' tone-quality may be the best to use. Usually this degradation above or below the optimum is quite slight, but in some pieces of music it can be considerable. There are various means of achieving tonal variety. It is controlled to some extent by breath delivery, to a lesser extent by tonguing, and to a much greater extent by fingering.

Variations in tone-quality: breath delivery

As we have seen in Chapter II, changes in the amount of air put into a recorder for any given note affect not only its pitch and volume but also its tone-quality. Generically, certain recorder tone-qualities are associated with loud notes and others with soft notes. According to what instrument and what music you are playing, the circumstances (solo, sonata, mixed-instrument ensemble, recorder consort, recorder orchestra), and the acoustics of the environment, you will need to select a median level of breath input which will constitute your *mf/mp* for the occasion, or even just the piece. The stronger the breath-level input you choose the more likely you are to activate the upper partials (harmonics) of the notes you play, giving a more penetrating tone-quality. If the median level is too high, your loud notes may develop a rasping, coarse tone, or even overblow. If the median level is too low, your soft notes may sound feeble and fluffy, or not be clearly audible.

You will have already tried to even out the varied tone-qualities of different notes by modulating breath input. But, conversely, you may wish to exploit these differences in tone-quality in response to the needs of the music you are playing. Practising music in remote keys, such as Schickhardt's sonatas in five or six sharps or flats, greatly increases awareness of the qualities of different notes, as well as exercising your fingering.

There has been considerable debate as to whether it is possible by using the mouth itself to alter the tone-quality of an ongoing note played with a given fingering and at a constant amount of breath input. The mouth cavity is of course itself a resonator, the sound chamber used by singers. The voicing and sound-producing part of a recorder, fixed by its maker, is, however, remote from the mouth by the length of the windway and the distance between the lips and the mouth cavity itself behind the teeth. Moreover, contact with the vibrating wood of the instrument is with the soft tissue of the closed lips, which dampens acoustic contact. It seems unlikely, therefore, that the mouth cavity can act as a coupled resonator. The matter can be determined by a simple experiment, for which you will need the help of an acute listener. You should play from the middle of a room towards a corner in order to reflect sound, and your listener should be closer in to the corner with his back towards you. Play at a constant breath input and velocity any note – treble C is a good one to choose, and then change the profile of your mouth cavity. Start the note with the mouth as rounded as possible, the chin stretched down low but without breaking the seal at your lips, and with the tongue at the bottom of the mouth, well out of the way, i.e. in the 'or' position. Then gradually raise the tongue to the 'er' position central in the mouth, bringing the chin up to feel natural and comfortable, but keeping the teeth apart; this makes the mouth less cavernous, but only slightly affects the rate of airflow through the mouth. You can then raise the tongue a little further towards the 'ee' position (here your lips begin to smile) but keep away from the point where the tongue starts to constrict the passage of airflow. Finish, if the remaining supply of breath allows, by moving the tongue back down to the 'or' position. Do this several times on the same note, and then repeat it with other notes. Before each note change, ask your listener if he has perceived any variations in the tone-quality of the note you have just played. John Martin's acoustic experiments and my own observations suggest that the answer will probably be 'no', although I am prepared to be open-minded about this controversial matter.

Of course if the tongue is raised further to the high-note 'ee' position where a constriction is caused, the velocity of the airstream reaching the labium edge will be increased; this changes the conditions of the above experiment. Dan Laurin (see Appendix 2) has conducted rigorous experiments both with oscilloscopes and with listeners to ascertain what changes might be made to tone-quality as between breath-deliveries of 'thick sound' ('or') and 'thin sound' ('ee'). His experiments take little or no account of the theory that the mouth cavity could act as a coupled secondary resonator, but they confirm that, with the same amount of airflow, the high position causes the upper partials to be more prominent in a note's acoustic make-up. Any perceptible changes in tone-quality that might be achieved by different configurations within the mouth, however, are likely to be slight in comparison with those that can be achieved by exploiting different fingerings.

These considerations in no way affect my advice in Chapter II on the importance of the tongue beyond its prime function of articulation. Its position in the mouth after articulation optimises tone production of the ongoing note and prepares for the next note. Because of their effect on the velocity of the airstream, the high tongue positions 'ee' and 'ü' favour high notes, and the low position 'or' favours low notes. But, as we have seen in Chapter VI, the 'ee' position, and even more so the 'ü' position above it, involves considerable strain upon the muscles at the side of the mouth, and the dropped chin for the 'ball in one's mouth' 'or' is hardly less comfortable; 'aa', where the tongue is a little higher than 'or', is more relaxed but less deliberate, and one needs to be deliberate in endowing low notes with their best tone-quality. For all intermediate notes, that is to say most of the recorder's compass, the most relaxed position is 'er'.

It also happens that these positions are ideal for the production of the tonguing consonants used in the different registers. The tonguing 'l' is often used for low notes, and also suits note production on bass recorders which need larger amounts of air. It is enunciated in most Western European languages on or below the teeth-ridge and its grazing effect is best obtained if the tongue approaches slightly from below, that is to say from 'or' or 'aa'. With 'ee' and 'ü' the tip of the tongue is very close to and slightly above the teeth-ridge, perfectly placed for a quick short downwards and forwards movement to the teeth-ridge or the upper front teeth to enunciate a light 't'. The central 'er' position provides a direct angle of approach for 'd' and 'r'. Ganassi suggests experimentation with vowel sounds following a tonguing consonant, and the above considerations would take us to 'loo', 'laa', 'der', 'rer', and 'tee' or 'tü'.

To suggest this is, however, slightly at odds with Ganassi's prime injunction to 'imitate the expression of the human voice', as this presupposes imagination of the employment of a full range of syllabic vocalisations throughout the whole compass of the recorder. It is the tongue, which, by its movements in the mouth, imitates the delivery of a singer. Although its effect on the recorder's tone-quality may, as we have seen, be only in the player's mind, it is the imagination of the player which gives life to the music he plays, and brings about its communication to an audience. The tongue, as it were, responds to your conception of the words which give meaning to the music, communicating their effect, or 'affekt'. If you feel you are making the recorder sing, you will be a better player.

Reverting to the non-imaginary, when the tongue is placed so high and close to the hard palate that eddies are introduced into the airstream, a palpable change in tone-quality will be perceived, as 'wind noises' will impinge upon the purity of the note, so degrading it. As we noted in Chapter II (p. 24), both breath pressure and the amount of eddy-created 'white noise' can be yet further increased by bringing the tongue right up to graze against the teeth-ridge or the upper front teeth. By this means an indeterminately pitched noise can be made with the recorder held away from the lips. Try this. A variety of white noise sounds can be mixed with a pitched note as the recorder mouthpiece opening is gradually brought back closer to the lips and up to its normal position. Such a constriction, but with much less white noise, or none at all, can be made by blowing through pursed lips with the windway at the edge of one's lips, so that articulation can be made with a soft 'p' consonant, as well as with more normal tonguings, or with aspirated 'h'. As the constriction requires breath input at a higher velocity, it helps steadiness of breath delivery in quiet music. This tone-quality is usable as a sort of 'lullaby sound', even in some baroque slow movements to which it may be suited. It also allows for an odd type of vibrato by slight trembling of the jaw to cause pulsation of the lips on the passage of the airstream.

These low-volume, high-pressure notes have less perceptible tonal degradation if one goes down to a very low breath input, so they are useful in keeping pitch steady in a decrescendo *a niente*. The gradual closing of the jaws and lips, and even the teeth, adds to the player's feeling that the sound is thinning out and disappearing. It also brings the tongue so close to the 'de' position that the final cutting off of all air supply at the end of the note can be managed with a fractional movement forward, quick and unnoticeable. The note might even be ended by closing the lips behind the opening of the recorder's windway. It is salutary to practise decrescendos with an electronic tuner – you will do well to keep the needle absolutely steady as the note whispers into nothingness.

Vibrato

Recorder vibrato is normally produced by the breath, or by the fingers, or exceptionally by the tongue. For a comprehensive consideration of 'Vibrato and Tremolo on the Recorder' see Nicholas Lander's article (with a bibliography of 45 items) within his Internet Recorder Home Page (see Appendix 2).

Breath vibrato The method of production of breath vibrato is described in Chapter II (p. 29). It undoubtedly opens up a vast range of different tone-qualities. These different tone-qualities are caused by variation in the amplitude of vibrato, in its frequency, and, above all, by how the two are combined (see diagram on the same page). 'Amplitude' refers to the band-width of vibrato, that is to say the range between the flattest pitch and the sharpest pitch in the cycle of each repeated oscillation. Amplitude may be wide (or 'prominent' or 'strong') at one extreme, or narrow (or 'shallow', 'light' or 'close') at the other. Because breath vibrato involves blowing alternately harder and softer, there is a pitch change across the oscillation but unavoidably this is accompanied by a corresponding volume change. A violinist by moving his finger on the string but keeping the speed and pressure of the bow-stroke steady can create vibrato without volume change. 'Frequency' relates to the number of oscillations per second, otherwise expressed as wave-length. Frequency can be slow (or 'low' or 'long' = long-wave) or fast (or 'high', 'rapid', 'quick' or 'short' = short-wave). The ways these two characteristics can be combined are legion, but long-wave vibrato tends to be associated with wide amplitude, and short-wave vibrato with narrow amplitude (see diagram). As the recorder's repertoire of tone-qualities is rather limited, players should, however, cultivate the use in appropriate contexts of all combinations, including those between the other extremes of fast wide oscillations and slow narrow oscillations.

As we saw in Chapter II, long-wave vibrato can be counted as so many oscillations or pulses per second. It is important that the oscillations should be evenly spaced; counting four, six or eight pulses to the second will assist control. Medium-wave vibrato involves counting faster, and beyond that the pulses are too fast to be counted at all. The effect of pulsation in a slow wide-amplitude long-wave vibrato is emphasised by the accompanying volume changes, a rather macabre effect which limits its usefulness in normal playing. Wide-amplitude short-wave vibrato (rapid 'h-h-h-h…') can have a very striking effect, however, giving a note or series of notes considerable prominence; the volume changes will then be too fast to be noticeable.

At the other extreme, high-frequency low-amplitude vibrato can be reduced to a point where the pitch (and volume) fluctuations are so narrow (to, say, within ten cents on either side of the central pitch) that, although the note will sound richer and warmer than the same note played at an absolutely steady breath input without vibrato, it will probably be perceived by an audience as a note being played at a constant pitch. This technique is very useful for keeping long notes steady – indeed, unless you have a supersensitive electronic tuner, the needle may not move as it will not react to the rapidity of the frequency. It is somewhat misleadingly referred to as 'tremolo-style' vibrato. A tremolo is a note of constant pitch with its pulsations (which can be slow or fast in frequency and which often change during the course of the note, beginning slowly and getting faster) being created by volume change alone. The tremolo was a fashionable ornament in early seventeenth-century vocal music, and can be imitated on a violin by keeping the fingers still but changing bow-pressure. It is difficult to produce on a recorder as volume change cannot be separated in variations of breath input from pitch change without very exacting and perfectly synchronised intonation-control finger movements. It is perhaps easier to attempt to imitate it with tongue vibrato, but it is an effect that is far less valuable in recorder playing than tremolo-style breath vibrato. This form of vibrato may be used in music where a perceptible vibrato might be considered out of place (see *PB*, Exx. 7 and 8). In well considered conjunction with plain notes, it is as important in enabling the recorder to be an expressive instrument as are the manifold varieties of perceptible vibrato. Perhaps this was the 'trembling breath' referred to in 1528 by Martin Agricola, which a century later Mersenne described as 'intoxicating the soul.'

It is particularly important to practise gradual changing of vibrato during the course of a long note between different frequencies and amplitudes, and (more usually) both, by whatever means the vibrato is produced, and to combine this with gradual dynamic change – crescendo or decrescendo, or both. This 'moulding' of notes and phrases is at the heart of musical expression. Some of my pupils have found it helpful to visualise an expressive long note by moulding it in a length of rolled-up plasticine, actually sculpting the shape of the note in their hands (an idea I derived from Roger North's diagrams – see p. 30 and *PRS*, p. 78), thereby adding tactile sensations to the process of achieving recorder expressivity.

When much time has been spent in mastering vibrato in all its subtle – and some less subtle – varieties, some players find it difficult to play a plain long note without vibrato. Others maintain that they have a 'natural' vibrato, like some ageing singers, but in recorder playing that is a misconception, however difficult it then may be to play a straight plain note. But most notes in recorder music are plain, especially in consort music. If this were not the case, vibrato would lose much of its expressive effect, and could no longer be thought of as a decoration. Visualisation of the progress of a note from its inception may help in returning to playing a plain note. Imagine a smooth-flowing river, or a straight line with a little dot of light moving slowly and steadily along it. Try blowing gently, though not too close, at a lighted candle to make the flame move away from you without flickering. Above all, hear the purity and simplicity of non-vibrato sound.

Command of breath vibrato is essential for playing twentieth-century music, although it should not be perpetrated in the manner of some singers who wobble excessively in an attempt to fill the large spaces of present-day opera houses, so that without reference to the orchestra it is difficult to know what note they are aiming at across a range of a semitone or more. String players were taught to shake their fingering hand from the wrist to achieve 'tone' and even Robert Donington in 1982 advocated a constant light vibrato for playing early music on bowed string instruments. Medieval and Renaissance musicians, it seems, used very accurate intonation, which vibrato would surely have ruined. But we know that some Renaissance singers used breath vibrato, not, however, always with approval as it was likened to the bleating of a goat. On the other hand, Ganassi instructs viol players to produce vibrato with the fingers, or with the bow, and in his book on 'The Vibrato of the Flutist' (see Appendix 2), Jochen Gärtner quotes as part of his section on the historical development of the vibrato (pp. 13–55) a verse by Martin Agricola (1528/1545) translated as follows:

> 'And if you wish a firm foundation
> So learn to play with trembling breath;
> For it is to singing most becoming,
> And to piping most flattering.'

As Agricola's 'piping' almost certainly includes recorder playing, this indicates that the use of breath vibrato was positively encouraged in the sixteenth century. But we do not know when and where it was employed in Renaissance music.

Roger North tells us that, in the seventeenth century, viol players played 'waived' notes' (p. 30 and *PRS*, p. 76) with vibrato during the centre of the note, and Donington's examples (*The Interpretation of Early Music*, pp. 232–3) show that string players from the sixteenth century onwards used wrist vibrato or finger vibrato (using the finger above the one creating the note) as an admired ornament or 'grace' on certain notes. As late as 1752, Quantz warns against using a trembling action in producing tone from the chest in flute playing, and to control intonation in a crescendo suggests 'making a vibrato with the finger on the nearest open hole'. But he, like Ganassi, also regards singers as a model; singers can only produce vibrato by breath (from the diaphragm), and it seems inconceivable that baroque singers did not occasionally use vibrato in the shaping of phrases, especially in emotional arias in operas.

Finger vibrato Finger vibrato has all the advantages of breath vibrato in variety of amplitude and frequency, and their many combinations, and it is easier to control. Moreover, the note is not affected by associated volume variations. It is, however, less vocal and more contrived in character than breath vibrato, and has the disadvantage of being on the flat side of a note and not equally spread between flat and sharp, unless of course the note is made sharper during the application of finger vibrato by increasing breath input, which also of course increases volume, or by using intonation-control fingering devices.

It seems that the finger immediately beneath the lowest closed hole was the one often used for finger vibrato, but this was on the side of the hole, impinging on the emerging air, rather than half-holing, which would usually have made a full rather than a close trill. Vibrato on bottom F was achieved by shaking the whole instrument – try it. The little finger beating beside its half-hole will produce a vibrato of low amplitude. Try it on C', gradually moving the finger across to cover all its half-hole, then back again to reduce the amplitude and revert to the unadorned note. As finger vibrato flattens a note, it is particularly effective to use it with a note which swells in volume, keeping the note in tune at the same time, possibly also with the help of some extra shading. Vibrato produced by beating the finger on a more distant open hole, and upon the edges of open holes, is referred to by Hotteterre; he provides instructions for each note. Once you become accustomed to finger vibrato you will find its tone-quality convincing, and fluctuations in speed and amplitude gratifyingly easy to control. With some fingers, vibrato can be applied at a very high frequency.

Other ways of producing vibrato for tonal effects Tongue-vibrato (y-y-y-y) is simple to manage, but there is no historical evidence for its use. It has great value as a form of tonguing (see Ch.III), but it is not readily acceptable to modern ears as a type of vibrato because it is too light to be convincing.

As we have seen before, vibrato can be produced by the lips, or even by shaking the whole recorder.

General Applying vibrato in any of its forms to a note, or to a few notes, within a phrase, makes those notes more prominent without needing to make them louder. In this way it shapes and moulds a phrase, as Lander puts it, 'creating the illusion of dynamic inflection'. It enriches a note, although overuse can sound soupy. It disguises hard edges of loud high notes, and it can even cover over some less than perfect intonation. By being able to make smooth gradations in frequency and amplitude of vibrato, a player can change the tone-quality of long notes during their duration, and such note coloration is particularly effective when combined with increases and decreases in dynamics. It helps to give equality to the recorder part when playing with louder instruments (see *PB*, Ex. 5). This effect can be enhanced by sounding a note close to its *forte* breaking point and using vibrato to take the note repeatedly up to the edge of its break but preventing it from actually breaking as it is pulled back from the edge in the wave of each oscillation; this enables notes to be played at their maximum volume. Vibrato can be made to express passions, such as boldness or anger or fright, or it can sound eerie.

Vibrato, however, is less fashionable than it used to be in the performance of early music, particularly in concerts and recitals with period instruments. Many recorder players, including myself, believe that their instrument sounds most pure and beautiful when playing a note that is perfect in intonation, absolutely steady in pitch, and clear in tone-quality with little or no wind noise. Unless tremolo-style vibrato as described on p. 93 is used where the pitch fluctuations are too small to be perceived by listeners, vibrato will inevitably be heard as a pulsating sound, thereby blurring intonation, even though it may be felt to be more ingratiating. Vibrato has many uses, and is an essential acquisition in a recorder player's palette of tonal coloration. Like an artist's colours, it needs to be employed with variety and sensitivity. Unremitting vibrato is as tiresome as over-ornamentation. A great asset, but to be used with caution.

Variations in tone-quality: tonguing

Strictly speaking, tonguing has relatively little physical effect on tone-quality, as it only affects the beginning of notes. But, as we have seen, articulation can change the entire character of a piece of music. For the player, it also has a psychological function, as less precise tonguings prepare the mind for a softer tone to match their 'unctuousness'. A passage can be made to sound different by varying only the level of the tonguing, but the difference in sound is one of attack rather than of tone-quality. Sometimes, however, attack is so marked as to change the overall quality of sound, e.g. 'chiff' in Renaissance dances. Strong tonguing at low breath input on staccato notes produces a damped and spongy texture effective in certain contexts. Bad tonguing, of course, can ruin the tonal quality of a piece: I have heard a whole passage of semiquavers played with a spitting sound at the beginning of each note due to over-strong tonguing.

On the other hand, extremes of tonguing form part of the tonal vocabulary of avant-garde music. Some composers have asked for a staccato note with so powerful a tonguing that it is spat rather than merely articulated – 'sputato'. Strange noises can be achieved by using tonguings such as 'th' and 'n', by placing the tongue directly on to the windway mouth, or by tonguing against the lips.

Variations in tone-quality: fingering

Fingering plays a more important part in achieving variety of tone in playing recorders than is the case with other wind instruments, and the references to tone in Chapters V and VI illustrate this. Differences in tone-quality are caused by differences in the pattern and intensity of the various overtones (harmonics or 'partials') and subsidiary notes that go into the making up of any note. The breathy undertone audible below thumbed notes on the recorder can coarsen tone-quality if the position of the thumb makes it discordant with the main note. The cross-fingerings so often used as alternatives have a pattern of harmonics different from plain-fingered notes, and produce a less dominating, more constricted quality of sound extremely useful in soft, contemplative music when their comparative thinness of tone gives a pleasing effect of distance. In consort music, these cross-fingerings are valuable in background parts when another player has the lead; they become essential if the notes in these parts are naturally rather prominent ones such as A on the descant, which in these circumstances would be fingered 0 1–3 45∅–. Other alternatives have a stronger and coarser tone than the normal fingering (e.g. treble alternative G' – 123 4567). These tonal variations of alternatives should be exploited in giving expression to music, as well as in avoiding obstacles to good expression sometimes inherent in the use of ordinary fingerings, for example the unwanted prominence of an A♭' in a C minor scale passage, or of an E♯ leading to an F♯' (better fingerings: ∅ 123 45∅–, and – 123 –––– respectively). The demands of the music may require a thin and distant D instead of the firm and beefy tone of the normal D: the alternative provides it.

More advanced players should explore in greater depth the recorder's potentialities in tone-quality variation which can be brought about by changes in fingering. Most alternative fingering tone-qualities are related to particular dynamic levels, mainly on the softer side, but, in the case of the closed G' fingering referred to above, on the louder side. It is fascinating to search out what tone-qualities are available for a note played at a constant volume. Start with a normal G', then play closed G', which will sound coarser and louder. It can, however, be brought back to exactly the same dynamic level as normal G' by slide-fingering 7 or by leaking 1, which gives it a less dominating tone-quality. Now play thumbed G' (∅ 123 456∤). This has an altogether thinner and reedier tone-quality; its propensity to sound quieter can, however, be modified by tighter thumbing, or by pushing 7 across to shade its other half-hole, feeding the note with some extra breath to stay in tune and bring it up to the volume of normal G'. Each finger movement produces

96

a change in tone-quality. Finally, play the soft G' – – –3 – – – –, so useful in *pp* passages. But this G' can be raised in volume to that of normal G' by shading with 1 and possibly some lower fingers; this gives a tone-quality which differs from the normal G' by having a slightly stronger element of harmonic overtones.

Now consider what other Ds there are other than the two mentioned above, aiming all the time at a constant dynamic level. This illustrates the effect of cross-fingerings on tone-quality. The 'one-and-a-half below' fingering for D is in fact a flattening of normal E. There is another D which is a flattening of F', i.e. 0 –23 45––, an extremely useful soft fingering. But gradually increasing the air input to make this louder will soon activate a harmonic so that the D breaks upward a fifth to A'. Flattening a note and then shading it to increase volume will certainly enlarge the recorder's tonal range, but it is also one of the means of obtaining multiphonics, where the breath input is held at the point at which a fundamental and a harmonic sound together. If you increase airflow to the flat C♯ 0 12– 456– you will at first change pitch, volume and tone-quality, but will soon approach the point where an approximate C♯ and D♯' (an odd mixture!) sound together, and with practised tonguing it is possible to articulate that multiphonic directly – and blowing harder will eliminate the C♯ altogether.

You will find other exciting tone-qualities by experimenting with half-holing; for example, note the tonal difference between normal E♭ and 0 1⁄2– – – – –. It is possible to half-hole with the first finger of the right hand curling round the upper edge of its hole so that the airstream emerging can be felt vibrating along the crease of the inside of the finger, almost as if you were extending the hole. This produces a rich and powerful sound for bottom B♮, and more especially upper octave B♮'. On some instruments, especially tenors, that upper octave note (tenor F♯') is rather weak with normal fingering, and this way of half-holing 4 serves as a loud alternative, with the notes immediately above and below accessible with fingers 3 and 6. And try the effect of shading half-holed notes.

While there seems to be no limit to experimenting with recorder fingerings, being able to use these special fingerings with accuracy and confidence in a performance situation requires a considerable amount of practice. To ignore them, however, is failing to make the most of the recorder's potentialities.

Even defects of a recorder can be pressed into service when the context justifies it. The clicks made in changing registers sound very effective in a piece of sopranino bird-music (e.g. A' to G' slurs in Couperin's *Le Rossignol en Amour)*, and the sharp trills a recorder sometimes tends to perpetrate (e.g. B♭' to A♭') have an arresting tone-quality most suitable in a virtuoso solo piece.

But, apart from breath, tongue and fingering, there is one more requirement to give life to those spirits which Francis Bacon said were contained within our instrument, and so create beautiful sound. This is the right attitude of mind. No player will produce good tone unless he knows what he wants and believes in the goodness of his instrument and the worthwhileness of the music he is playing. Conviction will carry a recorder player far. If he truly believes that the instrument he plays is 'une flûte douce', the chances are that it will be so.

RECORDER TECHNIQUE

Extended techniques

As stated in my preface to this book, I only wish to mention briefly a few of the variety of tone-qualities opened up by the avant-garde music of the later twentieth century, referring readers to Eve O'Kelly's book, especially Chapter 7. Some of these techniques I have already touched upon, such as flutter-tonguing, sputato tonguing, lip articulation, white noise and multiphonics.

Multiphonics Examples of multiphonics may be found by overblowing the bottom register of the recorder to activate harmonics, and then finding the exact articulation and breath input for getting between these notes at the break point so that they sound together, i.e. two harmonics, or a fundamental and a harmonic. Very steady breath is needed to keep the two notes equal in sound, but small changes will make one constituent more prominent than the other, so that you can blow harder or softer to make one note fade out altogether. The best results are obtained with most fingers covering their holes and others leaking, the amount of leak determining the pitch. We have already noted this effect with a C♯ variant fingering. Even more striking is to start with the slightly sharper C♯ variant 0 12– 45–7. With heavy shading, or just leaking, of the two uncovered holes it is possible on some recorders, by using tonguings and breath inputs of different strengths, to sound D', G" and B♮", even perhaps all three together. If by exact articulation, breath input and leaking fingerings, and possibly modifying the basic fingering, they can be made to sound in tune on your recorder, although individual recorders react very differently to harmonic fingerings, the top two will create the difference tone G, so producing a four-note root-position chord, which is a clever trick if you can manage to do it. Multiphonics come more easily on bass recorders.

Humming (or singing) Mersenne in 1636 noted that a duet could be played by humming or singing into the recorder, but this feature was not used in serious music until the avant-garde period. The vocalisation by the larynx creates eddies which somewhat degrade the quality of the recorder sound.

Playing two recorders at once …so recreating the medieval double-pipe (see p. 68).

Note-bending A technique widely used in non-Western music and in jazz, this involves raising or lowering the pitch of an ongoing note by breath input. It is easy to do if one allows for the resultant dynamic and tonal variation, but more difficult at a constant volume.

Glissandi A smooth pitch change from one note to another, covering all the intermediate tones, brought about by rolling or drawing a finger off its hole rather than lifting it. Easily done with small groups of notes within a register, e.g. C to G' – the whole hand slides backwards and outwards, or (allowing for a crescendo) using a multi-fingering fork such as 0 –23 45–– for D and sliding a finger at a time up to F'. But it is very difficult to do glissandi across register breaks. Glissando effects can also be obtained by moving a half-closed hand up and down over the recorder's window, or by taking off the head section and covering and uncovering by degrees the open end with the palm of the hand.

Percussive effects Hans-Martin Linde used a ring on his finger in his avant-garde pieces, which are spectacular. Ingenuity has no limits. Strong fingering on to open holes produces a soft but fascinating percussive effect with perceptible pitch. It need not be synchronised with tonguing. Some composers use it as a type of 'random fingering', which in its blown form, with rapid finger movements, is yet another avant-garde device.

Electronic effects A vast potential, a sound-world of its own (see p. 140).

Recorder harmonics This term is sometimes used for the soft notes produce by squeeze-thumbing the lower octave, but Markus Zahnhausen calls in one composition for a real recorder harmonic. This narrow-ranging register can be discovered by reducing breath input to a mere trickle, almost nothing. As breath input is difficult to control at so low a level, it helps to put the recorder at an angle at the side of the lips, almost closing them behind the windway, but allowing a needle of air at a higher pressure to get by in the furthermost corner of the windway opening. This will keep the harmonic steady. The two most accessible harmonics are on D and E. The tiny sound an octave higher (or a little more) that slowly forms is extraordinarily eerie and bell-like. It is the kind of note that normally lies concealed in the make-up of lower notes, giving them richness of tone-quality. This breath-input technique may be found useful to achieve steadiness with other long, very soft notes.

Although in isolation these and other effects may sound bizarre, good composers, such as Kazimierz Serocki in his *Arrangements* quartet of 1975/6 or Maki Ishii in *Black Intention* for one player (1975), can by mixing them judiciously with 'normal' notes (which are, however, sometimes played in extremely rapid groups) create a great deal more than surprise and wonderment, an affect which wears off with familiarity. Once one has learnt the vocabulary and the idiom, the merits of different compositions can be more carefully assessed, and one can give less regard to pieces where novelty and virtuosity seem to be ends in themselves rather than being a vehicle for the expression of new musical thought. It is perhaps at this point that one feels challenged to face up to the formidable difficulties of mastering extended recorder techniques.

The 1732 Walsh print of the last two movements of Handel's G minor recorder sonata. The word 'Adagio' is in itself often an invitation to ornament, and, as in Corelli's slow movements, the preponderance of minims and semibreves, and the intervals between them, confirm that challenge. The soloist must, however, keep within the harmonic patterns implied by the figured bass, for which modern editions provide a realised keyboard part. He should respect the outlines of Handel's melody, and should use Handel's own style of ornamentation.

In the last movement (see p. 117, and *PB*, Ex. 43 and p. 46) the Presto element is conveyed by the hyperactivity of the bass part, allowing the recorder to play at a speed suited to a Gavotte, and to ornament it in the repeats. Notice that there are no slurs (added editorially in the *PB* Ex.) in the first four bars of the repeat, nor indeed elsewhere on this page —but see *PRS*, pp. 26-7.

IX

ORNAMENTATION
A BRIEF INTRODUCTION

While a recorder player whose enjoyment of his instrument lies in consort and recorder ensemble music can probably get by with no knowledge of ornamentation, one who proceeds beyond this point to play baroque sonatas must begin to study this difficult and controversial subject. It is difficult because musical style has changed continuously down the centuries, sometimes rapidly, sometimes less so. Although music is a common language and composers moved freely from one European country to another, each country has its own national characteristics and musical style, so a mode of interpretation that may be correct in Italian music in 1700 may not be so in French music of the same date. Two styles may overlap at one time, however, or even within the works of one composer, e.g. Purcell wrote Fantasias for strings in a retrospective English style, while writing more Italianate vocal works, and J.S. Bach wrote both French suites and the Italian Concerto for harpsichord. And each composer who indicates how his own compositions may be ornamented, as did Bach, Handel and Telemann, all contemporaries, has an individual manner, even within Italian-style music, which would not quite suit the compositions of another composer. Different instruments have their own style of ornamentation to accord with their different expressive capacities; Bach's ornamentation for harpsichord is not the same as his ornamentation for violin, for example when he wrote versions of the same concerto for either instrument. Confusion is further compounded because writers on ornamentation do not agree among themselves, even in the same country or the same period. Therefore if one tries to derive general principles, one has to accept that they may be incorrect in a substantial minority of their applications. But one has to start somewhere.

There are excellent books on ornamentation, many of them being the result of profound scholarship: a selection is given in Appendix 2. Some are supported by extended examples of a composer's own ornamentation of his compositions. One of the soprano songs written by Antonio Archelei for the Florentine marriage festivities of 1589 was embellished by his wife Vittoria, one of the foremost virtuosi of the time, and the publisher, Malvezzi, printed her ornamentation. Ganassi's *Fontegara* (1535) is largely a treatise on free ornamentation for the recorder. At least from the sixteenth to the eighteenth centuries there is no shortage of source material. In the nineteenth century, composers came to expect performers to play what they had written, liberty only being granted in cadenzas. Today some composers, for example, of aleatoric music, have reverted to allowing performers liberties to such an extent that it is difficult to know within what conventions, if any, the player is bound.

Many soloists and early music groups cultivate authenticity in performance practice. There is now no shortage of recordings which are models of ornamentation, some of them the result of the performer's own considerable research. One of the best ways of learning about interpretation and ornamentation is by thorough and frequent listening to such performances, preferably with score in hand.

This chapter must therefore deal with ornamentation in a perfunctory and highly generalised way: you must go to specialist books on the subject to get the information you will need to give adequate performances of baroque music. But approach this immense subject a step at a time, reserving comprehensive volumes such as those by Donington and Neumann for a later stage and for reference. All this chapter can do is to help you to make a start, and to consider a few of the technical problems of playing ornaments on the recorder. Appendix 1 reiterates and develops much of the material in this chapter in the form of an extended exercise.

Renaissance ornamentation

The following general statements may be taken to be true for ornamenting music of the late Renaissance (approximately the latter part of the sixteenth century).

1 Ornamentation is a more or less continuous process of embellishing, usually in semiquavers, music written in longer notes (divisions and *passaggi*).

2 The process is based on formulae for dividing into semiquavers different intervals in the original melody. 'Memorise enough patterns in nine days, one day each for ascending and descending seconds, thirds, fourths, fifths, and one for unisons' (Conforto, 1593). These formulae were a legacy from the fifteenth century, perhaps earlier, of the processes of free improvisation of complete parts to a piece (e.g. a *basse danse*).

3 The movement of the ornamentation is steady and measured (this is an uncertain generalisation as Ganassi divides semibreves into 7s and 5s; but other writers are less rhapsodic). The semiquavers can themselves, however, be divided into shorter notes, or mixed with shorter notes (more true later in the sixteenth century).

4 The ornamentation must embellish the original melody, so that the main melody notes (i.e. those at chord changes) must be preserved. Passing notes in the original melody, however, may be ignored.

5 The ornamentation should itself be melodic in character, creating something new which, however, relates to and comments upon the original melody (the Spanish word for ornamentation is 'glosas' = gloss or commentary).

6 This new melody will tend to weave round, above, and beneath, the original melody note. It can, however, take the melody note up to an octave higher (or lower).

7 In ensemble music, parts do not ornament simultaneously (they do occasionally overlap in thirds in the process of making a continuous semiquaver web in the texture).

8 Each note must be articulated independently, even in faster-moving sections (see 3 above).

9 Only three specific ornaments ('graces') were regularly used in Renaissance music, though some special ornaments are associated with e.g. the voice or the lute. The three are:

mordent rapid movement to the note (a tone or semitone) beneath, or sometimes above, the note being played. Mordents may be shown by the sloping sign used in Renaissance keyboard music (ornament signs are not otherwise much used in Renaissance music).

tremolo rapid trembling (= a very fast trill – was it slurred?) usually taking up half the main note, more often the first than the second half. This very fast trill starts on the main note and can alternate with a semitone, tone, or even a third above, or somewhere between. Ganassi refers to a narrow tremolo as tender (*soave*), a wide one as lively (*vivace*). In a passage of descending equal notes, the first and every other note might be accorded a tremolo. A tremolo on a semiquaver is equivalent to an inverted mordent. The other kind of tremolo, on a single note, described on p. 93 is essentially a vocal ornament (confusingly called '*trillo*' in Italian).

groppo a prepared trill, being groups of semiquavers weaving in the manner described in 6 above, but leading on to the final note of a cadence by speeding up to eight demisemiquavers. The rhythmic emphasis of the eight demisemiquavers, which were tongued if possible, is on the note above the leading note, i.e. the upper auxilliary, as in most baroque trills. The last two notes were turned. The trill section of the *groppo* could be approached from below, i.e. (b) rather than (a)

10 Renaissance music can be played without ornamentation.

Towards the end of the sixteenth century, dotted notes began to feature more in patterns of ornamentation, and in addition, ornamentation became more rapid and showy – some said excessively so – by applying the principle referred to in 3 above. It thus became necessary for the sake of musical sense for some notes in the original melody to be left unornamented, so breaking up the stream of ornamentation and concentrating it upon elements of the melody. These shorter sections of faster ornamentation developed during the early seventeenth century into the more schematic ornaments of the baroque period. To quote Donington (see Appendix 2) 'An ornament is a short melodic formula which has formed in the tradition of free ornamentation as a crystal forms in a saturated solution.'

A suggested way of ornamenting the 'affetti' section of Fontana's Sonata Terza, illustrating the use of this type of ornamentation in Italy during the period before and after 1600, and including the use of vibrato as an ornament, is set out and discussed in *PRS*, pp. 108–11, as part of Chapter 6 on 'Ornamentation and Improvisation'. The chapter as a whole concentrates on late Renaissance ornamentation from which most baroque decorative styles developed.

103

RECORDER TECHNIQUE

Baroque ornamentation

Many of the principles of Renaissance ornamentation, particularly in free ornamentation, apply also to baroque ornamentation. But two major changes occurred. The first was that the process of 'crystallisation' developed to such an extent that much ornamentation in the baroque period is in the form of specific ornaments, known under a confusing variety of names in different languages. French baroque music depends for its effects on the tasteful use of specific ornaments, and many French composers preface their music with a table showing how to execute the ornaments which they represent by various signs.

The second change was the development of figured bass and with it the appearance of the appoggiatura, a discord against the concord represented by the figures of the thorough bass. Its dramatic use, especially in cadences, is a feature of baroque opera and instrumental music, and it replaced the mainly concordant semiquaver preparation for the trill in the Renaissance *groppo*.

We can now make some generalisations (i.e. more often true than false) about baroque ornamentation:

1 Baroque music cannot be properly played without ornamentation.

2 Some ornamentation, such as trills at final cadences of slower music, is obligatory, whether marked or not.

3 Further ornamentation is expected on repeats.

4 Ornamentation is an essential element in shaping phrases, to give emphasis to important notes; it enhances, not overlays, the melody.

5 One of the most important ornaments is the appoggiatura. In most contexts, this starts on the beat, and normally occurs from above the written note, though it can be played from below (see also *10* on the next page).

6 In common or duple time, the appogiatura at cadences takes half the value of the main note that follows it: in triple or dotted measures, it takes two-thirds of the value.

7 Trills are played slurred and fast, but at a speed to match the mood of the piece, i.e. slower trills in a *Largo*. All trills in the same piece, or section, should approximate to the same speed. Other than short trills, however, trills are not precisely measured: they may in some contexts speed up slightly towards their conclusion, if they last long enough.

8 Trills start on the beat, and with the upper auxiliary, which remains dominant during all or most of the trill.

9 Trills resolving upwards are turned. Passing trills (i.e. trills not on cadences) are turned if there is time (i.e. usually). It is especially important to turn them if they fall on an unaccented note (e.g. the second or fourth note of a 4/4 bar), even if, because of the speed of the piece, this means playing only four notes. Whatever is written in the music, the turn occurs at the same speed as the end of the trill (though it can get caught up in a *ralletando*). Cadential trills resolving downwards are not usually turned:

cadential trill

Count   1 2 3   4   1 2

passing trill

10 While appoggiaturas at cadences, and mordents or half-trills, start on, not before, the beat, much baroque ornamentation consists of lightly played notes between the beats of a melody. The slide or *coulé* (or passing appogiatura) connecting descending thirds, takes place before (and is slurred on to) the note on the beat. Ornamentation was played with great individual freedom.

11 Ornamentation which moves through a succession of notes should take account of the prevailing harmony; e.g. a flourish should be in scale-notes of the key of the piece and should change direction only on a note belonging to the chord being played. Chromatic runs only became common in the classical period of the later eighteenth century (e.g. in Mozart piano concertos), and ornamentation in triplets belongs to later rather than earlier baroque practice.

The purpose of ornamentation

The prime purpose of all ornamentation is to make beautiful music yet more beautiful by bringing out its shapeliness or emphasising its liveliness. Ornamentation should arise out of an appreciation of the qualities of the music being played. Ornamentation has a secondary effect of making the music even more pleasing, or more exciting to an audience.

The display aspect of ornamentation is secondary, and this should affect your approach to playing ornaments. Never push them. Remember ornaments have an element of discord. This is usually sufficient in itself to attract attention. In particular, do not deliberately accent appoggiaturas, which are always discords. But eighteenth-century writers are inconsistent in this respect – some say place a small accent on the appoggiatura to help your audience to feel that it is a discord; others say place a slight emphasis upon the following note to announce your arrival on the concord. Compromise is generally the right answer – let the appoggiaturas just speak for themselves, taking whatever weight falls upon them in the natural musical rhythm. An appoggiatura should be stressed, therefore, when it occurs on a note that would normally be stressed if it were not an appoggiatura, for instance, a note in a hemiola (i.e. the treatment of two bars of triple time as if they were one bar with three beats in duple time). For an example, see the end of the second movement of Handel's C major recorder sonata.

Some ornaments, such as the mordent, have a bite of their own. Again there is usually no need to emphasise it. If you find you are emphasising ornaments in your playing without good musical reason (your teacher will tell you if you are) deliberately unstress them.

Ornamentation may take place between notes (or even replace notes that are not essential to the harmonic or melodic framework). It should then be played lightly, with delicacy and freedom. Or it may belong to a particular note, often with an ornamentation sign above it. It should then be played with rather more precision and deliberation.

It is not easy to lay down general rules as to when and when not to ornament, as so much depends on the style of the piece. Early eighteenth-century French music, which is often not very melodious, depends for its effect on its being performed with 'taste and propriety', in other words, with appropriate ornamentation, and therefore demands more frequent and deliberate ornamenting than a piece in the Italian style in which ornaments are less frequent and more subservient to melody. On the other hand, Italian-style Adagios are often an invitation for considerable ornamentation (see p. 100), as shown by Corelli's ornamentation of his own slow movements, and, much later, by Quantz's long chapter 'Of the Manner of Playing the Adagio'. The effect of ornamenting a given note is to draw attention to it: it has the same result as a dynamic accent or as vibrato (which is a sort of ornament). It should therefore be related to phrasing, decoration being accorded to notes in a phrase which need bringing out. A secondary effect of an ornament, particularly one ending with a turn, is to give music a forward impetus; this is partly because part of every ornament is a discord and the ear anticipates its resolution. The leading note of a cadence is generally improved by decoration, and except in fast pieces its decoration at the final cadence of a whole section of music is obligatory. 'Embellishments', to quote C.P.E. Bach, 'make music pleasing and awaken close attention'; the variety they lend to a repeated section of music, played first only with cadential trills and such shakes and mordents as are essential to the phrasing, is particularly delightful. Slides and flourishes are particularly effective in Sicilianas and other movements in triple or dotted time. Rapid trills and flourishes also have the effect of making music more exciting. This quality is both an advantage and a danger. It is good to be able to compel the attention of one's audience, but sheer pyrotechnics, which often sound much harder to execute than they are, can make nonsense of music. The criterion to adopt is, 'can each ornament be justified musically?'.

References are made in Appendix 2 to books which give examples of ornamentation, often from original sources. As a starting point, however, study the second half (pp. 37–58) of Freda Dinn's *Early Music for Recorders* (but see the reference to this book in Appendix 2) which not only gives fully written-out examples of ornamenting whole movements, but in the text explains why particular ornaments have been used in particular contexts. She takes the reader through Handel's G minor Recorder Sonata, the Sonata da Camera by Thornowitz, and a French suite by De Caix d'Hervelois. Next extend your knowledge of French ornaments by reading and playing Leonard Lefkovitch's edition of Hotteterre duets with the composer's own explanation of the ornaments. Note that Hotteterre treats vibrato – finger-vibrato – as an ornament ('*flattement*') and says it should be used on nearly all long notes, slower or quicker according to the tempo and nature of the piece'. His *Principes* show how to finger it on each note of the recorder; these fingerings indicate the use in his time of quite a wide amplitude of vibrato. At this point you will be ready to broaden your knowledge of ornamentation by reading, and playing examples, from the more thorough-going books on ornamentation listed in Appendix 2.

For making a start on Renaissance ornamentation, I advocate playing the ornamented descant part in Bernard Thomas's edition of fifteen dances by Demantius. Having got the 'feel' of this kind of ornamentation, study it more thoroughly in Howard Mayer Brown's excellent book on the subject.

When you play music with much ornamentation (e.g. Renaissance divisions) try and keep the original melody in the back of your mind. However delighted your audience may be with your decoration, it is the original melody they should go away humming.

Execution of ornaments

The best way to begin learning how to play ornaments is with the turned trill. Practise slowly the second trill on p. 105, first as it is written, on the note D (i.e. E–D–E–D–E–D–C–D E). It should be enunciated 'Dhee–er–ee–er–Ee–er–or–er Dhee', perhaps using 'y' tonguing in accurate synchronisation with the finger movements as an extra method of control. This is the slurred baroque turned passing trill. Now play it with light tonguing for Renaissance use – 'Dhee–rer–lee–rer–Dhee–rer–lee–rer Dhee'. This is the first trill on p. 105; but practise both examples – the second starts 'Dhor–rer–lee–rer...' etc. Now repeat the exercise on F', i.e. starting with G', the note above, and using alternative fingering for the E turn (PB, Ex. 57). Next try it on B♮' starting on C'.

This is the point when you should turn to Appendix 1, ' 'Three Blind Mice' and Baroque Trills', where you will meet these same three turned trills in their slurred baroque version in a musical context. The first two are in the form of cadential trills resolving downwards to C and to E, while those in bars 3, 4 and 5 are passing trills. Work your way through the whole Appendix, but being absolutely sure that you have mastered the first section and worked up some speed without compromising accuracy, before embarking upon the second section.

When starting to learn to trill, trills should be executed with a hammering action and, unless there is need to shade the trilling hole, the trilling finger(s) should be lifted high between each blow: at this stage you may find that with light fingering, trills tend to speed up and run out of control. Although the trilling finger is somewhat tensed in its hammering movements, the other fingers should remain as relaxed as possible, all energy being concentrated, as it were, into the trilling finger. At a later stage, when you are confident that you can manage all trills with precision, you should make your fingering movements in trills and other ornamentation as light and economic as in your recorder playing generally. For trills on half-holes (e.g. A to G♯) swivel the wrist back so that the trilling finger remains in a comfortable position rather than bent up.

Once the trill is thoroughly mastered, other schematic ornamentation is simple if it can be regarded as a part of a turned trill. A mordent is taken 'Dhee–er–eee...', or 'Dher–or–eer' for low notes; it is rapidly tongued 'Dhee–rer–leee...' in Renaissance usage. A turn is equivalent to the last four notes of the turned trill, but with the last note held on. Mordents, shakes, and turns are usually played diatonically, though semitone chromatic mordents are also common.

mordent

(Renaissance unslurred)

shake, or half-trill

turn

In modern music, trills begin on the lower note except in pieces written in the style or form of old music, e.g. Herbert Murrill's Sonata.

The technical advice I have given in this chapter is no more than a beginner's guide to ornamentation. It is designed to help you through the first essential stage of acquiring control in ornamentation, with clean and accurate fingering and tonguing. If you do not feel a sense of control over your ornamentation, if you do not know where you are, the effect will be sloppy and ugly. You must first master the basic grammar, and gradually gain experience of using the elementary patterns suggested in this chapter and in Appendix 1 in your sonata playing (*PB*, Ex. 62). But to apply only these basic formulae would be far too rigid an approach to the supple and ingratiating art of ornamentation. As your control and confidence develops, and as by listening critically to good examples and by reading the books listed in Appendix 2 you gain a greater historical sense, you should begin to be more flexible, adventurous, and imaginative, though always within the bounds of the melodic and harmonic structure of the music, and above all in a manner that interprets the basic mood or 'affekt' of the piece. With much practice and experience, your ornamentation should become relaxed, *soigné*, and as natural as if you were inventing it as you went along. Only then will it sound 'authentic'.

X

PRACTICE

Amateurs generally have neither the time nor the incentive to spend long hours in regular practice, but on the other hand no self-respecting amateur could be satisfied with not being able to play music as he wants it to sound, and the only way of acquiring the technique upon which expression depends is by practice. Many players spend time simply playing through one piece of music after another: enjoyable though this may be, it is less profitable in improving one's playing and understanding of music than systematic practice and concentrated work on a single composition, a process which eventually gives deeper enjoyment than aimless sight-reading.

An amateur recorder player's practice should arise mainly out of working at a selected piece of music and the desire to interpret it sensitively. Technical difficulties present themselves in almost any piece, for even apparently easy music becomes hard if perfection is aimed at. Hypercritical listening to one's own playing of a simple tune brings salutary realisation of deficiencies in intonation, articulation, tone-quality, volume, and variation and control of vibrato, while in more complicated music, such considerations as unevenness of fingering in obstinate semiquaver passages, 'clicks' on slurs, and untidy ornamentation are added to these aspects of technique. So long as nothing short of the highest standards is accepted, the preparation of a piece of music for performance will reveal technical weaknesses, and it is upon these that practice should be based. The difficult passages in a piece should be ringed in pencil for special attention: play the passage slowly with meticulous accuracy, then gradually work up speed. When mastered, you can rub out your pencil marking. It is a less rigorous code of practice than would be followed by the professional, but as enjoyment is the be-all and end-all of amateur playing, the improved playing of a chosen piece of music is more satisfying than the drudgery of fundamental practice with its less immediate results. The clue to success in such a practice method is to choose for performance only pieces which are within one's capabilities. But if you feel technical exercises will help you, and you enjoy the challenge of, for example, playing rapid F♯ major scales, by all means mix them with your work on 'real music'.

Of course some exercises are 'real music' – one has only to think of Chopin's *Etudes*. Some recorder players have devised exercises which are both technically effective and enjoyable to play; some can even serve as recital solos. Examples are Hans-Martin Linde's 'Modern Exercises for Alto' (Schott 4797), Frans Brüggen's '5 Studies for finger control' (Recorder Music*Mail* BRP 0712), and Alan Davis's 'Fifteen Studies for Treble Recorder' (Schott 11480). Davis's second study is a jolly exercise in articulation, his third engages lugubriously in low-note half-holing (see p. 58), while the last five introduce avant-garde techniques.

RECORDER TECHNIQUE

Breathing and tonguing

A well-known oboe player due to play in the St. Matthew Passion once asked to be provided with a studio for two hours' practice: he spent the whole of his time playing one note, over and over again, loud, soft, distant, commanding, with all grades of vibrato from the plain statement of fact to the most passionate and dramatic, notes which started plain and soft and worked themselves up to a frenzy of volume combined with wide, slow vibrato which narrowed and speeded up until the note died away in quiet calm. The chapters on breathing and volume (Chapters II and VIII) show how practice of this sort can be planned. Long-note practice (*PB*, Exx. 1 and 2) gives the player the opportunity of knowing the character of each separate note on his instrument – its tone-quality and how it varies with differing breath inputs, how it responds to different types and strengths of tonguings, the amount and kind of shading it needs at different volumes, and, in relation to other notes, its intonation and how best it can be controlled (Chapters III, IV, VII and VIII).

The tonguing practice mentioned in Chapter III of playing B♭ with the fingering 0 −23 4567 is aimed at encouraging light tonguing and it should be used regularly as a reminder of what light tonguing is. Other exercises are suggested in that chapter (also *PB*, Exx. 9–17). Technical difficulties involving tonguing may arise from music with passage-work on high notes (as in the Second Brandenburg Concerto – *PB*, Ex. 46), where tonguing, thumbing, and breath inputs and pressures must be practised until all are right on every note (Chapters II, III and VI). Articulation exercises are cited in Appendix 2.

Fingering

Scale passages are so frequent in recorder music that the practising of scales out of context, although desirable, is not a necessity. Certain common sequences of notes, particularly those involving E♭ or B♭, tend to unevenness because of the disparity of finger movement; a three-finger move, especially if it involves the fingers of two hands or the sluggish third finger of the left hand (the finger that Schumann tried so disastrously to strengthen), tends to take longer than a one-finger move, and a one-finger move on a first finger can easily be skipped in a fast scale passage. 'Five-finger exercises' (from tonic to dominant and back) in keys such as F major, C minor, D major, A major, and F♯ major help to even out awkward sequences: they should be played separated, portamento, and slurred. Purely physical exercises, such as the independent moving up and down of those culprits the third fingers, or the sudden clenching and unclenching of the hand, spreading the fingers as wide as possible when unclenching and pressing them tight together when clenching, balance the strengths of the fingers. Softening the web between the fingers with olive oil and massaging the back of the hand between the knuckles also helps: if the fingers get tired with recorder playing, this rubbing, with the hand held absolutely limp, relieves tension. A player who habitually gets finger fatigue is almost certainly not relaxing his fingers and he should deliberately untense the finger muscles so that he becomes aware of the dead weight of his fingertips. But finger fatigue may simply be caused by practising for too long at a time – Quantz warned against too much practising.

If the fingers are getting tied up and not responding to what you want them to do, try this exercise: stop playing and put your recorder down, stand up, shut your eyes and let your arms hand limply from the shoulder as if they were pieces of string with a weight (the hand) tied to the bottom. Stay like this for at least a minute, thinking about nothing but those weights at the bottom of the pieces of string (your hands will begin to tingle). Then gradually set up a very slow and short pendulum movement from the shoulders, gently swinging the weights. After a few minutes, increase this so that the hands and all the fingers dangling from them shake around floppily, like a puppy shaking a rag. Follow this up with the clenching and unclenching exercise described above, and finally soothe each hand in turn by massaging outwards up the back of the hand between the knuckles. Then you can start playing again.

When speed has been gained by hammer-blow fingering in the early stages, fingering should gradually become lighter and looser, though no less rapid in movement; eventually the fingers should rest so gently on their holes that the vibration of the air in the instrument is felt on the pads of the fingers. In the hammer-blow stage of learning to finger, the fingers must perforce be held high, but a practised player who holds unused fingers high is wasting effort in making his fingers travel farther then they need. If the fingers have farther to move, fingering is bound to be slower, so the ideal aim is to hold unused fingers just above the point where they begin to cause shading – if they are held too low they may unwittingly flatten a note. As a general rule the unused fingers should lie in a plateau not more than an inch from their holes. The weight of the instrument should be taken entirely by the right thumb against the thumb-rest. The feeling of the fingers of a practised player should generally be of buoyant lightness, rapidity, and independence of movement, of fingers dancing over the instrument yet scarcely touching it. Passages of semiquavers should trip along gaily, the fingers lilting with the music.

Nimbleness and lightness is just as important in lifting your fingers off their holes as it is in dropping them down. Imagine that there is a flat strip of metal suspended along and an inch above the recorder's finger-holes. When you lift a finger the finger-nail taps lightly upwards on to this strip of metal in the same way as the pad of the finger on the opposite side taps to cover its hole. The two actions are reciprocal.

Practice is the opportunity for experiment, and a player faced with a difficult passage to master should see whether it can be made easier by the use of alternative fingerings. Where an alternative fingering is available, practise it until you are familiar enough with it to make a fair judgment as to whether it is better than the normal fingering: when the difficulty is not significantly relieved by the use of the alternative, choose the normal fingering. When you work on the *Practice Book*, consider each of the alternative fingers marked in there. These are intended as suggestions, not injunctions. In some cases you may prefer to use normal fingerings, or another alternative than the one suggested, to which your instrument may not respond well. As you become more experienced, your way of playing will change, so a fingering which once looked exactly right to express the music may, several years later, on going back to a piece you had previously worked on, seem clumsy or inappropriate. I now make much more use of thumbed G' (∅ 123 456̸7) than I used to, having cultivated breath delivery techniques that endow it with flexibility and elegance so that it sounds much less 'stifled'.

RECORDER TECHNIQUE

Thumbing

Sudden jumps or slurs over wide intervals are difficult on most instruments, and the recorder is no exception. Success depends on speed of thumb movement and control of breath input especially when used with what may be called 'hidden articulations' such as 'h' or 'y'. The position of the thumb when it is closing its hole is critical. It should be so near to the octaving position that a fractional bending of the thumb-joint will bring it there: in fact the thumb-nail should touch or nearly touch the instrument even when the thumb-hole is closed. The thumb movement can thus be made quickly, a slightly increased semi-articulated stream of air put into the recorder, and octave slurs will come easily (PB, Ex. 35). The thumb must move quickly, yet be completely relaxed. Let the recorder rest lightly on the thumb – don't push the thumb up into it. If the thumb is tense with lack of confidence it cannot do its job so well.

Scales and all fingering and thumbing practice, may profitably (especially to a player who does not frequently play with a group) be carried out to the accompaniment of a metronome, however exasperating this practice is. But it would be masochistic to do all your practice with the aid of a metronome.

Ensemble practice

Recordings of sonatas, trio-sonatas and other ensembles, concertos and even some consort music are available in which a recorder part is missing (see Appendix 2 under 'Groskreutz'). They provide a full musical experience for recorder players who, for one reason or another, are unable to participate in making music with other congenial players of their own standard. Even though beats are given before each movement, it is surprisingly difficult to keep in time with other players whom one cannot see. This makes it all the more necessary to concentrate as much on listening to the other players as on playing one's own part. It is an excellent form of ensemble practice, even if it deprives you of choosing the speed at which each piece or movement should, in your view, be played.

Sight-reading

Apart from the technique of playing the instrument, the recorder player has to master the technique of reading music at different pitches and in various clefs, otherwise he is not fully equipped for playing consort music (PB, Exx. 63–5). A treble player should be able to read at pitch (involving familiarity with upper ledger lines), and from music printed an octave lower, where bottom F is on the third line below the clef; playing descant music on the treble is a good exercise in 'reading up' and in negotiating high notes. A tenor player and perhaps even a treble player, may be asked to play from a C clef, and he should also be able to read from the bass clef in close score (PB, Ex. 65). The bass player must be able to play from his usual bass clef, and also from treble clef both 'normal' and at Tr [8] (i.e. with ledger lines below the stave) when music arranged for that shrieking combination of two descants and treble is made to sound more beautiful on two tenors and a bass. In consort music played at 8-foot pitch a bass player will probably be asked to 'pretend' he is playing treble, and a great bass player to pretend he is a tenor. Bass and contra-bass players must also be adept at choosing the right moment to move an octave up when notes lower than F are looming in their parts. Recorder players may at least be thankful that the French violin clef (p. 78) is no longer used, but acquiring it (playing treble recorder as if reading bass clef – for G is on the bottom line) opens up the possibility of reading early eighteenth-century music from facsimile, thereby getting as close as possible to the composer's intentions. Some musicians evolve fascinating short cuts to cope with different clefs, but for the recorder player the best way of approaching a strange clef is to locate two or three notes to act as 'anchors' and then to read by intervals as a singer does. Thus a tenor player reading the alto clef locates G, C', and G': the piece starts on D', goes up by a third, then down a fourth, when the player checks he is playing C' (middle line). Common accidentals such as B♭ and F♯ also assist the player in finding his way around.

Learning to play a recorder outside the usual F and C pitches is best tackled the same way. Thus a player of a voice-flute (in D) might choose A, D' and A' as his anchors, reminding himself that C is fingered 0 1–3 4––– and F' – –23 456– (0' 123 45–– being F♯ '). He then reads by intervals ('one note up', 'three notes down', etc.) and checks that he is reading correctly each time he arrives at one of his anchor notes. Beginners on the voice-flute should start with familiar music in its home key of D and which are mainly in conjunct motion without wide intervals. Other unfamiliar recorders such as the alto in G, or the sixth-flute, may be approached in a similar manner.

An excellent clef transposing exercise is to sing the piece to note-names. This 'interval' method is better than any 'mechanical' process of reading, as the player must hear the interval in his mind, and this 'pre-hearing' of sound – knowing in advance the note, or sequence of notes, which must be produced – is the secret of good sight-reading. In sight-reading practice, deliberately keep the eyes ahead of the notes that are being played, and if they slip back force them forward again. Get a friend unexpectedly to snatch the music away from you while you are playing and see how far you can go on without it. The ability to read well ahead makes awkward turn-overs more manageable. It also gives you just enough time to move over to a common alternative to avoid a 'clickish' slur (PB, Exx. 38–9). Naturally, though, you would not use the more esoteric alternative fingerings in sight-reading – you must make do with normal fingerings for most of the time.

Take every opportunity of combining practice with pleasure. Use good music as your basis of practice: if you exhaust the technical difficulties in Handel and Telemann (and you will be a good player to do that) appropriate Bach's flute sonatas as recorder music (PB, Ex. 27), for the remoter keys – one movement is in C♯ minor – offer all sorts of new difficulties. Country dance tunes, and especially those from Ireland and Scotland (PB, Ex. 22), provide excellent material for finger exercises, and compel one to maintain a firm rhythm at the same time. To test the efficacy of your practice play the recorder for some country dance society – extra musicians are generally welcomed. Above all, be purposeful. The singling out of imperfections and their systematic elimination is the only way to progress. Your private practice should be such that if at any time someone interrupted you and asked to what purpose you were practising, you could give a cogent and unashamed answer.

Picart's engraving of a recorder player's hands shown in Hotteterre's *Principes* (1707). Note that the wrists are held low, which creates an obtuse angle (of about 150°) between the back of the hand and the forearm. The fingers are parallel, or as nearly so as is comfortable, conforming to the advice contained in *The Second Book of the Flute Master Improv'd* (c. 1730) 'Observe…that you keep your fingers on a Direct Line from ye holes they Stop, neither bringing your Nuckles higher or lower but eaven with your fingers ends which will give every finger a greater Comand of ye holes it stops & is much hansomer for Sight' (see *Intro*, p. 18). Lateral support is provided by the left-hand little finger. The right-hand little finger is covering its single hole (see p. 10); but when that finger is not being used for its main functions of bottom-hole coverage and of shading for the fine tuning of other notes, it should rest beside its hole, touching the decorative ring of a baroque recorder. This provides additional lateral support.

XI

PERFORMANCE

The preparation of a piece of music for performance is the main subject of my book *Playing Recorder Sonatas – Interpretation and Technique*, where the recorder parts of complete movements, and in two cases complete scores, are included to illustrate the application of technique to the process of interpretation. Different aspects of interpretation are considered in much the same order as *Recorder Technique* considers different aspects of its subject, although 'breathing' is thought of in terms of phrasing, and fingering problems are dealt with as they arise in the sonatas themselves. It is of course much more effective to explain how music is prepared for performance by doing so with actual sonatas in mind. Readers who have or can obtain my Clarendon Press (OUP) book (see Appendix II) are advised at this stage to turn to that volume, although they may still find the more generalised approach to performance in this present chapter to be of value.

Performance is not necessarily public, nor indeed need there be an audience at all. It is an attitude of mind, the putting over of the finished product. Through imagination and some self-discipline you can perform a piece of music written for solo recorder to yourself and enjoy it as if you were the audience. With two or more players, this 'private music' can be imagined as a dress rehearsal for an actual public performance.

There are three stages in playing music – reading, rehearsal, and performance. Reading is the process of familiarisation when an attempt is made to hear the music as a whole and to find what it is about; rehearsal is the section by section analysis of the music when decisions are reached on details of interpretation and how this interpretation may be expressed in terms of the technical potentialities of the instruments being used; performance is the final result, the exhibiting of music to a real or imagined audience. In performing music, the player is more emotionally alert to the music, for by then the reason for every turn of phrase and its relation to the meaning of the piece as a whole will have been worked out: in performance the players' understanding becomes the audience's experience.

In choosing music for performance it is important, therefore, to select a piece that is within one's understanding, and not of such difficulty that that understanding cannot truly be expressed. In fact, as far as technical difficulty is concerned, the music chosen should be such that the player regards it as 'easy' (a standard of difficulty varying with his technical proficiency); then his mind will not be distracted by questions of technique when he is actually performing the piece. The music chosen should be a piece the player likes well enough for him to want other people to hear and like it. It should also be one which, if there is a real audience, is likely to appeal to the tastes of that audience – their best tastes.

RECORDER TECHNIQUE

Preparation of music for performance

There is a definite order in which the preparation of music for performance should be carried out.

Style. First read the music (not necessarily playing it) to discover what it is about. It is absolutely essential at this and later stages of preparation to look at the whole piece of music – always start the process with the complete score, not with your own part. If the piece has more than one movement, find out what happens in the other movements before starting any preparation. When you begin marking up your part, keep looking back to the score to see what the other parts are doing. Ideally, you should play through each of the parts which make up the entire composition. Take every opportunity to discuss the music with the other players involved.

Unless your piece is 'programme' music, its real meaning will be in musical terms, but some attempt at extra-musical categorising should be attempted. Most music, for example, falls into one of the three categories of song, dance, or narration. If the music is song-like, that is to say amenable to a verse pattern of words and containing relatively few wide intervals, a clue to its interpretation is already given – it should imitate the flexible movement of poetry with groups of notes articulating the syllables of individual words. If the music is intended to accompany dance, certain notes should be played much shorter than their written value to give 'lift', and the rhythm should be deliberate and forward-moving so that it carries the dancers with it: in this connection it is important to know something about the steps of old dances (see Mabel Dolmetsch's two books *The Dances of England and France* and *The Dances of Spain and Italy*) or better still watch or take part in the activities of a courtly dance society. If the music is in an extended narrative form, it must be thought of as a complex of words, sentences, and paragraphs, of statements developed and carried to a conclusion. Music may easily have elements of each of these categories, but, more often than not, one predominates.

A second method of approach to music is to discover its prevailing mood; one should be receptive to any emotion it might express, or to a 'programme' or series of pictures or events it might suggest, for imagination engenders feeling, and to feel something about a piece of music leads to good phrasing. Such an approach accords with the theory of 'affekts' in which music is seen as conveying an emotion or abstract quality (e.g. 'boldness') to the audience (*PRS*, Chapter I). External indications such as the composer's title of a piece, or its context in, say, a cantata or an opera, provide a valuable guide to the mood of a piece of music.

Music can further be categorised by its period and its style. If a piece of eighteenth-century music can be recognised as, say, an overture in the French style, the player who (as every recorder player should) has listened to and read about the music of that time knows at once how to play it: dotted notes are held on, semiquavers shortened and double-tongued, the movement made slow and lurching, and the sonority noble and pageant-like. Is the whole piece in the French style? If so, the manner of ornamentation will differ from the Italian style, and the whole question of inequality will arise. Books such as Donington's (see Appendix 2) are essential to elucidate interpretational and stylistic matters. To know about music and, before playing a note, to think systematically about each piece that is to be performed, is the secret of playing it well.

The next stage in one's train of thought is to consider the *speed* of the piece. If the music is in dance form the steps of the dance may decide the speed (although some dances such as the sarabande varied in speed between different periods): if the music is song-like it cannot be too fast nor too slow for the proper articulation and expression of words, always keeping in mind the speed which a singer would choose to convey the affekt of those words. The time signature, taken in conjunction with the sometimes misleading Italian speed indication (Vivace, Largo, etc.) and the nature and frequency of the shortest-value note in the piece, supply the remaining objective guidance. It must be remembered that in old music fast movements were often slower and slow movements faster than in more recent music. Provided one is equipped to judge, one's own feeling as to how fast a piece should be matters more than anything, but even this should be modified by considerations as to how quickly, or slowly, one can play the piece, although if there is a noteworthy difference between the manageable speed and the ideal speed, the piece should be regarded as too difficult for present performance. When the speed of the piece has been decided upon, it should be found on the metronome and marked down on the score for further reference. In the latter stages of rehearsal the whole piece may be played through once or twice with the metronome going: this can be an interesting and salutary experience. You may subsequently have to retard the speed if you find the hall you are playing in is fairly resonant.

The importance of a soloist studying the bass line of a sonata is well illustrated by reference to the last movement of Handel's G minor recorder sonata (see facsimile on p.100, and *PRS*, Chapter II). This is marked Presto, Handel's fastest speed other than Furioso (*PRS*, p. 83), so, looking only at the recorder part, we tend to choose a fast to very fast speed. But then we will notice that the piece is a gavotte, the rhythm of the three opening two-bar measures, basically 'Der da dher, t Da ti dhee', being almost a stereotype of that dance-form. Even without being intended for actual dancing, there is a limit to the speed at which a gavotte can be played without compromising its elegant character. The Presto element of this movement is entirely in the bass part, which busily jumps around in an unremitting torrent of quavers. Try playing it on a bass recorder – its hyperactivity is intensified by the difficulty and uncertainty of seeing where breaths can be taken, though this is hardly a problem for a continuo cellist (although good phrasing in any ensemble will be enhanced if all the non-wind instrumentalists synchronise their breathing with that of the wind-players or singers). The limit of speed is now conditioned by how fast the bass part can be played while still phrasing it and communicating its sense. This inevitably slows down the solo part to a speed more suited to a gavotte (see my commentary on *PB*, Ex. 43). It also gives more time for the recorder player to add in decorations at the repeats so that, without jeopardising the elegance and shapeliness of the melody, he can participate in the general excitement of the movement as a whole.

Phrasing should now be thought about and the consequential breath marks pencilled in. Use a soft (BB) pencil and have a rubber handy as you are almost certain to change your mind during the process of preparing a piece. Breath marks may be made with curved ticks, thus √, the size of the tick varying with the size of the breath. Phrasing marks where no breath need be taken should be made with a comma. In consort music, entries should be marked thus ⌐—, the thickness of the lines varying with the importance of the entries; examples of how to set about this are in Freda Dinn's *Early Music for Recorders*. The horizontal line extends to where the subject gives way to another entry or a cadence.

Phrasing is dependent upon form. First of all, then, the player must examine the structure of the piece and mark it out into sections. In a sonata these will be statement, development, recapitulation, coda, etc.; in a rondo they will be theme and episodes; in a chaconne each section will be the length of the ground-bass motif; in a fancy the emergence of each new theme to be worked on marks the beginning of each section. Even if a piece has no obvious sections into which it can be broken up (double bars, etc.), a count of the total number of bars and their division by two, three, or four will probably reveal that the piece is, in fact, made up of sections with the same number of bars, usually eight, twelve, or sixteen. Each of these sections should be marked off with a big breath-mark lightly pencilled in. When this mathematical process has brought one down to sub-sections of four, six, or eight bars, the shape of the opening theme should be examined, and any modification of sectional breath marks made according to whether it starts on, before, or just after the bar, for generally the position in the bar at which the opening statement starts conditions the phrasing throughout the piece. Next, one must find where the first phrase ends: if this is not evident, it may be revealed by accompanying harmonies, or deduced from the treatment of the phrase later in the piece or in other parts. Once the opening phrase, the germ of the whole piece, has been ascertained, its enunciation should be marked down either by staccato, stress, and slur marks, or by writing over it a pattern of tonguings or words that will serve as a permanent reminder of its nature. A mixture of mathematics, reasoning by analogy, and good taste will decide the positions of all other breath marks that might be needed. If the music is fast, places where it is necessary to take breath may be too far apart to indicate intermediate phrasing points, so commas should then be used, following the same principles. In preparing for performance, nothing should be left to chance: performances which sound the most spontaneous are those which have been most carefully prepared.

Particular attention must be paid to phrasing in consort music. This is partly because phrases in consort music overlap, partly because their ends are indefinite. Players must decide between themselves when their part becomes less important than someone else's: a good way of preparing a consort piece is to go through it with only the preponderating part playing, the theme being thrown from one player to another. Another approach is for every player to play each part in turn, as if in a round. In Italian and English consort music in particular, one should expect to find breath marks occurring between notes of the same pitch, between two short notes, or between a dotted note and the following short note: phrasing on the beat is more often wrong than right. Players of consort music must depend more on analogy and less on mathematics. If the piece has an underlay of words they should determine the phrasing, and their meaning should tell you how to play the music.

Unless there is a rest, the time taken by breathing must come out of the note before the breath mark. The player must decide exactly how much time he can afford to give to each breath. If he takes too long he might spoil a phrase by cutting the last note short, or even endanger a chord: on the other hand if he does not inhale enough air he might spoil the following phrase. He must make allowance for frequent breathing, particularly as under the nervous conditions of performance he will need more breath than in rehearsal. In rehearsal, therefore, the lungs must always feel comparatively full: if they do not, more breath marks should be made in the music. Very long notes constitute a problem *(PB,* Ex. 2). If there are two or more players to a part, arrangements can be made to breathe at different times during the note. Otherwise the player must take a good lungful of air, and, using as low a breath input as possible, hope he lasts out: it is better to break a long note to breathe rather than to peter out in ignominy just before the end. Choose a 'soft fingering' for the note, which uses less breath input. Extended passages of semiquavers are also difficult: if all else fails, a solution is to leave out an occasional note, choosing those that are off the beat, that belong to the chord of the harmony, and that come at the end of decrescendos. The note(s) to be omitted should be ringed and a breath mark put above. If a recorder is playing with strings or keyboard, the other players will need to know where breaths are being taken and make the necessary allowances in time and phrasing.

Dynamics. If the editor has not already done so, go through the music marking volume indications, working on the principles that no repeat passage is played exactly the same way the second time as the first. In eighteenth-century music, echoes should be looked for and marked as such; in consort music each new theme should be announced in such a way that it sounds new – louder, softer, smoother, sprightlier, etc. In sets of variations or chaconnes each section should have its own dynamic level. When more than one player is taking each part, dynamic variations can be achieved by arranging for fewer people to play in the softer passages; if this is done the instructions to the players should be indicated on the music at the preparation stage – 'soli' and 'tutti', or something more complicated.

Tonguing. My tonguing pattern for a gavotte on p. 117 is a reminder that articulation is as important an element in the shaping of musical phrases and in the communication of affekt as are expressive dynamics and variations in note-lengths and tone-qualities. Yet even players who have a full linguistic command of articulation often omit to exploit it, reverting to unvaried 'd's. This makes any music, however well phrased, dull and monotonous. But those who always carefully consider what general level of tonguing is most suited to each piece under preparation (a lolling and lilting tonguing for a Siciliana? a taut and insistent tonguing for a Tambourin?), even down to the detail of working out the best tonguing for each note, will before long find they develop a varied and expressive vocabulary of articulation. They will feel that they are talking into their instrument, and recorders respond more gratifyingly than any other instrument to the enunciation of speech rhythms. But certainly for some of the pieces you are preparing for performance, especially French-style music, it is a good idea to work out complete tonguing schedules, at least for several movements. For examples including a commentary, see *PRS*, pp. 82–4, 91–2, and also pp. 68 and 103. In preparing a tonguing schedule it is particularly important to consider where half-tonguings are required to eliminate clicks from awkward slurs where, for one reason or another, such problems cannot satisfactorily be resolved by using alternative fingerings. A completed tonguing schedule can be put to the test of your own criticism by wearing ear-plugs, which greatly increases perception of articulations.

Ornamentation. First, is ornamentation needed at all? If it is, which ornaments are obligatory, which optional? It is well to play only the obligatory ornaments – cadential trills, etc. – at the first playing and to decorate more lavishly for the repeat. Obligatory ornaments might be marked in ink, optional ones in pencil. Every ornament should be marked down and nothing should be deliberately left to improvisation, even though some improvisations might be generated in the heat of performance. The length of appoggiaturas should be noted, especially when two players are trilling together, and for true precision the number of notes in each trill should be settled, unless the trill is a long one. Turned trills should be indicated with a pair of semiquavers showing the turn (the eighteenth-century convention). Pick out and practise the most difficult trills in the piece to bring them up to speed.

Alternative fingerings should be marked with a cross: failure to do so could easily cause a player to be left in panicky indecision with his fingers fluttering ineffectually. Unusual alternative fingerings might be written out in a memorandum at the bottom of the page or above the note. *Vibrato* may be marked with a wavy line, the undulations of which correspond to the amplitude and the wave-length of the vibrato, and *shading* or *slide-fingering* with a downward or upward line, the slope of which denotes the extent of the shading or sliding required. In a *ff* or crescendo passage when shading might be applied over a number of notes the shading line should be extended, sloping farther down as more shading is applied, and the word 'shade' marked in. Editorial phrase-marks or ill-judged slurs that clash with one's own interpretation of the piece may need crossing out or altering. All such markings should be made in pencil, otherwise the technical commentary on the music could easily obscure the notes themselves. Of all the technical apparatus that appears on a thoroughly prepared piece of music, however, nothing matters as much as those two or three guiding adjectives at the beginning of the piece that remind the player how the piece is to be played as a whole.

Memorising

If you are playing a solo, you may wish to know the music by heart. For a concerto performance, the audience will expect you not to be cut off from them by a stand and music. A good musical memory is a gift which can best be cultivated by achieving close familiarity with the music. Once they have gained confidence, some players play better without the music, because the sound itself reminds them of their own part while they can hear the music in its entirety in their memories. The other parts, especially the bass, remind the soloist of his own part, and in the process, much better ensemble playing is achieved. But a memorised performance, played standing up, is usually associated with music which has a dominant solo part. With the exception of eighteenth-century concertos, some solo sonatas of the period, and pieces for unaccompanied recorder, the recorder's repertoire consists mainly of ensemble music in which all parts are equal. While there are advantages to be gained by all the players knowing the music by heart, it is an unusual accomplishment and not one generally expected by audiences.

Leading

Understanding should be reached before performance on such important details as to who is going to give the lead to start a piece, and who should be watched for the finishing of closing notes (usually but not always the player of the top part); the leader can indicate the tempo of a piece by raising his instrument in time with the beat preceding the start of the music, or he can count out one or more beats with the little finger of the left hand. Before beginning, the leader should catch the eyes of all the other players to see that they are ready to start, and are not taken unawares with empty lungs right at the opening of a piece. Music should be marked as to who is giving a lead and an ending, and when two or more players are sharing a piece of music, who is going to turn over the pages. If a turn-over is so difficult that it is impossible to play the music without a break or mishap, it is legally permissible to photocopy a page to resolve the problem. It should be clearly written on the music when repeats are not to be observed, but generally they should be.

Final preparation for performance

When the music is prepared, the instrument itself should be looked at. Make sure that the windway is clear from dirt or fluff and that the bore is clean and dry. See that the foot-joint is in the most comfortable position for the little finger (p. 22). If a keyboard is being used, tune to its pitch with your recorder warmed up before appearing for performance: a consort of recorders should know how far, if at all, each recorder has to be pulled out to be in tune. Recorders should be warm before performance, and, if more than one is used, a table in a warm place in the room should be available: the head-joints of instruments which are to be most played on should be kept in one's pocket when not being used. If the recorder is warm, clean and dry, nothing at all need be done onstage before performance, except perhaps to tune with strings. It is possible that the room in which the performance is to take place is not as warm as it ought to be, or the atmosphere might be humid: in this case to avoid condensation the player must play as dryly as possible, using a slightly lower breath input and avoiding drinking soon before playing. To take a sea-sickness tablet of that type that lessens the flow of saliva is a good insurance against clogging. Choose to play in the corner of a room from which the sound can be thrown forward, but if a continuo bass or a piano is being used for accompaniment, be near to it; listen to the bass, as it is as important as your own part. For good ensemble, players should be as near to each other as is convenient, and should arrange themselves in the order of the parts they are playing – descant next to treble, treble next to tenor, and so on. Every player should be able to see every other player. Arrange music stands at a height and position so as not to obstruct the audience's view of you; ensure that all the music is on each stand in the correct order; and put a piece of thin, opaque, and neutral-coloured card behind all the music to support it, and to look more handsome from the audience's point of view. Be sure that there is sufficient light for you to see your music.

In the minutes before the actual performance, do four things. Look at the first piece of music you have to play and recall its mood, speed, and phrasing. While you do this, breathe deeply in and out to clear stale air from the lungs and to help you adopt a calm attitude. All the while keep moving the third finger of each hand up and down on their holes – this helps to ensure fluency and independence of finger movements. Remind your feet not to beat time.

All is now ready, and the point is reached where the players, for those few brief seconds, hear in their minds the sound of the opening bars played at their right speed and style, then set in motion that inward rhythm that is to govern the piece, and, picking up its imperturbable beat, begin. Now let the music carry you forward: subject yourself to it, and forget technique.

121

Concert in a Garden – detail of an engraving by Bernard Picart, dated 1709. This could be a rare depiction of the performance of an actual piece, an undated Sonata in G by J.F. Fasch for flute, two recorders and continuo – an unusual ensemble. Hermann Moeck suggested that this piece may have been written for a garden concert. Note how the players keep 'eye-contact' with each other.

APPENDIX I

'THREE BLIND MICE' AND BAROQUE TRILLS

The exercise below has four main purposes:

1. To establish neat, accurate, and reasonably authentic standard patterns of trills suited to many baroque contexts as a sound basis from which greater flexibility in trill ornamentation may then be developed; and, in particular,

2. to ensure that these standard patterns place the upper auxiliary of the trill on the beat;

3. to familiarise the correct use of long appoggiaturas; and

4. to employ the necessary alternative fingerings, especially on the seventh note of eight-note turned trills.

8-note turned passing trill (bars 1, 2, and 3)

Appoggiatura and turned trill (bars 4 and 5)

Cadential trill, unturned (with appoggiatura) on final cadence (bar 6)

	Key:	Starting on:	
PRACTISE on	C	E (as written)	
	B♭	D	
	F	A	Count slowly as shown, with metronome if necessary.
	G	B	Gradually increase speed until
	F (upper octave)	A′	the count can become four
	D	F♯′	minims with no loss of accuracy.
	E♭	G′	Finally speed up to two beats in
	A	C♯	a bar.

Try the effect of starting on C or F′ – but not until you have done all the others (see p. 129).

This exercise is based on 'Three Blind Mice', a simple and well-known tune that uses only the eight notes of a major octave scale. The advantage of using a familiar and simple tune is that it is quite easy to transpose it aurally into other major keys, and it will also work in minor keys. It is not then necessary to follow written notes—the tune with its three trill patterns can be played blind. You then concentrate entirely upon the sound produced, and in this particular exercise upon achieving a perfectly balanced trill, one with all the semiquavers of equal length and with the correct (but very slight) accentuation on the fifth semiquaver: note how the semiquavers are grouped in the exercise. Tonguing or vocalisation is given as an additional aid to achieving control and balance in the trills.

Seventeenth- and eighteenth-century teaching material provides so many different examples of trill patterns that the concept of standard patterns of trills is open to challenge. The three basic patterns in the exercise are starting-points, and they are good and necessary starting-points. They incorporate common factors in baroque practice, two in particular. The first is that ornamentation should, although it may sound extemporised, always be neat and controlled and relaxed, not messy or obtrusive. The second is that, for the shorter trills at least, the weight is upon the upper rather than the lower auxiliary note of the trill. This in itself implies that baroque trills start with the upper auxiliary upon a beat. An appoggiatura is a discord, and the listener is held in suspense awaiting the pleasure of resolution upon the concord, a sensation particularly in evidence in a full cadence. The trill is a discord trying to resolve itself, not a concord harking back to the discord of the appoggiatura. The trill acts therefore, with the utmost baroque *politesse*, as a transition, beguiling the hearer by extending the suspense of the appoggiatura, touching upon but just holding off its full resolution. In the case of the unturned cadential trill (last bar of the exercise), it holds off the final resolution of the chord sequence until the last possible moment, after a brief but vivid anticipatory rest. It is necessary to understand the purpose of trills to play them well (see Ch. IX). Even recorder players often play trills the modern way ('upside-down'), starting too soon and landing heavily with the lower auxiliary on the beat; baroque delicacy and pithiness are then lost. Perhaps the three blind mice will help players to remedy this common fault.

The exercise proposes three standard trill patterns. The first one to be learnt to perfection (in all keys) is the eight-note turned passing trill. Unturned passing trills, which in the first bar of the exercise might be represented by eight semiquavers E–D–E–D–E–D–E–D, occur, but probably less frequently. In contexts of rising minims, passing trills would generally be turned, especially where the trilled minim is a leading-note (e.g. B trill to C). Passing trills are normally short, and eight notes is perhaps the average length. Moreover, the same eight semiquavers, usually unslurred, with the turn, were a standard Renaissance formula at the end of the *groppo* (PRS, p. 108, bar 73), and would have been assimilated into baroque ornamentation as an inherited pattern. Furthermore, it is easier both visually and aurally to perceive the balance of an eight-note turned trill than a shorter or longer one. A six-note turned trill may, for the purpose of ensuring its accuracy, especially in starting with the upper note on the beat, be taught as two triplets, slurred as six: this gives a neat twist to the accentuation but is misleading, as the balance should be **Dee-er-ee-er-or-er**.

Bar 3 of the exercise reaches the highest note of the melody and consolidates the turned passing-trill pattern given in bars 1 and 2. Conveniently, the tune now repeats itself, so the feel and balance of a long appoggiatura followed by a turned trill, resolving upwards, can be conveyed by tying the minim C on to the first semiquaver C of the same trill. The only difference, but a most important one, is that the vocalisation changes from 'Dee— Dee-er-' etc. to 'Dee——Ee-er-' etc. This pattern is consolidated by its repetition in bar 5.

It is in the unturned cadential trill that the fault of starting the trill too soon, and on the lower auxiliary, is most common. If the first semiquaver D in bar 6 falls on the second beat, the weight of the trill becomes a concord. If one overcompensates by holding back the first finger-stroke on to the D too late, again it will threaten to fall into a concordant position (i.e. that of the third semiquaver of the pattern). It has to be just right. To assist in achieving exactness, the exercise models the final cadential trill as closely as possible upon the previous eight-note turned trills. In effect it is exactly the same as the turned trill until the sixth semiquaver when, like the mice, it has its tail cut off. At the sixth semiquaver the trill movement suddenly stops and that semiquaver is held on, becoming a quaver, unstressed but given importance by being very slightly held, as if the note were being pinned to the paper. This small piece of rubato just leaves time for the tiny articulatory rest and for a crisp, very short, eleventh-hour demisemiquaver, almost stuttering on to the final relaxed tonic minim. Note that the demisemiquaver happens at such speed that it is not possible to use 'd' tonguing. Only 't' or 'k', the fastest-speaking articulations, can be used. If the final demisemiquaver in cadential trills is made too long, the whole piece of music becomes limp; it loses its baroque tautness and precision.

The type of cadential trill here recommended as a starting-point may be called a 'three-stroke' trill because the second finger strikes D three times, the last time held down. Note that it strikes on the 'er' of the vocalisation, off the beats. This can be practised away from the recorder at any time which might otherwise be wasted by making the back-and-forth tongue movements in the mouth silently (for 'ee' the tongue is further forward than 'er') and synchronising a finger-movement with the three 'er's of the pattern. Thus for the 'Dee——Ee' hold the first finger firmly down (e.g. on a table). Then, exactly as the tongue goes back for 'er' put the second finger down; lift it for 'ee' (on a subsidiary beat), down for 'er', up for 'Ee' (the 'and' beat) and finally down for 'err'. A little press with the held-down first finger on the 'Ee' at the beginning of the trill will help in getting this movement exactly right. This three-stroke cadential trill pattern is the shortest that constitutes a trill, for with only two strokes the ornament would be a shake or half-trill. In fast music, however, a shake may be substituted for a trill after an appoggiatura. Many trills are of course longer than three strokes, where the music allows the time, or the appoggiatura is shorter. As some baroque tables of ornaments show, such trills, though beginning with the upper auxiliary dominating, may, rather than prolonging the implied discord, change their balance so that they end with the lower auxiliary dominating. This happens by insinuating a triplet into the course of the trill. Longer trills may not be even, for several baroque authorities talk of trills getting faster. But, initially, total mastery must be gained of the three-stroke regular trill before experimenting with the many variations that are called for in different musical contexts. To use this three-stroke pattern in all contexts would be committing the sin of inflexibility, which is almost as venal as the sin of inaccuracy or sloppiness; almost, but not quite.

If the mice become tiresome, there is excellent trill practice to be found in Handel's recorder sonatas. Try the first section of the last movement of the C major sonata. This is in 3/8, which often suggests a one-in-a-bar beat (as in a passepied), but here needs to be counted in a fast three to give the long semiquaver passages in the bass enough time to breathe. It is in effect a lively minuet, fast enough for eight-note turned trills (eight demisemiquavers) to be a valid interpretation, although regular twelve-note turned trills are better – but faster and more difficult to keep under control. The notes of the trills are the same as in the 'Three Blind Mice' exercise, complete with a fast cadential trill after a hemiola (then use three or two strokes for the trill). There is great opportunity for turned passing trills in rising minim contexts in the second movement of the D minor sonata, although at hornpipe-speed there may be time for only six-note, rather than eight-note turned trills. Some of them involve fingering problems.

The turned passing trill in bar 2 of the 'Three Blind Mice' exercise uses E as the seventh note with an F' on either side. Trills, and especially turns, are the natural habitat of alternative fingerings. This in fact is the only one in the exercise as written. Most recorder players will automatically in this context use 0 –23 for E rather than 0 1––. The latter requires the movement of two fingers in opposite directions, which is much less easy to accomplish neatly than moving one finger (3) only; moreover, the alternative leaves the normal F' fingering in place. When the exercise is played in other keys all sorts of fingering problems arise. The overriding purpose of the exercise, however, is to achieve accurate basic trill patterns, irrespective of key. It is therefore wise to pause at this point while you master 'Three Blind Mice' trilled in C major, and to leave the fascinating complexities of turned-trill fingerings in more distant keys for later study. So get out your metronome and set it to eight steady beats to the bar ($\downarrow$ = 92). Be sure that the final bar is accurate, and go straight back to the beginning without *rall.*, or pause. Then gradually speed up the count, maintaining absolute accuracy and balance in the trills. You are now taking the first steps to becoming trill-perfect.

Some trill fingerings

'Three Blind Mice' (hereafter TBM) bar 2 contains the most common alternative fingering, E 0 −23 −−−−, here used for the F'–E turn. It illustrates three maxims applying to alternative fingerings. The first is that, in using alternatives to simplify fingering and slurring in fast music (all trills are fast, though not uniformly so), aim at a one- or two-finger movement to replace the more complex movement involved in normal fingerings. The second is to use a normal fingering—F' in this case—as the starting-point before employing alternatives. This is especially true when, as here, the context is from a normal note to an alternative-fingered note and then back to the normal note. The fingering of the normal note should not as a rule have to be disturbed when going on to the alternative. The third is to revert to the normal fingering for a held note, here for the E minim after the trill. This, however, may not be necessary if the alternative is as good in quality and intonation as the normal fingering, which is the case with E on most recorders, or if the quality and intonation of the alternative is better suited to the particular musical context. Many alternatives are too poor for a held note, but they may be perfectly acceptable for the note of a turn or trill, which passes by so quickly that its weakness is not perceived.

The TBM exercise is set out in C major, but should then, as suggested, be memorised and played in other keys, starting with B♭ major as this key introduces, at the third trill, the important closed G' alternative. It starts with a D–C passing trill with a B♭ turn; that poses no problems, but the second trill and turn, F'–E♭ –D, does. It occurs frequently and must be mastered. Start with normal F'. Then add fingers until the F' is flattened a tone to E♭. 0 −23 4−6− may be the solution, but instruments vary. Taking off 3 will bring you almost back to F', near enough for you to trill F'–E♭ with that one finger. Avoid multi-finger trills if possible, as they are less precise. The turn on D may be achieved with 0 −23 45−−, involving a quite simple movement of 5 and 6. This is a poor quality, sharpish D, but it is useful slurred at speed, with a slight drop in breath input, in this type of context. So for the minim D of bar 2 after the trill you must revert to normal fingering. Note that during all this the F' fingering stays down, providing a firm foundation for the other finger-movements.

TBM bars 3, 4, and 5 played in B♭ major slur B♭'-A'-G'. Start with normal B♭' and trill to A' with the little finger, covering both half-holes. Now comes the problem. We are in the upper register and normal G' is on the other side of the register break, being the highest note of the lower register. To use it would cause those 'clicks' of crossing register breaks which are the recorder-player's chief enemy. You must therefore use the closed G' fingering—all fingers down, thumb off. This entails adding 5 and moving the thumb off from its 'pinched' position, and this movement itself can cause a slight click if not perfectly synchronised. But in fact the little-finger alternative A' fingering Ø 123 4−67 works without the thumb. The secret therefore is to remove the thumb during the A' on the way down to G' and to put it back during the A' on the way back up to B♭'. This needs practising slowly at first.

TBM in lower octave F has to be managed with normal fingerings on its first two trills, although the second can be trilled with just 4. The third trill needs alternative E, and the D for the turn can usually be found by adding two fingers, i.e. 0 −23 45−−, as given above, with a drop in breath input.

TBM in G, beginning on B, again has to be started with normal fingerings. It helps to hold 5 down firmly for the B–A–G turned trill in bar 1. The E turn after the F#' of the third trill responds to the device of 'adding fingers below', such as – 123 4–6–.

The upper octave F' TBM requires the closed G' for the A'–G' trill in the first bar. Whether one starts on little-finger alternative A' depends on how good that note is on your instrument in intonation (?too sharp), tone, and tonguability. It is certainly an advantage in the appoggiatura situation of bar 6 to get straight on to it, thumbed of course for better quality. Once the trill movement has started, leave the thumb off . Now comes the rub. To get to the F' turn you *must* cross the register break. This means that the fifth semiquaver, G', must be normal fingering. It may help in this difficult movement to press 2 down and almost throw the other fingers upwards in a bunch off the recorder. The same problem occurs with an F#' turn after an A'-G' trill, as in D major. The good management of the closed and open G' in trills and slurs is fundamental to recorder technique.

The C'–Bb'–A' turned trill calls for the little-finger alternative A' (thumbed). It is a matter of personal preference whether to trill C'–Bb' with both 4 and 6, or with 4 alone with 6 staying down which is neater but, unlike this trill in the bottom octave (see above), may make the Bb' too flat.

The turn of the high F"–E'–D' trill involves the crossing of the register break between E' and D', which with normal fingering is, with careful breath-control, just manageable on the way down, but decidedly clickish on the way back up. Some recorders, with careful thumbing, will, however, slur back up from D' to E', without crossing the register break, by lifting 2. The other, more usual, way is to add fingers on to normal E' in its own register, maybe with 67 in the right hand and shading with half 3 in the left, a little tricky.

The vital fingerings for TBM in D major are closed G' (see above), F#' as 0 ––– –––– (a Renaissance favourite) in the F#'–E trill after a normal F#' start, and Ø 12– 45–– for the B' turn after C#'. A slight drop in breath input over this turn may help, as it does with many other alternative-fingered turns.

The first trill in the Eb version, starting on G', calls for a quick move from the 0 –23 4–6– Eb turn to normal Eb. Next we encounter the problem of trills with Ab' (see p. 65). In this context the solution may be to play a slightly sharp Bb' by half-holing 6 (finger bent position) and then use the thumbed Ab' trilling with 5. 7 may then account for the G' turn. The turned trill Eb'–D'–C' is difficult because of the register-break at Eb'. Start with normal Eb'. For the Eb'-D' trill you will have to shade with half 3 and trill with 7, but you may want at the sixth semiquaver to go on to normal D' in readiness for the C' turn. This method becomes well-nigh impossible if you substitute Db' for D' by trilling with 3 and 7 together (or with 3 only, or even 2) because of the click on the slur down from Eb' to Db' when the normal fingering comes in. So stay on the trill-fingering Ø 12×3 4567 right up to the C' at the turn.

The first trill in TBM in A major is a problem. Normal fingering? or trill sharp with 3 on 0 123× –56–? The third trill loses its terrors if you are able to stay in the thumbed register and trill A'–G#' with the little finger—a useful alternative on many instruments, though rather sharp. The F#' turn may then work (with gratifying simplicity) with 6 (see *PRS*, Ex. 8.6). For trill problems in E major, see *PRS*, pp.141–2.

TBM in minor keys will show up the few remaining trill-fingerings of importance. C minor requires at the outset the 'one-and-a-half-below' fingering for D after E♭. This is 0 1–3 45ˣ6– with 5 trilling, but reverting to normal D at the sixth semiquaver before the C turn. E minor's first trill needs – 123 4–6– for the E turn after the G'–F♯' trill, and it then requires the thumbed G' ∅ 123 456⫽ for the turn in the second trill after B'–A'. The C♯' turn after the E'–D♯' trill in this key is best taken as ∅ 123 4567. In B minor the third trill requires ∅ 123 –5∮– for A♯', and the thumbed G♯' (add 4) for the turn. F minor starts on A♭' with normal fingerings – –23 456–. Add 1 and 7 for the G' trill (closed G') and trill with these together, or with 7 alone. Throw all the fingers except 2 off at the sixth semiquaver for open G' and the F' turn.

The innocent-looking challenge at the end of the TBM exercise ('Try the effect of starting on C or F") will take you into A♭ major (four flats) and D♭ major (five flats). These remote keys are the breeding-ground of alternative fingerings to enable you to manage turned trills smoothly. They do not, however, reveal principles not already covered here. Though you may therefore run yet further with the three blind mice, they may take you into blind alleys of recorder technique – it is better to concentrate on other things until a particular trill problem arises in preparing a piece of music. If you can maintain perfect accuracy and poise at a reasonable speed in the three basic trill patterns in the TBM exercise in the eight major keys listed in the exercise and the four minor keys mentioned above, you will have the technique to face up with confidence and equanimity to the teachings of baroque writers on ornamentation and their scholarly interpreters such as Mather, Donington, and Neumann. But you still have a long way to go!

Carving on the front of the organ-case in Christ's College Chapel,
Cambridge (my photograph was taken with permission of the Master
and Fellows of that College). The woodwork in the chapel is by John
Austin, completed by 1703, and the organ itself was installed in 1705.
This illustration shows the carving to the right of the console, with
two recorders and their music, and there is a similar pair to the left,
with music marked 'Sinphony Flauto Primo', which is shown on the
cover of *The Cambridge Companion to the Recorder*. Like most baroque
recorders, these have only a single finger-hole for the little finger (see
pp.10 and 114). The music of both 'Flauto Primo' and 'Flauto Secundo'
is perfectly legible, but is not complete in itself as a duet – presumably
it at least had an organ continuo part. Neither the music, nor the
person who appears on a medallion in the Flauto Primo carving, have
yet been identified. A considerable amount of research has still to be
done on all aspects of the recorder – its acoustics, its changing design
over the centuries, who played it, what it played outside music
designated for it, and, above all, performance practice at different
periods and in different countries.

APPENDIX 2

SOME SUGGESTED READING

As it is my hope that most readers of this book will also possess *The Cambridge Companion to the Recorder*, edited by the late John Mansfield Thomson with myself as Assistant Editor (Cambridge University Press, 1995 – available in an inexpensive paperback edition), and as Chapter 14 of that book, written by me in association with David Lasocki, is a 'Guide to Further Reading – A select bibliography of recent books and some articles in English of special interest to recorder players', I do not feel that there is a need to update the Selected Bibliography which appeared as Appendix II in the 1986 edition of *Recorder Technique* (pp. 153–164). Both lists contain brief critical commentaries of each book mentioned, but the longer *Companion* list is more comprehensive and up-to-date. The purpose of this Appendix, therefore, is to draw the attention of readers of *RT* to sources of information (in English) about the recorder generally which have become available during the last ten years or so, and to enlarge upon references made in the text.

Major sources of information on the recorder

Recorder players with access to the Internet are better served than players of any other instrument with source material on the web, largely through the indefatigable efforts, in his spare time, of Nicholas S. Lander, a botanical taxonomist who works as Principle Research Scientist with the Western Australian Department of Conservation & Land Management, and who is also Webmaster of 'The Recorder Home Page'. This site, which comprises many thousand pages, is at http://www.iinet.net.au/~nickl/recorder.html and is on open access. You will first see a list of some 20–30 headings, including 'Search' which finds contents by key words.

The heading 'Technique' connects with about forty other web-sites which deal with a variety of subjects related to recorder technique. But you will be better rewarded by browsing the Recorder Home Page itself; this reveals material not directly referred to in the headings, for example, an article on Vicenzo Galilei's Ricercares, with a very clear explanation of the modes as used in late sixteenth-century compositions, the understanding of which is a prerequisite to effective interpretation of much of the music of this period (see p. 142). The Recorder Home Page includes a comprehensive general recorder bibliography and several others on particular topics; in the case of 'Recorder Iconography' (a descriptive catalogue with over 4,000 entries), the bibliography runs to about 750 items. Of particular interest is Lander's article 'The Recorder: Instrument of Torture or Instrument of Music?' which includes a history of the instrument, well up-dated on a world basis.

Richard Griscom and David Lasocki, *The Recorder: A Research and Information Guide*. First published by Garland in 1994, but totally revised and updated for the edition published by Routledge, New York, in 2003. This now runs to 2,132 items in 31 chapters. It is very well ordered and indexed, and incorporates critical summaries evaluating each book or article. Lasocki updates it annually in *American Recorder* in overviews of recent publications, which include, like the book itself, articles and books in languages other than English.

Important articles on subjects of interest to recorder players, with extensive bibliographies, are contained within the second edition of *The New Grove Dictionary of Music and Musicians* (29 vols., ed. Stanley Sadie, Macmillan, London, 2001, but now OUP). The article on 'Recorder' was written by Lasocki. *New Grove 2* is available, by substantial subscription, on-line; this version is regularly updated.

For general background to the recorder's history and repertoire, the four main books in English are *The Cambridge Companion to the Recorder*; Edgar Hunt's *The Recorder and its Music*, first published in 1962, but now available, with some updating, from Peacock Press; Hans-Martin Linde's *The Recorder Player's Handbook* (2nd edn., tr. Deveson, 1992, Schott, Ed. 12322); and Kenneth Wollitz's *The Recorder Book* (New York and London, 1982). Both the latter books have useful sections on technique, but their main emphasis is on interpretation.

The four main English-language periodicals devoted to the recorder are *The Recorder Magazine*, a quarterly published by Peacock Press which is also the subscription journal for members of the U.K. Society of Recorder Players; *American Recorder*, the journal of the American Recorder Society with five issues a year; *The Recorder Education Journal* published annually by the American Recorder Teachers Association and the British and Dutch branches of the European Recorder Teachers' Association; and the oddly named biennial *'Cinnamon Sticks – The Recorder in Australasia'*. In addition to news and reviews, these journals include articles on recorder technique and interpretation. There are also many newsletter-type publications, often of more local interest, specifically for recorder players, and articles of importance to recorder players may also be found from time to time in the following journals:

> *Early Music* (OUP) - the main academic quarterly in this field
>
> *Early Music Performer*, published biennially by Ruxbury Publications for the U.K. National Early Music Association (NEMA)
>
> *Early Music Today* (Rhinegold; six issues a year)
>
> *The Galpin Society Journal* (annually)
>
> *The Consort* (the Dolmetsch Foundation annual journal)
>
> *FoMRHI Quarterly*, the membership journal for makers of historic instruments, including recorders
>
> *Early Music America* (quarterly)
>
> *Goldberg* (quarterly, bilingual English/French or Spanish; or, now, English only)

These and other journals are listed in the Directory section of NEMA's *The Early Music Yearbook* (Ruxbury Publications), an essential reference book for anyone with an interest in early music.

Increasingly, articles are being published with open access on the web. This is the case, for example, with Dan Laurin's important article on 'The relation between the vocal tract and recorder sound quality', available at http://www.danlaurin.com/research.html. Pointers to such publications can usually be found on the Recorder Home Page. Web articles have the advantage to the reader that they are available without charge, and to the author that they can be constantly updated.

Text references (with some others)

Chapter I - Knowing your Instrument   While John Martin's is the only book on the acoustics of the recorder, some excellent articles have been written on the subject by Raymond and Lee Dessy in *American Recorder* (e.g. June, 1992, pp. 7–14; March 1999, pp. 8–10). Instrument makers such as Bruce Haynes, Alec Loretto, Bob Marvin, and Fred Morgan have made important contributions in this field (see section on 'Construction and Design' in Griscom/Lasocki).

Michael G. Zadro wrote two articles in *Early Music* (April and July, 1975) on 'Woods used for woodwind instruments since the 16th century'. There is an analysis of woods used in making recorders in Hildemarie Peter's *The Recorder – its traditions and its tasks* (Robert Lienau, 1953, tr. Godman, Hinrichsen, 1958), a pioneering work which still has much of value, especially the charts on historic fingerings.   Another short consideration of recorders of different woods is on pp. 42–3 of Adrian Brown's *The Recorder – A Basic Workshop Manual* (Dolce Edn. 112, Brighton, 1989, obtainable from The Early Music Shop, Bradford), and there are good articles on the subject by Carlos Serrano Márqez in *American Recorder,* January 2000, pp. 7–9, and by Alec Loretto in *The Recorder Magazine,* June 1998, pp. 48–9.

Brown's book also advises on tuning recorders, as does Edward L. Kottick in *Tone and Intonation on the Recorder* (McGinnis & Marx, New York, 1974), which contains much good advice in a short space.

On recorder pitch, see Fred Morgan, 'Making recorders on historic models', in *Early Music,* January, 1982, pp. 14–21 (an issue devoted to the recorder), and other references in Griscom/Lasocki. And see also Bruce Haynes, *A History of Performing Pitch* (2002).

Jean-Claude Veilhan's bilingual *The Baroque Recorder* (Leduc, Paris, 1980) contains important source material, a helpful commentary, and extended practice examples from baroque music. I strongly recommend it.

Sylvestro Ganassi's *Opera intitulata Fontegara* (Venice, 1535), translated and edited by Hildemarie Peter (English tr. Swainson, 1956) is available as Hinrichsen Edition D1289. Pages 9–14, which are of exceptional value to all recorder players, are about recorder playing generally, and the book is then concerned with divisions, some of which are rhythmically difficult, up to the important closing words on pages 87 and 89.

The best source of information about the medieval recorder, with many iconographic examples, is Lander's article on the Recorder Home Page. See also Horace Fitzpatrick in *Early Music* (October, 1975), and other references in Griscom/Lasocki. A full account of the first documentation of the word 'Recordour' in 1388 is in my article in *Early Music Performer* (March, 2001), reprinted from the German woodwind instrument journal *Tibia* (Moeck, Celle, 2/2000). See also my articles in *American Recorder,* November, 1997, and

RECORDER TECHNIQUE

November, 1999.

Denis Bloodworth, Edgar Hunt and Constance Primus have, among others, written about bass recorders, including tutors such as Bloodworth's *Bass Recorder Handbook* (Recorder MusicMail NOV 110202). Two articles on bass recorders can be accessed through the Recorder Home Page under the section 'Technique'.

The Recorder Home Page has two articles on choosing recorders (click 'Articles' and look under Collins and Everingham). The Home Page also contains a constantly updated database of all contemporary recorder makers, with contact details, including websites.

David Lasocki's edition of Jacques Hotteterre Le Romain's *Principles of the Flute, Recorder and Oboe*, with Picart's engraving on p. 72 facing the chapter 'On the situation of the recorder and the position of the hands', was published by Barrie and Jenkins, London, 1968 (reprinted 1978).

Chapter II - Breathing and Breath Delivery There is an excellent article on breathing for recorder playing by Jeanette Hajncl called 'Don't Panic!' on pp. 10–11 of the March 1998 issue of *The Recorder Magazine*, based on Alexander Technique principles. It mentions other books; see also other references in Griscom/Lasocki.

I should like to take the opportunity at this point of referring to Walter van Hauwe's *The Modern Recorder Player* (Schott – Vol. 1 (1984) Ed. 12150, Vol. 2 (1987) Ed. 12270, and Vol. 3 (1992) Ed. 12361) as it is one of the few recorder methods which gives proper emphasis to breathing for recorder playing. The volumes are progressive, and form a well-presented distillation of the author's long experience in teaching at the Sweelinck Academy in Amsterdam, one of the most prestigious centres for producing recorder players and teachers. Van Hauwe's approach and manner, very different from that of *RT* and *PB* though covering the same ground, is stimulating and at times challenging and even controversial. There are of course many other excellent recorder tutors, for example Alan Davis's *Treble Recorder Technique* (Recorder MusicMail N1178), though most do not have amateur adult recorder players in mind as their prime readership.

Chapter III – Tonguing (Articulation) Historical tonguings are described in Veilhan (see under Ch. I), in Marcello Castellani and Elio Durante's multilingual *Del portar della lingua negli instrumenti di fiato* (SPES, Florence, 1979), and, with an excellent commentary, in George Houle's article 'Tongueing and Rhythmic Patterns in Early Music' in *American Recorder*, Spring, 1965, pp. 4–13.

French-style articulation is considered by David Lasocki and Betty Bang Mather, and more recently, in even greater depth, by Patricia N. Ranum (see p. 142), for example in her article '*Tu-Ru-Tu* and *Tu-Ru-Tu-Tu*: Toward an understanding of Hotteterre's Tonguing Syllables' in *The Recorder in the Seventeenth Century* (ed. Lasocki, STIMU, Utrecht, 1995). Another important article by her can be accessed through the Recorder Home Page under the section 'Technique'.

Reilly's translation of Quantz's 1752 *On Playing the Flute* is published by Faber (1966; 2nd edn 1985).

Masochistic recorder players might enjoy Kees Boeke's *The Complete Articulator* (Schott, Ed. 12261), a training programme of difficult exercises 'for the perfect control of articulation syllables', and Aldo Abreu's *Articulation Etudes for the Recorder* (Part 1, 2002 – Part II to follow) obtainable from Von Huene, Boston, Mass.

Chapter IV – Intonation The best introductory article is by Scott Reiss, 'Pitch, Control: Shading and Leaking' in *American Recorder*, November, 1987, pp. 136–9. Eugene Reichenthal has written on 'Partial Venting' in *The Recorder Magazine* (then known as *Recorder and Music*), June, 1976, pp. 193–5, and there is also my 'A Short History of Partial Venting' in the June 1995 issue.

Chapter V – Alternative fingerings Daniel Waitzman, *The Art of Playing the Recorder* (AMS, New York, 1978) is the only book I know about recorder technique which is not also a tutor. Although Waitzman advocates the use of a bell-key recorder, there is a great deal of good advice and commentary in this book which applies to recorder playing generally. The last part (pp. 73–106) is about fingering. There is an excellent article by Peter Wells on 'Fingering for expressive purposes in the music of the Baroque' in *The Recorder Magazine*, Spring 2001, pp. 8–11.

Chapter VI – High Notes See Waitzman, and Vetter (ref. p. 67). Griscom/Lasocki refers (items 1175-7) to three articles on recorder high-note fingerings in *The Galpin Society Journal* (1958, 1960 and 1961), and to Andrew Robinson's 'Leg Technique' in *The Recorder Magazine*, March, 1995.

Chapter VII – Volume (Dynamics) On p. 82 I refer to Thurston Dart's *The Interpretation of Music* (Hutchinson, London, 1954/5), e.g. to p. 72 and 73. This book has by no means become totally out-dated - it is full of insights and good sense. As the index shows, there are many references to dynamics.

Unfortunately the only book on recorder dynamics, a good one, has not been translated from German into English. This is Johannes Fischer's *Die dynamische Blockflöte* (Moeck, Celle, 1990).

Anthony Baines's *Woodwind Instruments and their History* was originally published in 1957 by Faber; this excellent book is now available as a Dover Editions paperback (New York, 1991). For voicing to increase volume see Alec Loretto's article 'Double chamfers' in *The Recorder Magazine*, Summer 2003, p. 50.

Lander's article on the Recorder Home Page on the history of the recorder (see under Ch.I) includes an account (pp. 8–15) of recorder modifications from 1930 to the present day, most of them designed to increase volume. See also references in Appendix 3 under 'Electroacoustic music'.

Chapter VIII – Tone See Kottick, referred to under Ch.I above. Griscom/Lasocki refers to articles where the harmonic structures of recorder notes with different tone-qualities due to varying patterns of upper partials are scientifically examined, and where undertones are similarly considered.

Dan Laurin's research referred to on p. 90 on the effect of the shape of the mouth cavity on recorder tone-quality was also the subject of an article in *American Recorder*, September, 1999, pp. 13-17.

Lander's article on 'Vibrato and Tremolo on the Recorder' can be accessed on the Recorder Home Page under the section 'Technique'. This is the best available treatment of the subject for recorder players. Jochen Gärtner's book on flute vibrato (tr. Anderson) is published (1981) by Gustav Bosse Verlag at Regensburg in Bavaria. It is physiological and scientific in its approach, but is interspersed with useful historical background and helpful hints.

Robert Donington's *The Interpretation of Early Music*, published by Faber, first appeared in 1963 but was revised periodically to 1977, and again for a paperback edition in 1989. At 766 pages it is longer even than Frederick Neumann's *Ornamentation in Baroque and Post-Baroque Music* (630 pp. – 'Vibrato' is on pp. 511–522; Princeton University Press, paperback, 1983), or his *Performance Practices of the Seventeenth and Eighteenth Century* (605 pp., Schirmer, New York, 1993). More for reference than casual reading.

Eve O'Kelly's *The Recorder Today* was published by Cambridge University Press in 1990.

Chapter IX – Ornamentation An enormous literature, including Donington and Neumann, and Dolmetsch and Dannreuther before them. But once your technique is in place, which the Three Blind Mice will see to, it is better to listen to good recordings and hear ornamentation rather than to read about it.

For Renaissance ornamentation I suggest the CDs 'Wordplay' (Musica Antiqua of London - Signum SIG CD 031) and Flautendo Köln's 'Ancor che col partire' (AM 1286-2), both with instrumental settings (mainly recorders) of madrigals and chansons. The first of these includes Philip Thorby's ornamentation of a Willaert madrigal in accordance with the precepts of Ganassi. And one small book – Howard Mayer Brown's admirable *Embellishing 16th–Century Music* (Oxford, 1976). Use London Pro Musica's series 'Ricercate e passaggi' (Early Music Shop, Bradford) for your practice.

Any recording of Telemann's *Sonate Metodiche*, and your own playing of the opening movements of these twelve sonatas (Dolce edn. 120-01), will introduce you to at least one composer's concept of baroque ornamentation. If at all possible, obtain through ERTA (Peter Bowman, tel. 01580 895177) or ARTA (Professor Eva Legêne at Indiana University) copies of *The Recorder Education Journal* Nos. 5 (1999) and 6 (2000) – a gold-mine for recorder players of information and advice on baroque ornamentation.

For French-style ornamentation I suggest that you listen to recordings of Couperin's music, especially pieces such as *Les Goûts-Réunis* which can be played on the (tenor) recorder. The best practical book on the subject is still Betty Bang Mather's *Interpretation of French Music from 1675 to 1775 for Woodwind and Other Performers* (McGinnis & Marx, 1973).

Mather and Lasocki's *Free Ornamentation in Woodwind Music 1700-1775* (McGinnis & Marx, 1976) and Ernest T. Ferand's *Improvisation in Nine Centuries of Western Music* (Arno Volk, Cologne, 1961) contain historical examples in the form of complete movements, 66 in the former, 39 in the latter, both with good introductions. Excellent practice material.

The 'Ornamentation' article in *The New Grove* 2nd edn, now by a team of writers, is thorough and informative, and is well supplied with examples of individual ornaments. It is organised on a country by country basis. Like Donington and Neumann, this is essentially a reference article (or series of articles).

Freda Dinn's *Early Music for Recorders* was published by Schott (Ed. 11155) in 1974. It is an excellent book, but do not accept her proposed ornamentation and phrasing uncritically – nor indeed mine, for the Handel G minor sonata is considered both in her book and in *PRS*, and one of the Byrd trios she expounds has also been the subject of an article by me in *The Recorder Magazine*, September, 1993. You should not even feel bound by a composer's ornamentation of his own music. Lefkovitch's edition of Hotteterre's *Duo and Rondeau* is Schott Ed. 11252. For Hotteterre's *Principes* see under Ch.I.

Christoph Demantius, *Fifteen Dances* 1601 ed. Thomas (London Pro Musica LPM GM2) is for recorder quintet (SAATB), with Bernard Thomas's suggested ornamentation in the top part.

Chapter X – Practice Griscom/Lasocki lists nine articles under 'Practising' (Nos. 1193-1201), mainly in *American Recorder*, each with a different approach.

Susan Groskreutz's 'Play-along discs for recorder students: an overview' is in *American Recorder*, September and November, 2001. Music Minus One (MMO) recordings are obtainable at Forsyth's, Dean Street, Manchester.

Chapter XI – Performance *Playing Recorder Sonatas* was published in hardback and paperback by Clarendon Press, Oxford (OUP) in 1992, and I envisaged it as the culmination of a three-part recorder method preceded first by *Intro,* and then going on to *RT* and *PB* taken together. *PRS* is permanently available on order from OUP. The 'method' is in a sense incomplete as there are as yet no books on playing recorders with other instruments and voice, and only two specifically on recorder consort playing. These are Paul Clark's *Adventures in Consort Playing* (1993) published by Roy Brewer's Allegro Press, Clifton, Bristol, who also publish my *Playing Recorder Duets* (1995), and Bert Spanhove's *The finishing touch of ensemble playing* (Alamire, Peer, Belgium, 2000). But perhaps the best way to learn about recorder consort playing is to work under an inspirational and experienced conductor, particularly of ensembles of recorders with other instruments and voices, such as, currently in the U.K., Peter Holman, Andrew Parrott, and Philip Thorby; there are many opportunities to do this. My own education in consort playing was in this way, under Walter Bergmann at Morley College, London.

Mabel Dolmetsch's books on courtly dances were published by Da Capo Press, New York (paperback) in 1976, having been originally published by Routledge, London, in 1949 and 1954. They cover dances during the period 1460 to 1600.

To the great benefit of early music performance, considerable scholarship has been devoted in recent years to performance practice. Here are references to nine books, and see also Neumann's 1993 book (listed under Ch. VIII), and there are others, and many articles:

Timothy J. McGee, *Medieval and Renaissance Music – A Performer's Guide* (University of Toronto Press, 1985).

Ross W. Duffin (ed.), *A Performer's Guide to Medieval Music* (Indiana University Press, 2000).

Howard Mayer Brown and Stanley Sadie (eds.), *Performance Practice – Music before 1600* (Macmillan, London, 1989).

RECORDER TECHNIQUE

Robert Donington, *Baroque Music: Style and Performance* (Faber, London, paperback, 1982).

George Houle, *Meter in Music 1600–1800* (Indiana U.P., 1987)

Steven E. Hefling, *Rhythmic Alteration in Seventeeth- and Eighteenth-Century Music* (Schirmer/Macmillan, New York, 1993).

Mary Cyr, *Performing Baroque Music* (Scolar Press, Aldershot – now Ashgate, 1992).

Peter le Huray, *Authenticity in Performance – Eighteenth-century case studies* (Cambridge U.P., paperback, 1990).

Rachel Brown, *The Early Flute: A Practical Guide* (Cambridge U.P., paperback, 2002).

For some others, see p. 142.

APPENDIX 3

FURTHER REGIONS

When you have worked your way all through *Recorder Technique* and can play all the Exercises in the *Practice Book* with accuracy and panache, and have also carefully studied *Playing Recorder Sonatas* and performed the music in it, you may rightly regard yourself as an advanced recorder player. At that point you might wish to improve your abilities across the whole range of music that can be played on the recorder, but, like most professionals, you may decide to specialise. This Appendix offers a selection of further regions to conquer.

You are likely to discover, however, that some of these areas require even more than the hard work of frequent (ideally, daily) practice in new ways of recorder playing. In some cases, considerable study of scholarly writings on the subject is essential, for example in the books listed at the end of Appendix 2, together with your own research in libraries with original early printed music and manuscripts. Some professional groups, having espoused an area such as medieval music, are so taken up with the struggle to earn a living by getting concert engagements and the disruption this causes that their interpretations may be thought to be less than satisfactory for lack of unremitting scholarly background. In other areas you may need to have skills as an acoustician or micro-electronic engineer. Or you may need to cultivate styles where improvisation and non-written communication has long been the traditional means of making music.

In most, but not all, of these areas you will need to work with like-minded and experienced enthusiasts to attain the utmost in ability and enjoyment.

Avant-garde compositions

Rather as the term 'art-nouveau' is a label for a past period of architecture and design, 'avant-garde' refers to a type of composition fashionable over several decades in the second half of the twentieth century. Avant-garde composers were preoccupied with the use and developments of extended techniques as described in Eve O'Kelly's *The Recorder Today* in 1990. A seminal book was Bruno Bartolozzi's *New Sounds for Woodwind* (Oxford, 1967,) and, specifically for the recorder, Michael Vetter's *Il Flauto Dolce ed Acerbo* (Moeck, 1969, Ed. 40009), with a recording of the same title. The protagonists were mainly from central Europe and Japan, and being able to read German is a considerable advantage in getting to know this music.

One of the advantages of avant-garde music to the lone recorder player is that most of the compositions are for unaccompanied recorder. Communicating the sounds they had in mind in written notation, however, was a problem for composers, who devised their own vocabularies of signs and symbols (see Peter Wells's article in *The Recorder Magazine*, Summer, 2000, pp. 59–62), and some publications of avant-garde music have more pages explaining how to play the piece than of the music itself. The explanations have to be learnt before the music can be performed. The problem is compounded when the music is notated as a graphic score (O'Kelly, pp. 72–7). Some composers recorded their music, but this was more likely to be an example rather than a model of performance, all the more so where the composition has an aleatoric element of improvisation. Certain notational conventions became generally accepted, however (see Ursula Schmidt's book, Moeck 4022, in German), and they represent the sounds which have entered the vocabulary of present-day composers.

Australian composers in particular have developed a type of composition which incorporates dramatic action into the music.

A start towards playing avant-garde music may be made by working through Volume III of Walter van Hauwe's *The Modern Recorder Player* (Schott Ed. 12361), which goes a little beyond the scope of *RT*. Michael Vetter's *Il Flauto Dolce ed Acerbo* (which is in English) will take you further still. Alan Davis's Studies (p. 109) provide another gateway to avant-garde music, and after that I suggest you work on Konrad Lechner's *Spuren im Sand* for tenor recorder (Moeck 1526); the footprints lead you gradually, with interesting music and clear explanations (in English), to a point where you might tackle multiphonics in Hans-Martin Linde's *Music for a Bird* (Schott OFB 154) which has become a sort of primer for advanced students, though his other pieces, such as *Amarilli mia bella* (Schott OFB 133), are in my view better – but more difficult – music, and his 1990 CD (WER 6191-2) can be used as a model. But this is not for the faint-hearted.

Electroacoustic music

Michael Vetter's 60's LP (Moeck) included two pieces where the recorder was accompanied by prepared tapes, and this opened up a new field of electronic compositions with recorder, described up to 1990 by O'Kelly (pp.77–81) and more recently in *The Recorder Magazine* by Philippe Boulton (March, 1998) and Peter Bowman (Autumn, 2000), and in *American Recorder* by Cesar Villavicencio (January, 2002) who uses a MIDIfied version of a square-designed Paetzold contra-bass recorder. In the same issue Ray and Lee Dessy and others discuss microphone positioning in recorders. Inevitably, music for electronic recorders tends to be personal to its composers, and experimentation and improvisation is of the essence.

Jazz

While recorders have occasionally appeared in pop groups, they have had little place in serious jazz music until recently, but there is no shortage of jazz-based compositions for recorders, some very attractive, and variously demanding, by composers such as Andrew Charlton. Developments in the field of recorder jazz are discussed in Pete Rose's regular columns in *American Recorder*. But jazz is not generally written down, as it is an improvisatory form based upon familiar chord sequences (like so much baroque and earlier music) in which rhythmic inequality (as in French baroque and earlier music) and devices such as note-bending play an important part. Although the recorder seldom features in mainstream jazz, in principle it might come to do so for players with both electroacoustic skills, good technique and musicianship, and irrepressible enthusiasm. This does not mean to say that jazz music cannot be played on a recorder without built-in amplification, even with a harpsichord, as in Evelyn Nallen and David Gordon's

'Respectable Groove' CD. *American Recorder* in September 1996, featured 'The Recorder Blues' (Ray and Lee Dessy – 'happiness is found in playing the blues. Here's how to get started'), with more on blues and crossover music by Scott Reiss.

Microtonality

Quarter-tones, which may be regarded as an interval of fifty cents, and microtones (i.e. other ways of dividing the interval of a tone) are used in several highly-regarded Japanese avant-garde compositions, but the main proponents of microtone music are the composer Donald Bousted (who wrote a series of six articles in *The Recorder Magazine*, Autumn 2001 to Winter 2002), and the recorder duo of Kathryn Bennetts and Peter Bowman. Together they wrote the tutor, *The Quarter-Tone Recorder Manual* (Moeck, 1998, Ed. 2084), which gives fingerings, and the duo has recorded some of Bousted's music – the CD is obtainable from The Early Music Shop, Bradford.

My suggestion is to start by listening to that CD. You may get hooked.

I will now slip back some eight centuries and pick out several other 'Further Regions' chronologically.

Medieval music

Several (but an increasing number of) versions of medieval music may be found in recorder catalogues, mainly trios, as three-part music (referring to the Trinity, or perfection) was common from Pérotin (c.1200) to Dufay (d.1474); and recorder players from David Munrow onwards have revelled in the few estampies and other dances which were written down in the thirteenth and fourteenth centuries. But there is a wealth of fine trio music contained in MSS such as the Squarcialupi Codex (including Landini) and the Buxheimer intabulations (Paumann, Dunstable, Binchois etc.). Some of it, especially the fourteenth-century music (Machaut etc.), is rhythmically very demanding, as is the fast-moving continuous ornamentation. Even though much of it is available in scholarly editions, a very considerable amount of knowledge of medieval music – its style, notation, principles of word-setting, performance practices – is needed to do justice to it. Furthermore, its spirit is more likely to be discovered by mixed groups of recorder, lute, harp, medieval fiddle and – especially – voices, than by a recorder trio - so you will need to be versatile. And there are problems of suitable types of recorders and their sound and pitch (usually high-pitch), and the use of probably rather limited percussion. But this is far too fascinating and beautiful a repertoire to be disregarded. Start with the later period and then work backwards.

16th- and 17th-century consort music

Byrd, Holborne, Gibbons and others are favourites among recorder groups, along with recorder versions of music for voices and organ, and are deeply enjoyable played in this way. But advanced players may wish to delve more deeply by knowing more about the principles upon which Renaissance polyphonic composition at different periods was based, by playing in the notation of the time from facsimiles of printed music, often in unfamiliar clefs, by learning where ornamentation might have been added, by studying word-rhythms in different languages (being able to sing, especially at sight, is an advantage) and by improvising additional parts. All this will bring them closer in spirit to the music-making of the time. Morley is an excellent teacher in his *A Plaine and Easie Introduction to Practicall Musicke* (1597), but simple introductions to the modes and the gamut are contained in Lander's Galilei article (see p. 131) and in Thurston Dart's *Invitation to Madrigals* Book 4 (duets) (Stainer and Bell, London, and Galaxy, New York, 1967).

They will also need to play Renaissance-type recorders (including an alto in G) at the pitch of voices or viols, so the use of descants is a rarity. Other than lively dances, Renaissance music, especially pieces composed with viols in mind, sounds best at eight-foot pitch on recorders all made by the same maker.

French baroque music

Much of this music, including some by Couperin, suits recorder. But acquiring the style needs a knowledge of the French language and how it was set to music, of performance practice, of ornamentation (such as ornamented Brunettes), of inequality, and, above all, articulation. *PRS*, Ch. 4 offers a taster, but you need to study much more deeply the books and the practice material mentioned on p. 136, and also Mather's *Dance Rhythms of the French Baroque* (Indiana U.P., 1987) and Ranum's *The Harmonic Orator – The Phrasing and Rhetoric of the Melody in French Baroque Aires* (Pendragon Press, 2001).

Flute (and some other) music (see *PB*, p.i)

From the late seventeenth century, the voice-flute (tenor recorder in D) was used to play music composed for the violin (see my article 'The Coalman Reveal'd' in *The Recorder Magazine*, Winter 2002, pp.142–4), and voice-flutes were still being made in the nineteenth century in continuation of the practice of some amateurs of playing flute music without having to learn flute embouchure. A certain amount of flute music, however, can be played with or without transposition, on the treble recorder; the common transposition, as provided for by Telemann, was to transpose a minor third up, not that difficult if you think bass clef (or the French violin G clef) and adjust accidentals. The voice-flute becomes difficult to play well in three or more flats, but such music is quite likely to fit on to a tenor recorder, particularly if you can manage to get high notes by bell-shading.

The rewards of this piracy are enormous – J.S. Bach's flute sonatas including the solo sonata, and his organ trio-sonatas, and more sonatas by C.P.E. Bach including another great solo sonata; Leclair's violin sonatas where he gives flute as an alternative, and Rameau's *Pièces en concert*; Giuseppi Sammartini and John Stanley; many pieces by Haydn, mainly trios; Mozart's Flute Quartets and sonatas (the Andante K.315 and the oboe quartet can be played on treble); and even Weber's flute sonatas and Schumann's *Three Romances*. It is better to avoid music written in a showy flute idiom, as exemplified by some of Quantz's concertos and many later flute duets. Simple arrangements for flute of twentieth-century pieces (e.g. Elgar) become available, and Benjamin Britten's *Metamorphoses* for oboe solo is not out of reach for tenor players.

Csakan music (or czakan)

The csakan (see Lander's 'History'), said to derive from a Hungarian folk instrument but probably invented around 1807 by Anton Heberle, quickly became fashionable in Vienna and later across Germany. The Viennese composer and virtuoso Ernst Krähmer, with Heberle and others, created for it a repertoire of romantic Biedermeier music. The instrument was in A flat, and keyed, but keylesss versions existed, occasionally in C so it was then virtually a descant recorder, and termed 'flûte douce'. Some players, such as Piers Adams, specialise in this very attractive music – he is editing it for Dolce edition. Quite easy pieces were composed for amateurs, but most of the repertoire is much more virtuosic. It is tremendous fun – puff pastry with lashings of cream.

You could play it on a csakan of course. Copies are made by Paetzold, of Ebenhofen, Germany.

The modern British repertoire

The nucleus of what to me is an extremely attractive repertoire was formed in 1940-50 with a group of sonatinas written by then young British composers, such as Lennox Berkeley, Walter Leigh and Alan Rawsthorne, written at the instigation of Manuel Jacob, a pupil of Edgar Hunt (see Eve O'Kelly, pp. 38–40). It was added to with many commissions by Carl Dolmetsch (see Andrew Mayes, *Carl Dolmetsch and the Recorder Repertoire of the 20th Century*, Ashgate, Aldershot, 2003), and works by Malcolm Arnold, Arnold Cooke, Gordon Jacob and Edmund Rubbra, among others. This tradition is being continued by John Turner in a series of pieces which can be heard on his CDs, including compositions by William Alwyn, Leonard Bernstein, Gordon Crosse, Edward Gregson, Peter Crossley-Holland, Timothy Moore and Philip Wood. Avant-garde effects are used only in moderation, and the level of difficulty ranges from fairly difficult to virtuoso.

World music

In their final degree term my students studied 'world music', which they greatly enjoyed; but it was designed to get them to exploit some of the extremes of the recorder's tonal potentialities, such as blowing at an angle across the windway. The recorder is versatile as a mimic, and direct-blown flutes of different kinds are used in many countries. To name some, there is the Japanese shakuhachi, the Romanian naiu (panpipes), Andean pipes such as the Bolivian pinkillu and the Incan quena, North American Indian flutes, the Arabic ney and the Irish tin-whistle. Each country has its own way of making music, and it is not easy to capture indigenous styles, particularly in ornamentation, in complex and elusive rhythms, and in language-related expression. Irish ornamentation differs from the accented 'graces' derived from the bagpipe music of its Celtic neighbour Scotland, in rather the same way as Irish dancing differs from Scottish dancing, and I suspect the same applies to different countries in South American - written arrangements of music from Bolivia, Brazil and Argentina for recorders tend to homogenise such characteristics. And in any case, much of the original music is improvised, almost spontaneously.

RECORDER TECHNIQUE

Current interest in world music, and deeper respect for the music of distant nations, has led to 'crossover music', and the merging of diverse musical traditions. A recent example is Ronald J. Autenrieth's *Alab & Drive* for tenor and bass recorders and plucked double bass (Moeck, ZfS 761, 2002). 'Alab' is the rhythmically free and contemplative introduction preceding an Indian raga; 'drive' stems from jazz music. The recorder, with its direct-blown flute relatives throughout the world, is an ideal instrument for music of this kind, and the example I have quoted (which is not particularly difficult to play, though all too brief) also bodes well as one of an increasing number of compositions where recorders are associated on equal terms with other instruments. To quote Eve O'Kelly (p. 126), 'the ingredients are present for a bright future'.

Two areas not included in this list, the recorder orchestra and recorder solo music, are dealt with more fully in two articles in *The Recorder Magazine*, Spring and Summer, 2004.

INDEX

This index covers both *Recorder Technique* and *The Practice Book* ('*PB*'), where references are to page numbers not to Ex. Numbers.

Main entries, and others of special importance, are in bold. In *PB*, each Ex. is indexed by composer in bold, with a reference also to the relevant page of the updating commentary, whether or not it mentions the name of the composer.

Indexing is conceptual, not only by keyword. Thus 'gradually getting softer' is indexed as 'decrescendo', and cadential trills within the music of *PB* Exx. are indexed as such.

Semicolons in the more extended listings indicate a change in the chapter referred to.

Names of persons are generally those of composers, unless shown otherwise.

Fingerings in both books are for the treble (alto) recorder, unless otherwise stated.

A

Printed in August 2021
by Rotomail Italia S.p.A., Vignate (MI) - Italy